INTERFACES AND DOMAINS OF CONTACT-DRIVEN RESTRUCTURING

The Afro-Hispanic Languages of the Americas (AHLAs) present a number of grammatical similarities that have traditionally been ascribed to a previous creole stage. Approaching creole studies from contrasting standpoints, this groundbreaking book provides a new account of these phenomena. How did these features come about? What linguistic mechanisms can account for their parallel existence in several contact varieties? How can we formalize such mechanisms within a comprehensive theoretical framework? How can these new datasets help us test and refine current formal theories, which have primarily been based on standardized language data? In addressing these important questions, this book not only casts new light on the nature of the AHLAs but also provides new theoretical and methodological perspectives for a more integrated approach to the study of contact-driven restructuring across language interfaces and linguistic domains.

SANDRO SESSAREGO is Associate Professor of Linguistics in the Department of Spanish and Portuguese at the University of Texas at Austin and a member of the Rapoport Center for Human Rights and Justice. He works primarily in the fields of contact linguistics, sociolinguistics, syntax and human rights. He has published a number of books on law and linguistics; his most recent one is Language Contact and the Making of an Afro-Hispanic Vernacular (2019, Cambridge).

CAMBRIDGE STUDIES IN LINGUISTICS

GENERAL EDITORS: U. ANSALDO, P. AUSTIN, B. COMRIE, T. KUTEVA, R. LASS, D. LIGHTFOOT, K. RICE, I. ROBERTS, S. ROMAINE, M. SHEEHAN, I. TSIMPLI

In this series

123 NIINA NING ZHANG: *Coordination in Syntax*
124 NEIL SMITH: *Acquiring Phonology*
125 NINA TOPINTZI: *Onsets: Suprasegmental and Prosodic Behaviour*
126 CEDRIC BOECKX, NORBERT HORNSTEIN and JAIRO NUNES: *Control as Movement*
127 MICHAEL ISRAEL: *The Grammar of Polarity: Pragmatics, Sensitivity, and the Logic of Scales*
128 M. RITA MANZINI and LEONARDO M. SAVOIA: *Grammatical Categories: Variation in Romance Languages*
129 BARBARA CITKO: *Symmetry in Syntax: Merge, Move and Labels*
130 RACHEL WALKER: *Vowel Patterns in Language*
131 MARY DALRYMPLE and IRINA NIKOLAEVA: *Objects and Information Structure*
132 JERROLD M. SADOCK: *The Modular Architecture of Grammar*
133 DUNSTAN BROWN and ANDREW HIPPISLEY: *Network Morphology: A Defaults-based Theory of Word Structure*
134 BETTELOU LOS, CORRIEN BLOM, GEERT BOOIJ, MARION ELENBAAS and ANS VAN KEMENADE: *Morphosyntactic Change: A Comparative Study of Particles and Prefixes*
135 STEPHEN CRAIN: *The Emergence of Meaning*
136 HUBERT HAIDER: *Symmetry Breaking in Syntax*
137 JOSÉ A. CAMACHO: *Null Subjects*
138 GREGORY STUMP and RAPHAEL A. FINKEL: *Morphological Typology: From Word to Paradigm*
139 BRUCE TESAR: *Output-Driven Phonology: Theory and Learning*
140 ASIER ALCÁZAR and MARIO SALTARELLI: *The Syntax of Imperatives*
141 MISHA BECKER: *The Acquisition of Syntactic Structure: Animacy and Thematic Alignment*
142 MARTINA WILTSCHKO: *The Universal Structure of Categories: Towards a Formal Typology*
143 FAHAD RASHED AL-MUTAIRI: *The Minimalist Program: The Nature and Plausibility of Chomsky's Biolinguistics*
144 CEDRIC BOECKX: *Elementary Syntactic Structures: Prospects of a Feature-Free Syntax*
145 PHOEVOS PANAGIOTIDIS: *Categorial Features: A Generative Theory of Word Class Categories*
146 MARK BAKER: *Case: Its Principles and Its Parameters*
147 WM. G. BENNETT: *The Phonology of Consonants: Dissimilation, Harmony and Correspondence*

148 ANDREA SIMS: *Inflectional Defectiveness*
149 GREGORY STUMP: *Inflectional Paradigms: Content and Form at the Syntax–Morphology Interface*
150 ROCHELLE LIEBER: *English Nouns: The Ecology of Nominalization*
151 JOHN BOWERS: *Deriving Syntactic Relations*
152 ANA TERESA PÉREZ-LEROUX, MIHAELA PIRVULESCU and YVES ROBERGE: *Direct Objects and Language Acquisition*
153 MATTHEW BAERMAN, DUNSTAN BROWN and GREVILLE G. CORBETT: *Morphological Complexity*
154 MARCEL DEN DIKKEN: *Dependency and Directionality*
155 LAURIE BAUER: *Compounds and Compounding*
156 KLAUS J. KOHLER: *Communicative Functions and Linguistic Forms in Speech Interaction*
157 KURT GOBLIRSCH: *Gemination, Lenition, and Vowel Lengthening: On the History of Quantity in Germanic*
158 ANDREW RADFORD: *Colloquial English: Structure and Variation*
159 MARIA POLINSKY: *Heritage Languages and Their Speakers*
160 EGBERT FORTUIN and GETTY GEERDINK-VERKOREN: *Universal Semantic Syntax: A Semiotactic Approach*
161 ANDREW RADFORD: *Relative Clauses: Structure and Variation in Everyday English*
162 JOHN H. ESLING, SCOTT R. MOISIK, ALISON BENNER and LISE CREVIER-BUCHMAN: *Voice Quality: The Laryngeal Articulator Model*
163 JASON ROTHMAN, JORGE GONZÁLEZ ALONSO and ELOI PUIG-MAYENCO: *Third Language Acquisition and Linguistic Transfer*
164 IRINA NIKOLAEVA and ANDREW SPENCER: *Mixed Categories: The Morphosyntax of Noun Modification*
165 ABRAHAM WERNER: *Modality in Syntax, Semantics and Pragmatics*
166 GUGLIELMO CINQUE: *The Syntax of Relative Clauses: A Unified Analysis*
167 SANDRO SESSAREGO: *Interfaces and Domains of Contact-Driven Restructuring: Aspects of Afro-Hispanic Linguistics*

Earlier issues not listed are also available.

INTERFACES AND DOMAINS OF CONTACT-DRIVEN RESTRUCTURING

ASPECTS OF AFRO-HISPANIC LINGUISTICS

SANDRO SESSAREGO
University of Texas, Austin

CAMBRIDGE
UNIVERSITY PRESS

University Printing House, Cambridge CB2 8BS, United Kingdom

One Liberty Plaza, 20th Floor, New York, NY 10006, USA

477 Williamstown Road, Port Melbourne, VIC 3207, Australia

314–321, 3rd Floor, Plot 3, Splendor Forum, Jasola District Centre, New Delhi – 110025, India

103 Penang Road, #05–06/07, Visioncrest Commercial, Singapore 238467

Cambridge University Press is part of the University of Cambridge.

It furthers the University's mission by disseminating knowledge in the pursuit of education, learning, and research at the highest international levels of excellence.

www.cambridge.org
Information on this title: www.cambridge.org/9781108833820
DOI: 10.1017/9781108982733

© Sandro Sessarego 2021

This publication is in copyright. Subject to statutory exception and to the provisions of relevant collective licensing agreements, no reproduction of any part may take place without the written permission of Cambridge University Press.

First published 2021

A catalogue record for this publication is available from the British Library.

ISBN 978-1-108-83382-0 Hardback

Cambridge University Press has no responsibility for the persistence or accuracy of URLs for external or third-party internet websites referred to in this publication and does not guarantee that any content on such websites is, or will remain, accurate or appropriate.

Per Gianna e Marino

Contents

List of Figures	*page* xi
List of Maps	xii
List of Tables	xiii
Acknowledgments	xv

1	**Questioning a Long-Lasting Assumption in the Field**	1
1.1	The Creole Debate	8
	1.1.1 My Two Cents	10
	1.1.2 Degrees of Contact-Driven Restructuring	16
1.2	Second-Language Acquisition and Creole Formation	19
1.3	Vernacular Universals	21
1.4	Theoretical Assumptions	23
	1.4.1 The Framework	23
	1.4.2 Interfaces and Second-Language Development	26
1.5	Domino Effects	29
1.6	Overview	32

2	**The African Diaspora to the Andes and Its Linguistic Consequences**	35
2.1	Divergent Views on the Origins of the Afro-Andean Spanish Varieties	35
2.2	A Sociohistorical Sketch of Black Slavery in the Andes	37
	2.2.1 First Arrivals	38
	2.2.2 The Second Wave	44
	2.2.3 The Gradual Path to Social Emancipation	48
2.3	A Closer Look at Three Afro-Andean Communities	50
	2.3.1 Yungas, Bolivia	51
	2.3.2 Chota Valley, Ecuador	53
	2.3.3 Chincha, Peru	55

3	**Reconciling Formalism and Language Variation**	57
3.1	Synchronic Variation in Traditional Generative Grammar	58
3.2	The Sociolinguistic View on the Matter	59

3.3	Synchronic and Diachronic Attempts to Reconcile Variation and Formalism	60
3.4	Variation and Minimalism	62
4	**Variable Phi-Agreement across the Determiner Phrase**	**66**
4.1	Fieldwork and Data Collection	67
4.2	Agreement Configurations Based on Both Grammaticality Judgments and Sociolinguistic Interviews	69
4.3	Quantifying Variation	74
4.4	Reconciling Variable Outputs with Invariable Syntax	80
4.5	On the Persistence of Default Values at the Morphology–Syntax/Semantics Interface	91
5	**Partial Pro-Drop Phenomena**	**99**
5.1	A Testing Ground for the Null Subject Parameter	99
5.2	Two Partial Pro-Drop Varieties in Ibero-Romance	102
5.3	On the Nature of Partial Pro-Drop Phenomena in the AHLAs	107
5.4	Rethinking Parameters	110
5.5	Along the Morphology–Semantics and the Syntax–Pragmatics Interfaces	111
6	**Early-Peak Alignment and Duplication of Boundary Tone Configurations**	**125**
6.1	Theoretical Background	125
6.2	Methodology	128
6.3	Prosodic Findings	130
	6.3.1 Pre-nuclear Position	130
	6.3.2 Nuclear position	132
6.4	An Analysis along the Pragmatics–Phonology Interface	135
7	**Final Considerations**	**140**
References		145
Index		169

Figures

1.1	Sample F0 contours for *Porque ya no da manera ... tengo propiedad* 'Because there is no way ... I own property' in Chocó Spanish	*page* 7
1.2	Sample F0 contours for *Yo siempre más harto que todo ellos* 'I am always much more than all of them' in Yungueño Spanish	7
1.3	A continuum of outcomes involving degrees of substrate and L2 input	18
2.1	A Spanish *conquistador* with his black servant	40
4.1	Gender agreement evolution across the Yungueño Spanish DP	78
4.2	Gender agreement evolution across the Chota Valley Spanish DP	78
4.3	Gender agreement evolution across the Chincha Spanish DP	79
6.1	Frequent pitch accents in Spanish	127
6.2	An F0 contour for *Después había que hacer camani* 'Later one had to do work' in Yungueño Spanish	132
6.3	An F0 contour for *Allí yo estaba pues, yo le criaba a sus hijitos* 'There I was, well, I would take care of their children' in Chincha Spanish	133
6.4	An F0 contour for *Quieren saber el tiempo de antes* 'They wanted to know about the past' in Chota Valley Spanish	134
6.5	Common Spanish broad and narrow-focus strategies (via phonology with the possibility of phonetic upstep)	137
6.6	Suggested Afro-Andean broad and narrow-focus strategies (via phonetics only)	137

Maps

1.1 The Afro-Hispanic varieties of the Americas 2
2.1 Three Afro-Andean communities: Yungas, Chota Valley, Chincha 51

Tables

1.1	Developmental stages in English interlanguage syntax	*page* 20
1.2	Lenition of velar plosives	30
2.1	Demographic figures for the city of Potosí (1611–1832)	43
4.1	Gender agreement configurations found in Yungueño Spanish, Chota Valley Spanish and Chincha Spanish	72
4.2	Cross-generational variable rule analysis of the contribution of Grammatical Category and Generation to the probability of lack of gender agreement in the Yungueño Spanish DP	75
4.3	Cross-generational variable rule analysis of the contribution of Grammatical Category and Generation to the probability of lack of gender agreement in the Chota Valley Spanish DP	76
4.4	Cross-generational variable rule analysis of the contribution of Grammatical Category and Generation to the probability of lack of gender agreement in the Chincha Spanish DP	77
4.5	Variable rule analysis of number agreement variation in the Yungueño Spanish DP	80
4.6	Grammatical hierarchy of gender agreement in Afro-Hispanic vernaculars compared with classroom students of Spanish	95
4.7	Variable rule analysis of number agreement variation in the Puerto Rican Spanish DP	96
4.8	Variable rule analysis of number agreement variation in the Popular Brazilian Portuguese DP	96
5.1	Evolution of inflectional paradigms in Brazilian Portuguese	104
5.2	Evolution of the pronominal paradigm in Brazilian Portuguese	104
5.3	Variable rule analysis of the contribution of internal factors to the probability of lack of subject–verb agreement in Yungueño Spanish	108
5.4	Variable rule analysis of the contribution of external factors to the probability of lack of subject–verb agreement in Yungueño Spanish	109

6.1 Methodological summary for declarative intonation in Yungueño Spanish, Chota Valley Spanish and Chincha Spanish — 129
6.2 Pre-nuclear pitch accents in Yungueño Spanish, Chota Valley Spanish and Chincha Spanish — 131
6.3 Nuclear configurations in non-IP-final ips in Yungueño Spanish, Chota Valley Spanish and Chincha Spanish — 133
6.4 IP-final configurations in Yungueño Spanish, Chota Valley Spanish and Chincha Spanish — 134

Acknowledgments

This project is based on more than ten years of research fieldwork in Afro-Latino communities across Ecuador, Bolivia and Peru. Hundreds of people (informants, colleagues and friends) have contributed to its creation, and I owe my gratitude to all of them. In particular, I wish to thank Lorenzo Sangiacomo, Luis Delgado, Fabio Lazzaro, Olga Palacios, Paola Palacios, Anahí Landazuri, Rolando Palma Quiroz, Alessandro Garro and Jocelyne Couchy for assisting me during the data collection, as well as colleagues Nicolas Quint, Stefano Manfredi, Rita Eloranta, Ugo Corte, Anu Raunio, Eeva Sippola, Angela Bartens, Salikoko Mufwene, Enoch Aboh, Damián Blasi, Stefan Pfänder, Bernd Kortmann, Marlyse Baptista, Donald Winford, Terrell Morgan, Carol Klee, Armin Schwegler, Bettina Migge, Michel DeGraff, Kofi Yakpo, Leonie Cornips, Peter Bakker, John McWhorter, Miguel Gutiérrez-Maté, Adrián Rodríguez-Riccelli, Dale Koike, Jacqueline Toribio, Barbara Bullock, Chiyo Nishida, Sergio Romero, Orlando Kelm, Manuel Díaz-Campos, Julio Villa-García, Iván Ortega-Santos, Adriana Orjuela, Ignacio Satti, Federca D'Antoni, Don Walicek, Margot van den Berg, Rajiv Rao, Mario Soto and Myungji Yang for the constructive conversations we had on a number of aspects of this study.

Writing this book would not have been possible without the backing of several institutions which have provided me with research support that allowed me to focus on this project for the past three years. For this reason, I wish to thank the University of Texas at Austin (UT), the Centre National de la Recherche Scientifique (CNRS), the Netherlands Institute for Advanced Study (NIAS), the Helsinki Collegium for Advanced Studies (HCAS) and the Linguistics Summer School Bolivia (LSSB). My research has especially benefited from the following support: the UT Provost's Authors Fellowship Travel Fund, two UT Supplemental Research Fellowships, the CNRS LabEx Fellowship, the NIAS Individual Fellowship, the HCAS Fieldwork Grant, the HCAS Core Fellowship and the LSSB Excellence in Linguistics Research Award.

Some ideas and parts of chapters that appear in this book have also been enriched by the feedback provided by reviewers working for academic journals and edited volumes in which I have published studies related to Afro-Hispanic linguistics during the past decade. In particular, I should thank the anonymous reviewers of *Diachronica, Journal of Pidgin and Creole Languages, Language Ecology, Spanish in Context, Lingua, Sintagma, Humanities & Social Sciences Communications, Cuadernos de la Asociación de Lingüística y Filología de América Latina, Studies in Hispanic and Lusophone Linguistics, Isogloss, Revista Internacional de Lingüística Iberoamericana, Iberia, Papia* and *Folia Linguistica,* as well as those involved in the peer-review process of book chapters that appeared in a number of edited volumes published by John Benjamins, Routledge, Elsevier, de Gruyter and Iberoamericana. I am also indebted to my colleague and friend David Korfhagen (University of Virginia) and three anonymous reviewers who have commented on different drafts of this book. Special thanks go to Helen Barton, Isabel Collins and all the Cambridge University Press team for their help and professionalism during all the steps of this publication process.

Last but not least, I would like to express my deepest gratitude to all the Afro-Ecuadorians, Afro-Bolivians and Afro-Peruvians who participated in my research and who warmly welcomed me into their communities. Thank you!

1 *Questioning a Long-Lasting Assumption in the Field*

In accounting for the origins of several of the Spanish and Portuguese contact varieties spoken across the Americas, Africa and Asia, Granda (1968: 202–203) claimed that the grammatical similarities found among all these vernaculars should not be ascribed to the "independent production of exactly the same simplification processes,"[1] since that would be as absurd as the "parallel invention of the same alphabetic system in multiple and distant geographic locations."[2] Thus, according to his view (the Monogenesis Hypothesis), all these contact varieties must have developed from a common root, a proto-language, a once-spoken creole language, in this specific case. In fact, Granda proposed that an Afro-Lusophone creole would have formed around the fifteenth century along the western coasts of Africa, from the early contacts between Portuguese traders, explorers and missionaries, and the local African populations (see also Thompson 1961; Valkhoff 1966). This early contact language would then have been taken to several regions across Asia and the Americas during the following phase of European colonial expansion and, subsequently, its lexicon would have been systematically substituted with words proceeding from the European languages spoken in those colonies, thus essentially preserving its core grammatical structure. This would explain – in his view – why all those contact vernaculars share several linguistic traits.

In his analysis of Afro-European language evolution in the Americas, Granda also tried to address another important question: Why are Spanish creoles only spoken in two highly circumscribed regions of the Americas, in sharp contrast with the relative abundance of English- and French-based languages of this type? Indeed, the only two reported varieties that have traditionally been classified as Spanish-based creoles are Papiamento (spoken

---

[1] Original version in Spanish: "producción independiente de procesos de simplificación, exactamente coincidentes."
[2] Original version in Spanish: "invención paralela de un mismo sistema alfabético en múltiples y distantes puntos geográficos."

2 *Questioning a Long-Lasting Assumption in the Field*

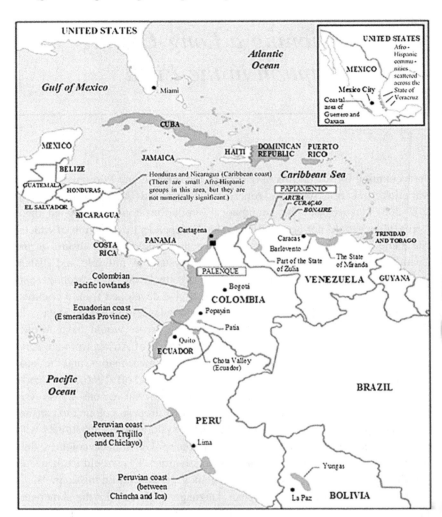

Map 1.1 *The Afro-Hispanic varieties of the Americas*

on the Caribbean islands of Aruba, Bonaire and Curaçao, Netherlands Antilles) and Palenquero (used in the small former maroon community of San Basilio de Palenque, Colombia). In order to account for the paucity of Spanish creoles Granda (1978) argued that the vast majority of the Afro-Hispanic varieties of the Americas (see Map 1.1, adapted from Klee & Lynch 2009: 6) went through a process of decreolization (Whinnom 1965), an incremental approximation to

Spanish, which would have taken place during the nineteenth century after the abolition of slavery, since the former slaves gradually obtained more and more access to the standard language (Decreolization Hypothesis).

According to what may be described as Granda's Monogenesis-Decreolization Hypothesis, therefore, Spanish slavery would have been quite comparable to the forced-labor systems implemented by the other European powers in the Americas, and, consequently, it must have generated similar creole languages. He summarizes his view on the origin of the Afro-Hispanic vernaculars of the Americas in four main points (1978: 335):

(a) Hispanic and non-Hispanic colonies were characterized by similar social structures. For this reason, Spanish creoles must have formed in Spanish Americas, as they did in other European colonies.
(b) Such Spanish creoles must have developed from a common Afro-Portuguese root.
(c) The current paucity of Spanish creoles in the Americas must be due to a contact-driven decreolization process, which took place during the nineteenth century.
(d) The deviant grammatical features found across these Afro-Hispanic dialects are the remaining traces of such a previous (de)creolization phase.

Granda's Monogenesis-Decreolization Hypothesis had a huge impact on the field of Afro-Hispanic linguistics and, even though today it is unlikely that any linguist would subscribe to its more radical version, which assumes that all Atlantic and Pacific creoles derived from one single proto-language (but see McWhorter 2000 for a somewhat similar proposal for English- and French-based varieties), the idea that the Afro-Hispanic dialects of the Americas developed out of a creole via decreolization is still quite common among linguists.

In fact, such a model has been proposed over and over, by several authors, to account for a number of the linguistic features found in almost every contemporary Afro-Hispanic variety. For example, Schwegler (1993, 1996), Otheguy (1973) and Megenney (1993) support a potential decreolization process for Caribbean Spanish. In this regard, Otheguy (1973: 334–335) could not be more explicit when, after analyzing several grammatical traits encountered across these dialects, he stated:

> In summary, the data presented here strongly suggest that the 'habla bozal' spoken in the Spanish Antilles (and possibly throughout the Caribbean) during colonial times was a Creole ... Given this, the sample points of

coincidence presented here between features which are shared by most Creoles but which are peculiar to Caribbean Spanish cannot be discarded as coincidence and must be taken into account in any explanation of the historical genesis of this major dialect type.

Granda (1977) and Schwegler (1991a, 1991b) propose a similar evolutionary path for Chocó Spanish (Colombia). Álvarez and Obediente (1998) indicate the same for coastal Afro-Venezuelan Spanish, Schwegler (1999) for Chota Valley Spanish (Ecuador), and Lipski (2008) and Perez (2015) do so for Afro-Bolivian Spanish. Schwegler (2014), in a more recent study, has further backed the hypothesis of a now-extinct Afro-Iberian creole for the black vernaculars spoken in Cartagena (Colombia), Chota Valley (Ecuador), Yungas (Bolivia) and Palo Monte (Cuba).

The most recent instance I have encountered of this long-lasting claim on the origin and evolution of the Afro-Latino varieties of the Americas is Guy (2017: 72), who selects Afro-Bolivian Spanish (ABS) to exemplify this hypothetical (de)creolization process, which, in his view, affected many other Afro-Hispanic and Afro-Lusophone vernaculars, including Popular Brazilian Portuguese (Guy 1981, 2004). He states:

> Its history of linguistic isolation implies that ABS must be more basilectal, closer to the speech of the earliest generations of Africans in the Americas, than Brazilian Portuguese and Caribbean Spanish. This in turn implies a historical trajectory by which all of these varieties started out as creoles, or at least restructured varieties tending toward the creole end ..., and then acquired their present form through differing degrees of standardization.

From a historical point of view, Granda's proposal does not seem to be based on solid ground. Several scholars have shown that the sociodemographic conditions for Spanish creole formation were not present in a number of former Spanish colonies (see, for example, Mintz 1971, Laurence 1974, Lipski 1993 and Clements 2009 for the Caribbean; Sessarego 2011a, 2013a, 2014a, 2015, 2019a for Bolivia, Ecuador, Peru and the Colombian Chocó; Díaz-Campos & Clements 2005, 2008 for Venezuela). Thus, on a case-by-case analysis, the (de)creolization model does not appear to be feasible.

Recent investigations have tried to provide a more comprehensive framework to account for the paucity of Spanish creoles in the Americas. By adding a legal dimension to this debate, it has been claimed that the relative scarcity of Spanish creoles in the Americas is, to a good extent, related to the peculiarities of the Spanish legal system in matters of black slavery, and, in particular, to the fact that the Spanish slave was the only one who was granted legal personhood and all the rights that the status of legal person implied. (See the Legal

Hypothesis of Creole Genesis, Sessarego 2015, 2017a, 2017b, 2018a.) This would have provided the Spanish slave with more access to the colonial language as well as more chances of achieving manumission and integrating into free society. This model has also been used to explain why the only Spanish creoles spoken in the Americas are actually found where Spanish law never applied: in the Netherlands Antilles (where Papiamento is spoken) and in the Colombian village of San Basilio de Palenque, a former maroon community, where, by definition, the Spanish Crown never managed to impose its rule (Sessarego 2018b, 2018c).

Conversely, the literature in support of the Decreolization Hypothesis has, for the most part, paid little attention to the sociohistorical and legal evidence available for colonial Spanish America. Rather, the (de)creolization proposal rests, first and foremost, on linguistic analyses, or on the idea that, since the contemporary Afro-Hispanic dialects of the Americas share several non-standard features, such grammatical elements must have derived from a common creole root. This approach is due to the traditional methodology creole studies inherited from the fields of dialectology and comparative historical linguistics. Schwegler (1991a: 74) provides a very precise picture of the logic behind this way of reasoning when he states:

> When we examine related dialects, such as Dominican Spanish, Cuban Spanish, Chocó Spanish or Cartagena Spanish/Palenquero, ..., the general dialectological and comparative historical linguistic practice is to assume that such dialects used to belong to an ancient diasystem, and that, for such a reason, they are not the result of independent innovations. As we have just suggested, the Afro-Portuguese creole hypothesis provides such an original diasystem ...[3]

Examples (1)–(5) and Figures 1.1–1.2 illustrate the most commonly mentioned "creole-like" traits that characterize these contact varieties. These features are exemplified here with data from a number of studies on Afro-Latino linguistics, which indicate their parallel presence across all of these vernaculars (see also Sessarego 2013b, 2019b and references therein).

---

[3] Original version in Spanish: "Cuando examinamos dialectos relacionados como el español dominicano, el cubano, el chocoano o el cartagenero/palenquero, ..., la general práctica de la dialectología y la lingüística histórica y comparativa es de suponer que tales dialectos pertenecían a un antiguo diasistema, y que, por lo tanto, no son el resultado de innovaciones independientes. Como acabamos de sugerir, la hipótesis criolla afroportuguesa proporciona tal diasistema de base ..."

(1) Use of non-emphatic, non-contrastive overt subject pronouns
   a. Yo tando muy pequeña yo conocí a una señora
      I being very young I knew to a woman
      'When I was young I met a woman.' (Barlovento Spanish, Megenney 1999: 117)
   b. Cuando él hace en la casa de él, me llama él
      when he makes in the house of he me call he
      'When he makes it at his house, he calls me.' (Chocó Spanish, Rodríguez Tocarruncho 2010: 61)
(2) Invariant verb forms for person and number
   a. Yo sabe
      I know.3.SG
      'I know.' (Afro-Puertorican, Álvarez Nazario 1974: 194)
   b. Yo quiele sé diputá
      I want.3.SG be deputee
      'I want to be a deputee.' (Afro-Peruvian Bozal Spanish, Lipski 2005: 253)
(3) Lack of subject–verb inversion in questions
   a. ¿Onde tú taba, mijito?
      where you was my-son
      'Where were you, my son?' (Barlovento Spanish, Megenney 1999: 118)
   b. ¿Qué ella dijo?
      what she said
      'What did she say?' (Chincha Spanish, Sessarego 2015: 58)
(4) Lack of gender agreement in the Determiner Phrase
   a. Nuestro cultura antiguo
      our.M culture.F old.M
      'Our old culture.' (Yungueño Spanish, Lipski 2008: 89)
   b. Mugué malo
      woman.F bad.M
      'Bad woman.' (Afro-Puertorican, Álvarez Nazario 1974: 189)
(5) Lack of number agreement in the Determiner Phrase
   a. Tan chicquito puej mij nene
      are little.SG well my.PL baby.PL
      'Well, my kids are little.' (Afro-Mexican Spanish, Mayén 2007: 117)
   b. Cuatro hermano joven
      four brother.PL young.SG
      'Four young brothers.' (Chota Valley Spanish, Sessarego 2013a: 70)

Figures 1.1 and 1.2 depict constructions showing pitch-accent configurations that present early-peak alignment with the stressed syllable (Sessarego 2019a: 120; Rao & Sessarego 2016: 56).

This book is about contact-induced language change. In particular, this study strives to provide a formal account for the parallel presence in the Afro-Hispanic languages of the Americas (AHLAs) of the aforementioned

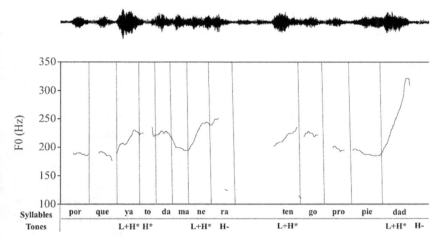

Figure 1.1 *Sample F0 contours for* Porque ya no da manera ... tengo propiedad *'Because there is no way ... I own property' in Chocó Spanish*

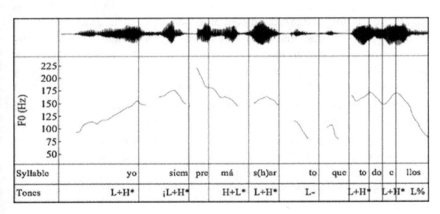

Figure 1.2 *Sample F0 contours for* Yo siempre más harto que todo ellos *'I am always much more than all of them' in Yungueño Spanish*

linguistic features, without falling back on the traditionally assumed proto-creole explanation. The questions to be answered are as follows: How did those features come about? What are the linguistic mechanisms that can account for their parallel existence in several contact varieties? How can we formalize such mechanisms within a comprehensive theoretical framework? How can these new datasets help us test and possibly refine current formal theories, which have primarily been based on standardized language data?

The analyses presented in this study to answer these questions are primarily based on data from three specific AHLAs: Yungueño Spanish (YS), from Bolivia; Chota Valley Spanish (CVS), from Ecuador; and Chincha Spanish (CS), from Peru. These data were collected over the past 10 years during a number of fieldwork visits to the local Afro-Latino communities (Sessarego 2011a, 2013a, 2014a, 2015). In this study, I refer at times to all of these varieties with a single umbrella term, "Afro-Andean Spanish." I do this for the sake of simplicity, even though CS is not technically spoken in the Andes, since Chincha is located on the Peruvian coast. For the same reason, I often refer here to Ecuador, Bolivia and Peru as Andean countries or as territories belonging to the Andean region, and when describing the sociohistorical development of these dialects I talk about "the African Diaspora to the Andes." This is done with the goal of providing the reader with a set of broad terms to refer to these Afro-Hispanic vernaculars and to the regions in which they are spoken as entities belonging to the same group, since they share a common historical and linguistic background.

Given the grammatical parallelisms encountered across these three dialects and the rest of the AHLAs, the model proposed here can be generalized to all such contact varieties, thus accounting for the commonalities traditionally ascribed to the (de)creolization of a hypothetical creole diasystem. Moreover, as we will see in the following chapters, such features are not actually only exclusive of the AHLAs; rather, they tend to appear in most varieties of Spanish in contact with other languages. Thus, this indicates that they are not necessarily the effect of a specific set of African substrate languages. Conversely, these grammatical phenomena are driven by common, contact-induced processes, which are related to processing constraints affecting the interfaces between different language modules; hence, they are universal and depend on the nature of the architecture of the language faculty (Sessarego 2019b).

1.1 The Creole Debate

For the past 30 years the field of contact linguistics has been characterized by a heated debate, recently labeled the Creole Debate (McWhorter 2018a), which focuses on the structural and typological status of creole languages. On the one hand, some scholars have claimed that creoles may be classified according to their structural properties (Bickerton 1981) or as a typological class (Bakker et al. 2011, 2016; McWhorter 1998, 2001; Seuren & Wekker 1986). In particular, McWhorter (1998) proposed a "Creole Prototype," according to which a creole would be generally characterized by: (1) minimal inflectional affixation; (2) minimal use of tones; and (3) semantically transparent derivation. McWhorter (2001: 5) even claimed that creoles should be seen as "the world's simplest grammars," since, having developed out of pidgins just a few hundred years ago, they would not have had the time to enrich their systems with the structural complexities – often resulting from long processes of grammaticalization – which appear to characterize older languages.

On the other hand, other scholars have rejected these analyses and prefer to depict creoles as by-products of their shared sociocultural history, often related to black slavery and plantation societies (DeGraff 2003; Mufwene 1997), thus claiming that creoles do not show anything exceptional from a strictly linguistic point of view (DeGraff 2005), and that describing them as "simpler" is just a controversial statement, which may be unconsciously derived from the racist bias that the European colonizers had about the Africans' cognitive skills to learn European languages (Aboh & DeGraff 2016: 5).

A recent contribution to the Creole Debate is the proposal offered by Aboh (2015), who conceives of these languages as mixed grammars. In his view, a creole, like any other contact variety, would be the result of a combination of features proceeding from the pool of languages that were in contact, according to a competitive mechanism driven by environmental and/or ecological factors (Mufwene 2001). Aboh (2015: 8), therefore, argues that creoles are not at all "exceptional;" rather they "represent a normal instance of language change resulting from the contact between typologically different and genetically unrelated languages (e.g., Romance/German vs. Kwa/Bantu [Niger-Congo])." This would be the only reason why the structural changes observed in creoles tend to be more contrastive than in other contact varieties.

The most recent study on this ongoing debate has been published by Blasi, Michaelis and Haspelmath (2017: 723), who, after running several R simulations on a database of 44 creole languages and 111 non-creole languages (R Core Team 2016), concluded that "while a creole profile can be detected statistically, this stems from an over-representation of Western European and West African languages in their context of emergence," so that "grammars are robustly transmitted even during the emergence of creole languages," which calls into "question the existence of a pidgin stage in creole development and of creole-specific innovations." Blasi et al. (2017), therefore, echo Aboh's (2015) proposal in that they suggest that creoles are essentially a mix of Western European and West African features, while it also appears to provide quantitative support for the claims against both the simplicity of creole grammars and the loss of grammatical features during creolization.

Deconstructing the notion of "creole" and taking sides in the aforementioned debate is neither the topic nor the point of this book. Nevertheless, I will summarize in a nutshell the problems I see with the way this debate has been carried out and, after presenting my personal opinion on the matter in Section 1.1.1, I will offer a working definition of "creole" in Section 1.1.2 to help readers better understand why I do not think most AHLAs went through any (de)creolization phase.

1.1.1 My Two Cents

First of all, as recently explained in Sessarego (2020), I have to say that I do not think that *grammars are robustly transmitted during the emergence of creole languages* (in contrast with Blasi et al. 2017), since certain core aspects of language (e.g., bound morphology and tones) tend to be reduced during creolization; at the same time, I would not say that *creoles are the simplest languages in the world* (against McWhorter 2001, 2018a), since in other aspects of their grammars (e.g., syntax, phonology and semantics), they may inherit a fair number of overt distinctions, which would make them quite complex, from an overall comparative perspective.

In order to understand why the varieties we call "creoles" today look the way they look, it is of fundamental importance to figure out what cognitive processes were at work in the minds of their creators. Without a serious reflection on such mental processes (and the nature of the grammatical restructuring they imply), counting the number of features that creoles may have inherited from one language or another does not help much. It would be a purely *descriptive exercise*, not an *explanatory analysis*. Even the most recent publication on this topic, Blasi et al. (2017), is quite limited in this sense. In fact, the study tries to provide statistical support in favor of this supposedly "robust" grammatical transmission without offering any possible explanation for why that may be the case. The authors acknowledge this shortcoming. Thus, they conclude by admitting that they do not know the reasons behind their findings (2017: 5):

> Why such a complex human behavior can be successfully transmitted even in the typical (intricate and multilingual) contact situations of creoles is still unclear ... Either way, our results reflect the astonishing resilience of language transmission.

In order to cast light on this apparently mysterious issue, it is crucial to acknowledge that creole formation involves – to a good extent – adult second-language acquisition (SLA) processes in a context of intense language contact.

This being said, it becomes relevant to the analysis to distinguish between *two different types of grammatical transfers*, which characterize the speech of any adult trying to acquire a foreign tongue. To do so, I rely on the classification of Winford (2003), who adopts van Coetsem's (1988) notion of language agentivity. Thus, I distinguish between *borrowing*, which primarily affects lexical items and occurs under Recipient Language (RL) agentivity, and *imposition*, which concerns structure (syntax, phonology and semantics) and is driven by Source Language (SL) agentivity. With these notions in mind, it appears reasonable to expect creole varieties, which were predominantly created by adult speakers of African languages, to present a significant number of syntactic, phonological and semantic features proceeding from those substrate African languages, while displaying lexical features from the European languages (the "lexifiers"). In addition to these two different transfer types, there is at least one more fundamental process that applies during SLA, *grammatical reduction*. This tends to significantly affect bound morphology and tones (i.e., morphological and tonal features), which are often conceived in the SLA literature as the "bottleneck of acquisition" (Slabakova 2008, 2009). Unlike *borrowing* and *imposition*, which *result in the transfer* of syntactic, semantic, phonological and lexical features, *grammatical reduction* implies a *strong tendency not to transfer* morphological and tonal features.

Any study claiming that "grammars are robustly transmitted even during the emergence of creoles" (Blasi et al. 2017: 723) should show how *all* of the aforementioned components of grammar get transmitted. Blasi et al. do not do so, since as can be observed in their appendix (see Blasi et al. 2017, Supplementary Table 3, pages 8–11), they do not account thoroughly for the morphological and tonal features of the lexifier and substrate languages. Of the 92 features I counted in Blasi et al.'s dataset, 30 belong to the domain of syntax (e.g., order of adjective and noun), 27 to semantics (e.g., indefinite articles), 12 to phonology (e.g., schwa), 7 to the lexicon (e.g., *pequenino*), 15 to morphology (e.g., gender in independent personal pronouns) and 1 to tones (e.g., presence of tone). The sample is obviously highly skewed toward syntactic and semantic features, which together make up some 62 percent of the dataset. On the other hand, morphology and tones, which are at the core of the Creole Debate, make up only 17 percent of the data. Going back to our theoretical assumptions, this means that 83 percent of the features here analyzed belong to the processes we identified as *borrowing* and *imposition*, which, as indicated, consist of *two different types of transfer*.

Given that these computer simulations per se do not explain the processes at work in creolization, there are infinite ways in which the feature database could be built to back one theory or the other. Blasi et al., consciously or not, have created a feature pool that supports a theory of creolization in which pretty much any ancestor feature is perfectly *transferred* to the creole language. They achieved that by (randomly) excluding tones and morphology from the dataset. Obviously, if such features were added to the code, the R simulation would tell us a completely different story. For a paper that is aimed at casting light on the Creole Debate, this looks quite puzzling, since most of the tensions in the literature have actually gravitated around those features (McWhorter 1998, 2001; DeGraff 2003, 2005; Bakker et al. 2011, 2016; Aboh 2016).

Quite surprisingly, at the beginning of Blasi et al.'s study, the authors indirectly admit that morphology is significantly reduced during SLA, since they state that "languages with larger populations tend to have simpler morphology, presumably due to the larger number of non-native speakers" (2017: 723). For this reason, one would expect that at least morphology would be coded into their computational model. However, toward the conclusion of their study, it becomes obvious that that was not the case. Indeed, on the last page of their paper they state that, according to their feature database, creoles do not present any significant innovation with respect to their substrates and lexifiers, but that this may not necessarily be the case for all aspects of grammar, since some areas, "such as morphology" were "not well covered by [the] data" (Blasi et al. 2017: 727).

Given this particular feature selection, which was in part constrained by the availability of data in the atlases, the results obtained by Blasi et al. should be expected. They essentially offer a complex computational model to provide quantitative evidence for something that would appear quite intuitive to most people working in linguistics: the lexical features of creoles mainly proceed from their Western European lexifiers (as the word "lexifier" already suggests); some of the structural features of creoles are transferred from their West African substrate languages.

This account, therefore, *describes* (some of) the data, but *does not explain* them. It presents two main fallacies: (i) it does not distinguish between the two types of feature transfer (*borrowing* vs. *imposition*), and consequently it does not explain why the lexicon tends to come from one group of languages, while structure is derived from the other group; and (ii) it does not account for the *grammatical reduction* of morphology and tones, and therefore does not clearly acknowledge that some aspects of grammar are *not* robustly transmitted during creolization.

Not acknowledging the presence of these three distinct processes during creolization, and therefore treating all features in the same way, is misleading, since it reduces creole formation to a random mix of features, which would be grouped together without any systematicity. That is not how creoles developed. The problem with Blasi et al.'s (2017) study is that it seems to forget altogether that the kind of grammatical restructuring that shaped creoles was necessarily mediated by SLA processes. The vast majority of creole creators, in fact, were not proficient bilinguals of African and European languages. For this reason, equating creoles to mixed languages cannot possibly be sustained from a cognitive perspective, since the processes at work in the formation of these two types of contact varieties are necessarily different.

Mixed languages, such as Media Lengua (Muysken 1997: 365), are the result of proficient bilinguals who voluntarily decide to combine two languages they speak, usually for identity and/or ludic reasons. In (6), it can be observed how Media Lengua consists of Spanish lexical items systematically embedded into Quichua morphosyntax. This is only possible because the creators of Media Lengua were proficient speakers of both Spanish and Quichua, and thus they could freely "mix and match" their lexicons and structures. Thus, as is clear from (6), the morphological richness of Quichua is well preserved in Media Lengua. Conversely, the same cannot be stated for the creole Palenquero (7) (McWhorter 2018b: 9–10), in which the morphological richness of Kikongo and Spanish has been lost.

(6) a. Shuk fabur-da mana-nga-bu shamu-xu-ni   Quichua
       one favor-ACC ask-NOM-BEN come-PROG-1
       'I come to ask a favor.'
    b. Vengo para pedir un favor   Spanish
       come-1 to ask-INF a favor
       'I come to ask a favor.'
    c. Unu fabur-ta pidi-nga-bu bini-xu-ni   Media Lengua
       one favor-ACC ask-NOM-BEN come-PROG-1
       'I come to ask a favor.'

(7) a. O ma-tadi ma-ma ma-mpembe ma-mpwena   Kikongo (Bentley 1887: 526)
       AUG C8P-stone C8P-DEM C8P-white C8P-big
       i ma-u ma-ma tw-a-mw-ene
       COP C8P-that C8P-DEM we-them-see-PERF.
       'These great white stones are those which we have seen.' (C8P = noun class 8 plural)
    b. Est-a-s piedra-s grande-s y blanc-a-s   Spanish
       DEM-FEM-PL stone-FEM-PL big-FEM-PL and white-FEM-PL
       son las que hemos visto.
       COP-3P DEF-FEM-PL REL have-1PL see-PP
       'These great white stones are those which we have seen.'

c. Ese ma piegra blanko é ese ke suto a miná Palenquero
   this PL stone white is this REL 1PL PAST see
   'These great white stones are those which we have seen.'

This is because the creators of creole languages were not bilinguals in African and European languages who decided to mix those grammars for ludic and/or identity reasons; rather, they were, for the most part, adult speakers of African languages, who acquired some aspects of the European languages (primarily the lexicon) to create a new means of interethnic communication, on which they inevitably *imposed* some aspects of their L1s (primarily the syntax, phonology and semantics).

While both Media Lengua and Palenquero can be *described* as displaying features from Spanish, Quichua or Kikongo, the *explanation* for why they look so different from one another cannot certainly be the same. The reason for this is that grammars are not robustly transmitted during creolization, since morphology and tones are particularly hard to master during untutored SLA, as we will see in more detail in Chapters 4–6 of this book. On the other hand, in the context of mixed languages, which is characterized by a more balanced level of bilingualism, those components of grammar are more easily preserved and passed on to the newly created contact variety.

At this point, I wish to stress that my analysis is not meant to be polemic, and that I can certainly see how Aboh's proposal can be understood as suggesting that *all* contact situations involve some degree of hybridization. This being said, I think we really need to be clear on the fact that somewhat similar results may have been created by very different processes. In particular, it would be a mistake to treat the processes that shaped mixed languages like those behind creole formation. While mixed languages originated in communities with a high level of bilingualism, creoles developed in multilingual contexts in which the access to the European languages was much more constrained and the motivations to develop a new, hybrid variety were significantly different.

The data so far presented have shown that, owing to the process of *grammatical reduction*, creole languages tend to present fewer morphological and tonal complexities than their lexifiers and substrate languages. Nevertheless, I think it would be a mistake to claim that they are actually "the world's simplest languages" (McWhorter 2001: 5). This is because processes of borrowing and imposition can introduce overt distinctions in these languages that make them relatively complex. This is particularly evident for the aspects of the grammar that tend to be more significantly affected by imposition phenomena (e.g., semantics, syntax and phonology). I will exemplify these complexities by analyzing Sranan Tongo, an English-base creole from Suriname with a strong Gbe component among its substrate languages. This language has been defined as a "radical creole" on multiple occasions (Bickerton 1981; Winford 2000), and thus it would be extremely simple according to McWhorter's proposal.

It is not uncommon to detect in creole languages certain semantic distinctions that exist in substrate languages but are absent in their lexifiers. This means that, in such aspects of their grammars, creoles may actually be conceived as more complex than their ancestor European languages. For example, Gbe presents a rich copula system, which distinguishes among predicative noun phrases, adjectives and locative phrases. As can be observed in (8), the Sranan copula system preserves such distinctions, which do not exist in English.

(8) a. Den. tu man **na** skowtu
 the.PL two man COP police
 'The two men are policemen.' (Wilner 1992: 47)
 b. A pikin Ø siki
 DET child sick
 'The child is ill.' (Winford 1997: 238)
 c. A owru **de** baka a doro
 DET machete COP back DET door
 'The machete is behind the door.' (Wilner 1992: 18)

This example, therefore, shows how African language speakers, while creating Sranan, imposed their semantic L1 categories on the means of interethnic communication they were targeting (Baker 1990). This resulted in a copula system that presents more overt distinctions than the English one, and that, consequently, may be classified as more complex.

Certain syntactic structures found in creoles appear to have been transferred via imposition from their substrate languages, even though they may be considered typologically marked. One clear example is serial verb constructions, which, again, can be encountered in Sranan and Gbe and are not present in English. Thus, besides the English-like verb constructions, Sranan also displays Gbe-like serial verbs. This richness in verb configurations may be conceived as an additional layer of complexity belonging to Sranan that English does not show.

(9) a. Kofi **hari** a pikin **komoto na** ini a olo
 Kofi pull DET child come-out LOC in DET hole
 'Kofi pulled the child out of the hole.' (Winford 2008: 33)

b. Kofi **teki** a nefi **koti** a brede
Kofi take DET knife cut DET bread
'Kofi cut the bread with a knife.' (Winford & Migge 2008: 710)

When pronouncing words in a foreign language it is inevitable that one imposes on such lexical items some of the phonological patterns of their L1. Such a process may result in the simplification of certain aspects of the target language phonological inventory, as well as in the complexification of others, especially if the creole creators are multilingual in a number of African languages and the lexical items to be acquired come from a variety of grammatical systems. An instance of this in Sranan may be exemplified by the existence of four nasal phonemes /m, n, ɲ, ŋ/, while English presents only three /m, n, ŋ/, as shown by the minimal pairs in (10) and (11).

(10) Sranan
    a. /**m**a/ 'but' vs. /**n**a/ 'to be'
    b. /**ɲ**an/ 'to eat' vs. /**m**an/ 'man'
    c. /toŋo/ 'tongue' vs. /toko/ 'trouble'
(11) English
    a. /tʌŋ/ 'tongue' vs. /tʌn/ 'ton'
    b. /mæm/ 'mam' vs. /mæn/ 'man'

To conclude, this section has provided an overview of the so-called Creole Debate and its most recent developments. As I have indicated, my position is on neither side of this controversy. Rather, I think the best way to cast light on the nature of creoles (and of any other contact variety, for that matter) would be to focus on the cognitive processes that shaped them. Conversely, counting the number of features that creoles may have inherited from one language or another – selecting them randomly, without discriminating among them, and without understanding the processes behind their formation – does not appear to be of much help to explain how creoles came about. Important to the goals of this book is to notice that native-like morphosyntactic and prosodic patterns are particularly hard to master in SLA and, for this reason, the reduction and subsequent reorganization of features in these aspects of grammar are not only present in creole languages. Rather, these phenomena are also highly persistent in *advanced* L2 varieties and, consequently, can be commonly detected in most contact languages. They clearly belong to the AHLAs, which, as it will be shown, have been shaped by advanced SLA processes.

1.1.2 Degrees of Contact-Driven Restructuring

Having summarized in a nutshell some of my main objections to both sides of the Creole Debate and having highlighted three key processes operating in contact-driven restructuring, I wish to offer a working definition of "creole" (at least from a structural perspective), which will help better understand why I do not believe most Afro-Hispanic varieties went through a (de)creolization phase.

Part of the reason why defining the notion of creole linguistically is so difficult is that it has to do with interpreting a historically specific sociocultural concept as a typological class. Indeed, a peculiarity of our field, creolistics, is that there is no common consensus among scholars on what creole languages are. As illustrated in Section 1.1, while some colleagues have tried to describe creoles according to certain grammatical features (Bickerton 1981; Seuren & Wekker 1986; McWhorter 1998, 2001, 2018a; Bakker et al. 2011, Bakker, Levisen & Sippola 2016), others have rejected any kind of typological approach, arguing that there is nothing exceptional about creole grammars, since it is only their social history – often related to black slavery and colonization – that makes them somehow "different" or "special" (Mufwene 1997, 2001; DeGraff 2003, 2005). A third, middle-ground, approach to creoles, which probably describes how most of our colleagues feel about the subject, is presented by Schwegler (2010) in an article reviewing the current standing of pidgin and creole studies. He suggests that it is the "combination of internal linguistic features and shared external history that gives creoles exceptional status" (2010: 435), and for this reason, "conceptual terminology such as 'creole,' 'creolist,' 'creolistic,' 'creolization' and so forth continues to be applied without hesitation by most creolists, including those who reject the possibility of defining 'creole' as a class" (2010: 438).

Besides this wide range of conceptual definitions, it must also be said that under the "creole umbrella" there are varieties that appear to have undergone more grammatical restructuring than others; some present stronger traces of the African input, while others more closely resemble the European lexifiers. Given this heterogeneous situation, additional terms, such as "semi-creole" (Holm 1992) or "intermediate creoles" (Winford 2000), have been coined to classify vernaculars that would be placed somewhere along what may be viewed as a "creole thermometer" (Lipski 2008: 183). These contact languages, therefore, could be located – just for practical convenience – along a continuum of "creoleness," ranging from close approximations to the lexifiers to varieties presenting extreme substrate retention (see Alleyne 1980: 181), as illustrated in Figure 1.3 (adapted from Winford 2000: 216).

For the sake of practice and the need to employ a more stable metric of comparison across these vernaculars, I will adopt the structural distinction drawn by McWhorter (2000) between "creole" and "dialect." Indeed, even though this author acknowledges that contact-driven restructuring operates

```
←Slight substrate retention ←→Moderate←→ Extreme L1 retention→
```

```
Advanced ←→ 'Indigenized' ←→ Intermediate ←→ Basilectal ←→ Radical
Interlanguage     varieties           creoles              creoles         creoles
```

Figure 1.3 *A continuum of outcomes involving degrees of substrate and L2 input*

along a continuum, he highlights how such a range does "not invalidate the usefulness of a perceptual distinction between dialect and creole" (McWhorter 2000: 10). Thus, according to this distinction, creoles tend to show more radical signs of contact-driven restructuring (i.e., highly reduced inflectional morphology, abundant presence of substrate structures, etc.), which make them significantly diverge from their lexifiers, while dialects present fewer signs of contact (i.e., more moderate morphological reductions, some African lexical borrowings, etc.) and thus converge more closely with the European varieties to the point of being mutually intelligible. Given this broad distinction between creole and dialect, contact vernaculars like CVS, CS, YS and most AHLAs, in contrast to varieties such as Papiamento and Palenquero, would be better classified as belonging to the second group. In fact, they would be located on the leftmost side of this hypothetical continuum (see Figure 1.3), since they present minimal substrate retention as well as traces of advanced SLA processes (see also Perez, Sessarego & Sippola 2017).

Some colleagues may wonder if it would be feasible to treat the aforementioned non-standard phenomena characterizing the AHLAs as archaisms, and thus assume that they were already present in colonial Spanish and were preserved in some rural and/or isolated Afro-Hispanic communities, while disappearing from other Spanish dialects. This hypothesis, I think, is highly unlikely for two main reasons: first, there is no evidence that the aforesaid grammatical traits ever existed in the history of Spanish (Nebrija [1492], 1981; Bello [1847], 2011; Lapesa 1981; Penny 2002); second, as will be shown in this book, these features appear systematically in Spanish contact vernaculars, and are even common in contemporary Spanish contact varieties that have nothing to do with colonial Spanish, such as the speech of advanced L2 classroom learners (Montrul 2004; Geeslin 2013). That being said, the question left to be answered is: Were these AHLAs "creoles" that became "dialects" after an intense process of decreolization, or were they "dialects" (i.e., relatively similar to what they are now) in the first place?

According to the supporters of the Monogenetic-Decreolization Hypothesis, these vernaculars would have become dialects after a gradual approximation to Spanish. This assumption, I suggest, is not on the right track, since neither linguistic nor sociohistorical evidence appears to support it. Conversely, the available information for these vernaculars indicates that, with all probability, these AHLAs did not change much from their original inception (Sessarego 2011b, 2013c, 2014b, 2014c, 2016a, 2017b, 2017c, 2017d, 2017e, 2019c). In this book, I argue that the so-called AHLA "creole-like" features, on which the Monogenetic-Decreolization Hypothesis has been built, should not necessarily be ascribed to a previous (de)creolization phase; rather, they can perfectly be explained as the expected by-product of *universal interface-driven processes of advanced SLA*, which were nativized and conventionalized by subsequent generations of speakers (Sessarego 2013b, 2019b).

1.2 Second-Language Acquisition and Creole Formation

Among the first scholars to highlight the connection between SLA processes and creole formation are Schumann (1978) and Andersen (1980, 1983), who suggested that pidginization resembled in a number of structural aspects the early stages of untutored SLA. During the past few decades, the study of how SLA processes may have shaped the formation of pidgins and creoles has received significant attention, which resulted in a fruitful cross-fertilization between the fields of language acquisition and creolistics (Kouwenberg & Patrick 2003; Lefebvre, White & Jourdan 2006; Siegel 2008).

A relatively recent proposal that attempts to combine aspects from these two fields to cast light on the nature and evolution of creole languages is the Interlanguage Hypothesis of Creole Formation by Plag (2008a, 2008b, 2009a, 2009b). This hypothesis adopts insights from Pienemann's (1998, 2000) Processability Theory, at the core of which is the quest for why there appears to be a *common universal sequence in the development of second languages*, independently of the speakers' native languages (L1s). Processability Theory, which assumes psycholinguistic models of speech production along the lines of those designed by Kempen and Hoenkamp (1987) and Levelt (1989), addresses this problem by proposing that language processing procedures obey a hierarchy of activations in language generation that, in turn, determines their order of acquisition.

Pienemann (2000) illustrates this developmental path with data from English as a second language (L2). Indeed, studies on SLA have repeatedly shown that L2 learners, independently of their L1s, tend to follow a specific sequence of

Table 1.1 *Developmental stages in English interlanguage syntax*

Development	Structure	Example
Initial state	One-word utterance	Ball
	Canonical word order	Bob kick ball (SVO)
	Neg + V	He no like coffee
	Adverb fronting	Then Bob kick ball
	Topicalization	That I didn't like
	Do-fronting	Do you like it?
	Yes-No inversion	Has he seen you?
	Copula inversion	Where is John?
	Particle verbs	Take the hat off
	Do/aux 2nd	Why did he sell that car? Where has he gone?
Target	Cancel inversion	I wonder why he sold that car

acquisition in English, as shown in Table 1.1. They begin by producing one word at a time to increasingly form more complex structures, according to a hierarchical sequence. In some cases, they manage to achieve higher proficiency levels, and thus become able to generate more processing-demanding structures, such as the canceling of inversion in subordinate interrogative clauses.

Plag's Interlanguage Hypothesis embraces the notion of a hierarchy of second-language development – on which Processability Theory is built – to suggest that certain common aspects of creole grammars (i.e., highly reduced inflectional morphology, the unmarked nature of many syntactic structures, the conflation of phonological categories, cases of circumlocutions, etc.) may be conceived of as the structural traits of *conventionalized interlanguages of an early stage* (Plag 2008a: 115). Thus, the contact varieties Plag is referring to in this case are those that would be placed on the rightmost side of the creole continuum, like basilectal and radical creoles (see Figure 1.3).

Without delving into the details of Plag's model here, there is a notion of his proposal that I wish to highlight, since it appears to also be highly relevant to the current project on the AHLAs: there is a *universal hierarchy of SLA* that constrains language development and thus shapes the grammars of all contact varieties. This aspect of L2 development, I argue, is the key to understanding the nature and origin of the Afro-Hispanic "creole-like" elements. In fact, as it will be explained in the following chapters, these features can be conceived of as the result of *advanced* SLA processes. For this reason, as far as these specific structures are concerned, most AHLAs could be classified – to adopt Plag's terminology – as *conventionalized advanced second languages* (Sessarego 2013b).

1.3 Vernacular Universals

A thorough analysis of the emergence and conventionalization of the "creole-like" elements encountered in the AHLAs cannot be exclusively restricted to the SLA processes that generated them; rather, it should also include a sociolinguistic model capable of casting light on why they were adopted by the members of these communities and maintained in their speech until the present day. A model that may provide us with proper insights into the aforementioned issues is the theory of Vernacular Universals (Chambers 2003, 2004). According to Chambers' proposal, in fact, a reduced set of phonological and morphosyntactic features tend to characterize vernaculars, no matter where they are spoken. He calls such features "vernacular roots" and suggests that, in some sense, these non-standard traits are easier to produce and thus *more natural* than their standard counterparts (Chambers 2003: 266–270).

The idea that vernaculars may be conceived of as more natural systems, since they present constructions that tend to be artificially removed from the monitored prestige variety by prescriptive processes of standardization, is nothing new in sociolinguistic theorizing (Mühlhäusler 1986; Weiss 2001). In fact, Kroch (1978: 18), building on Labov's (1966, 1972a, 1974) work in the formulation of his phonological theory of social dialect variation, already highlighted how the prestigious variety "characteristically resists normal processes of phonetic conditioning (both articulatory and perceptual) that the speech of non-elite strata regularly undergoes." Chambers (2004: 128), however, goes a step further, claiming that these vernacular roots are the natural by-product of "the species-specific bioprogram that allows (indeed, requires) normal human beings to become *homo loquens*." Chambers (2004: 128–129) claims the universality of such features since they "occur not only in working-class and rural vernaculars but also in child language, pidgins, creoles and interlanguage varieties" and provides a list of the most common ones for English:

- (ng) or alveolar substitution in final unstressed *–ing*, as in *walkin'*, *talkin'*, and *runnin'*.
- (CC) or morpheme-final consonant cluster simplification, as in *pos'office*, *han'ful*.
- Final obstruent devoicing, as in *hundret* (for hundred), *cubbert* (for cupboard).
- Conjugation regularization or leveling of irregular verb forms, as in *Yesterday John seen the eclipse*, or *Mary heared the good news*.
- Default singulars, or subject–verb non-concord, as in *They was the last ones*.

- Multiple negation, or negative concord, as in *He didn't see nothing*.
- Copula absence, or copula deletion, as in *She smart* or *We going as soon as possible*.

I personally find it a bit overstretched to claim that these features should be understood as "the natural outgrowths ... of the language faculty" (2004: 128). Moreover, Chambers' formulation of his proposal is reminiscent of Bickerton's (1981) Bioprogram Hypothesis on the formation of creole languages, which has been proven wrong on a number of sociohistorical and linguistic matters (see Winford 2003: 304–357 for an overview). Nevertheless, I think that Chambers makes a very good point when he claims that pidgins, creoles and interlanguages tend to share a number of vernacular traits. This is because features that imply less processing and metalinguistic control are acquired first, and thus they tend to appear both in contact languages and in unmonitored speech. As a result, all of these varieties will share structures that tend to be easier to produce and acquire and, in this sense, are "more natural" or "less marked" (Battistella 1990).

Determining the naturalness of linguistic phenomena is not always an easy task, not even for the aforementioned vernacular forms listed by Chambers. Indeed, while consonant cluster simplifications may be analyzed as the effect of more economic motor-articulatory movements, which can be measured (Chambers 2003: 258–259), it is not so easy to demonstrate, for example, that negative concord is more natural than single negation (2004: 129). In fact, it is true that double negation tends to be found in most English vernaculars, but before claiming that it is more natural or less marked, further linguistic evidence should be provided, such as establishing whether it is really less costly to process and easier to acquire in L2. Nevertheless, as for the "creole-like" features characterizing YS, CVS, CS and the rest of the AHLAs, there is enough evidence showing that these forms are easier to process than their standard Spanish counterparts. In fact, they are even commonly detected in the speech of advanced L2 speakers, who often do not achieve the proficiency level required to master the most complex target language (TL) forms (Montrul 2004; Geeslin 2013).

The theory of Vernacular Universals combines aspects of sociolinguistics and cognitive linguistics. From a sociolinguistic point of view, the vernacular roots represent the features characterizing the basilect or non-prestigious variety; from a cognitive perspective, they are related to processing strategies and principles of articulatory motor economies. As Chambers puts it (2004:

130), "unifying the functional principles into a few empirical defensible cognitive strategies may be too much to ask of any branch of linguistics at this time, important though is to try." In this regard, I would add that this objective may be achieved, at least in part and for the Afro-Hispanic contact varieties, if we integrate proposals from other linguistic branches, such as SLA (e.g., Pienemann's Processability Theory) and creolistics (e.g., Plag's Interlanguage Hypothesis), into this model.

Chambers' (2003: 254) proposal echoes Kroch's when he says that "the standard dialect differs from other dialects by resisting certain natural tendencies in the grammar and phonology"; he goes even further when he states that "the basilectal form is primitive, part of the innate bioprogram, and the standard form is learned, an experiential excrescence on the bioprogram" (2003: 286). This last idea is also much in line with Gadet and Pagel's (2019) notion of "natural" in ecological linguistics. The authors, in fact, elaborate on Mühlhäusler's (1986: 61–62) notion of a prestigious variety as a "cultural artefact" to claim that "naturalness decreases as the pressure of social and cultural forces increases, which is a path followed by all languages" (Gadet & Pagel 2019: 63).

I am not in the position to say whether all of the features Chambers (2003, 2004) indicated as English vernacular roots would emerge spontaneously in cases of standard L1 acquisition. Nevertheless, as far as the AHLAs and other contact varieties are concerned, it is definitely possible to affirm that a certain set of grammatical traits are easier to acquire/process than others, and unless social pressure pushes them out of language, there is no reason why they could not be adopted and conventionalized at the community level, becoming – in this way – part of the contact grammar that would be natively acquired by the following generations of speakers. As I will argue in the rest of this book, the rural Afro-Andean communities of Yungas, Chota Valley and Chincha represented the perfect locations for such a conventionalization to take place, since they were – until recently – isolated farming villages far from the social pressure posed by formal education, standardization and the linguistic norm.

1.4 Theoretical Assumptions

1.4.1 The Framework

The primary theoretical framework adopted in this study is the one provided by the Minimalist Program (Chomsky 1995, 2000, 2001). A central concept embraced by minimalism is *economy*. A theory of Universal Grammar (UG)

(Chomsky 1965 et seq.) has been built around this notion. Thus, the Minimalist Program tries to achieve descriptive and empirical adequacy while keeping to a minimum theoretical abstractions and stipulations. Another idea at the core of this research program is that the language faculty, the innate and universal human cognitive capacity for language, can be conceived of as an optimal Computational System (Comp.S), so that it can be minimally characterized by a reduced number of syntactic operations: *Merge*, *Move* and *Agree*.

Merge and *Move* apply cyclically to build constituent structure. *Merge* assembles the entries selected from the Numeration (i.e., the collection of lexical and functional items, which contain formal features), while *Move* creates a copy of a given entry and merges it in a different location of the syntactic tree. The created syntactic constituent is associated with meaning and sound. Such an association occurs at the point of Spell Out, where the computation splits and thus yields to two independent representations: Logical Form (LF) and Phonological Form (PF).

LF and PF belong to the Conceptual-Intentional (C-I) and Articulatory-Perceptual (A-P) systems, respectively. After Spell Out, Comp.S no longer has access to the created structure, which is shipped to the C-I and A-P systems. Along the A-P path, several morphological and phonological processes apply, leading to a PF representation; along the C-I path, logical operations take place, which contribute to the semantic interpretation of the syntactic structure and yield to an LF representation (12).

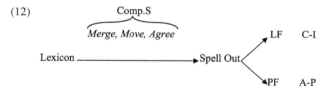

Agree is a formal operation that, in contrast with *Merge* and *Move*, does not create syntactic constituents. It satisfies the purposes of valuating certain features (unvalued) and deleting others (uninterpretable) in the narrow syntax (before Spell Out). According to Chomsky (2001, 2002, 2006), in fact, syntactic derivations are driven by processes of feature valuation and checking. A useful proposal that has been put forward and implemented by the Minimalist Program is the distinction between interpretable and uninterpretable features (Chomsky 1995; Frampton & Gutmann 2000; Pesetsky & Torrego 2007). Interpretable features are readable at LF, and thus they carry semantic information that can be interpreted by the C-I system. Uninterpretable features, on the other hand, do not carry any semantic import, and thus these features are present in the derivation only to satisfy a purely syntactic purpose: they trigger the necessary syntactic operations during the computation, and are eventually deleted via *Agree* before Spell Out. *Agree*, therefore, eliminates uninterpretable features, which are unreadable at the LF/PF interfaces and – if not removed – would cause the derivation to crash.

The Minimalist Program rests on the assumption that cross-linguistic variation concerns the lexicon and its formal features (Borer 1984), while syntax is universal and, therefore, invariable (Chomsky 1995; Brody 2003). Given this approach, cross-linguistic variation is mostly conceived of as a matter of feature distribution across lexical entries in the different human languages. Baker (2008: 156) has labeled this idea the "Borer–Chomsky Conjecture," which may be better understood by looking at the two following passages taken from Borer (1984: 2–3, 29):

> Interlanguage variation would be restricted to the idiosyncratic properties of lexical items. These idiosyncrasies, which are clearly learned, would then interact with general principles of UG in a particular way.
>
> It is worth ... reiterating the conceptual advantage that reduced all interlanguage variation to the properties of the inflectional system. The inventory of inflectional rules and of grammatical formatives in any given language is idiosyncratic and learned on the basis of input data.

While the acquisition of lexical items, and thus of their respective grammars, is conceived of as natural and "instinctive" during normal L1 development (Pinker 1994), it is well known that L2 development is often incomplete and lacks spontaneity, since the acquisition device becomes increasingly less flexible as children get older (White 2003a). In line with Herschensohn (2000), I assume that the acquisition of L2 features is gained through a *gradual* phase of L1–L2 transition. This fact may be formalized by saying that, during the acquisition process, certain features, after having lost their L1 values, are *unspecified* and will incrementally gain new L2 values, thus giving rise to variation or *optionality*. This process consists of the progressive mastery of the TL's functional and lexical categories, through the gradual acquisition of its lexicon (Herschensohn 2000: 81).

A number of authors suggest that the availability of UG is not limited to L1 acquisition; rather, it drives L2 development through a set of possible, acquirable grammars, and therefore it is fully accessible during L2 acquisition (see Epstein, Flynn & Martohardjono 1996; Schwartz 1996, 1998; Schwartz & Sprouse 1996). In Herschensohn's words: "L2 grammars are constrained by universal principles in that intermediate and final-state grammars are possible human languages" (2000: 80). The advantage of this approach over previous generative attempts – such as the Principles & Parameters model (Chomsky & Lasnik 1993) – is that parameter resetting is no longer considered to be the fundamental difference accounting for L1 vs. L2 development. Rather, this distinction is now explained as an incomplete command over a language-particular lexicon, which interfaces with other linguistic modules.

Instead of a "yes/no" parameter switch, the gradual acquisition of features naturally accounts for the variability encountered in all second languages. L2 acquisition happens gradually and the most peripheral morpho-lexical items, as well as the phenomena implying high processing demands on the linguistic interfaces, will be the last ones to be mastered, since the learner constructs the grammar "from the core to the periphery" (Herschensohn 2000: 81).

1.4.2 Interfaces and Second-Language Development

A well-known hypothesis of L2 development, which was explicitly formulated to account for *the residual optionality found in very advanced stages of SLA*, is the Interface Hypothesis (IH) (Sorace & Filiaci 2006; Tsimpli & Sorace 2006; Belletti, Bennati & Sorace 2007). The IH proposes that constructions that concern an interface between syntax and cognitive domains external to the core of the language machinery (i.e., discourse) would be more difficult to acquire in L2 than constructions that do not involve such an interface. This proposal was then applied to the early stages of first language (L1) attrition and to bilingual L1 acquisition, which show parallel instances of optionality, to offer a more comprehensive framework for the study of bilingualism (Sorace 2011: 1).

Much of the research concerning the IH has focused on the study of the syntax–pragmatics interface, which, according to Sorace and her associates, is conceivably one of the most challenging aspects of L2 development, and may possibly never be fully mastered by L2 speakers, nor even by near-native speakers (but see Montrul 2011 and Slabakova & Ivanov 2011 for a different perspective on this point). This proposal was originally put forward after examining the use and interpretation of subject pronouns in near-native L2 Italian speech (Sorace & Filiaci 2006; Belletti et al. 2007). Findings showed how, compared to native speakers, the near-natives significantly preferred overt subject pronouns in contexts that would require a null subject (*pro*), thus leading to the production and acceptance of constructions that would sound pragmatically odd to the ear of a native speaker, such as the use of overt anaphoric subject pronouns after topical subjects, as in (13b) and (14b) (Sorace 2011: 2).

(13) a. Perchè Giovanna non è venuta?
'Why didn't Giovanna come?'
b. ?Perchè **lei** non ha trovato un taxi.
c. Perchè ___ non ha trovato un taxi.
'Because she couldn't find a taxi.'

(14) a. La vecchietta$_i$ saluta la ragazza$_j$ quando pro$_{i/?j}$ attraversa la strada.
b. ?*La vecchietta$_i$ saluta la ragazza$_j$ quando lei$_{?*i/j}$ attraversa la strada.
'The old woman greets the girl when ø/she crosses the road.'

A parallel phenomenon was also detected by Tsimpli, Sorace, Heycock and Filiaci (2004). In that study, the authors analyzed similar patterns in the speech of Italian and Greek speakers who had acquired near native-like proficiency in English and thus were starting to experience attrition on their L1. The informants also tended to accept overt subject pronouns in contexts that would require null subjects. Given these results, the authors concluded that structures involving high processing demands at the syntax–pragmatic interface appear to be the last ones to be acquired in L2 development and the first ones to be eroded in cases of attrition (see also Romero & Sessarego 2018 on this point).

In an attempt to formalize the detected overuse of overt pronouns and the resulting optionality characterizing these grammars, Tsimpli et al. (2004: 264) proposed that in these contact varieties the [+/−Topic Shift] feature, which generally distinguishes between overt subjects and *pro* in null subject languages (NSL) like Italian, Greek and Spanish (Cardinaletti 1997; Philippaki-Warburton 1987; Ordóñez & Treviño 1999), would no longer be systematically associated with such pronouns, owing to the influence exerted on these categories by English, a language in which null subjects are typically not allowed (see also Grimshaw & Samek-Lodovici 1998 on this point). In a more recent analysis of that formalization, Sorace (2011: 13) has schematically represented the differences between a native and an attrited/near-native grammar in this respect (15)–(16). Thus, as shown below, attrited/near-native overt subjects would be the locus of optionality, since they may be variably associated with [+/− Topic Shift] features.

(15) Monolingual grammar:
OVERT ⇔ [+Topic Shift]
NULL ⇔ [−Topic Shift]

(16) Attrited/Near-native grammar:
OVERT ⇔ [+Topic Shift]
OVERT ⇔ [−Topic Shift]
NULL ⇔ [−Topic Shift]

In recent years, the literature on SLA and interfaces has seen a proliferation of studies. A number of authors, in fact, have proposed models to explain the nature of mapping between language modules and the inherent challenges that the L2 learner faces when dealing with different interfaces. In particular, since the original formulation of the IH, much debate has focused on whether it is correct to identify the syntax–pragmatics interface as the main locus of instability and optionality in L2 development. (See Rothman & Slabakova 2011 for a review.)

On this point, Sorace and colleagues have been quite determined to show that, while other interfaces certainly present challenges to L2 acquisition (e.g., syntax–semantics, syntax–morphology, etc.), the interface that outranks all others in terms of acquisitional barriers remains the syntax–pragmatics one (Sorace et al. 2009; Serratrice et al. 2009). In their view, while interfaces like the syntax–semantics one are "internal" to the language machinery, the syntax–pragmatics interface is "external" to it, and thus would be harder to master, since it requires the coordination of linguistic and non-linguistic domains (Sorace & Serratrice 2009). This concept is clearly expressed by Tsimpli & Sorace (2006: 653) when they state:

> The distinction between the two interfaces is based on the assumption that the syntax–discourse interface is a 'higher' level of language use, integrating properties of language and pragmatic processing, whereas syntax–semantics involve formal properties of the language system alone.

On the other hand, some authors have questioned the idea that the syntax–pragmatics interface should be conceived of as the most challenging aspect of SLA (White 2011; Ivanov 2009; Rothman 2009; Montrul 2011). In particular, Slabakova (2008, 2009, 2013, 2016, 2019) has advanced the Bottleneck Hypothesis (BH), which offers a different account to explain "why some linguistic features and constructions are easy or difficult to acquire in a second language" (2013: 5).

The BH claims that the L2 learners' greatest challenge resides in the morphology–semantics interface, where meaning is mapped onto overt morphemes. This criticism to the IH is built – in part – on studies suggesting that a number of structures requiring the coordination of the syntactic and pragmatic modules are not particularly problematic for advanced speakers and near-natives, thus showing that not all syntax–pragmatics phenomena are inherently challenging in L2. (See Valenzuela 2006, Donaldson 2011 and Ivanov 2012 for clitic left dislocation in Spanish, French and Bulgarian, respectively.)

The fundamental assumption on which the BH is built is that during L2 acquisition "syntax and semantics flow smoothly" (Slabakova 2008: 100), since syntactic and semantic principles are universally provided by UG; what represents the real "bottleneck" of acquisition has to do with associating such semantic concepts to L2 inflectional morphemes. (See also Lardiere 2005 on this point.) Slabakova, in fact, embraces a view on language diversity that steams out from the Borer–Chomsky Conjecture (Baker 2008) and then applies it to L2 acquisition. Thus, according to Slabakova, given that cross-linguistic variation depends on the distribution of different formal features in the lexicon (i.e., the idiosyncratic rules of inflectional systems) (Borer 1984), while syntax and semantics remain the same across languages (Chomsky 1995), then what is challenging in L2 acquisition "is what is dissimilar from the native language" (i.e. morphology), since "the universal parts can transfer in a direct manner" (Slabakova 2019: 158).

Slabakova has backed her proposal in a variety of studies in which she systematically showed how bound morphology, and especially agreement markers, appears to be particularly challenging to master for basic, intermediate and even advanced L2 speakers (Slabakova, 2008, 2009, 2013). In replying to this type of criticism moved by the BH against the IH, Sorace (2011: 26) has argued that showing that the semantics–morphology interface is challenging for L2 learners is actually missing the point of the IH, which is not a proposal meant to account for the different developmental stages of L2 acquisition. Rather, it is a hypothesis put forward to explain why there is residual optionality in pronominal subject use at the highest level of ultimate attainment (i.e., near-nativeness) when – in Sorace's view – speakers no longer show as much morphosyntactic variability.

As far as the current book is concerned, it is of little importance to decide which hypothesis of SLA and interfaces provides the most accurate predictions to account for near-nativeness or other L2 stages. What really matters here is to keep in mind that interfaces have been a major area of research in the field of SLA due to the high challenges that they pose to the development of L2s. Thus, this study will show how all of the so-called Afro-Hispanic "creole-like" traits can actually be conceived of as by-product of interface-driven SLA strategies, common to both advanced L2s and near-native varieties, and which, therefore, do not necessarily support any of the long-assumed (de)creolization processes (Sessarego 2013a, 2015, 2019b).

1.5 Domino Effects

Central to my proposal is the notion of a language *system*, or the idea that each language has its own internal equilibrium. Each time something is added to or removed from a given system, the other elements belonging to it must inevitably reorganize to reach a new point of balance. This process is constantly at work in all languages and can be clearly traced diachronically. A well-studied instance of such a balancing process, which applied in the history of the Spanish language, is lenition, a consonant shift that has taken place across the lexicon in the evolution of the language from Latin to Old Spanish. Penny (2002: 74–75) uses these words to describe it:

> An increase in spoken Latin of the incidence of geminates ... led to an unbalanced consonantal system, an imbalance which was redressed by the simplification of the geminates, a process which had the consequence of causing a chain-reaction of further changes (voicing of voiceless intervocalics and fricatization/loss of voiced intervocalics) ...
>
> Geminates were reduced to simple intervocalic consonants ...; e.g. /kk/ > /k/. This simplification put pressure on preexisting intervocalic consonants to change, causing the simple intervocalics (if they were originally voiceless) to become voiced (e.g. /k/ > /g/), in order to maintain, by other means, the original contrast between geminate and simple. In turn, the voicing of voiceless intervocalic phonemes threatened merger with the pre-existing voiced phonemes, and the latter (if originally plosive) became fricative (e.g. /g/ > [γ]) in order to avoid the merger. The chain-reaction was completed when, in order to avoid merger with the new voiced fricatives, the pre-existing voiced fricative /j/ ... was eliminated from the words in which it occurred.

This series of interrelated modifications is summarized in Table 1.2, in which the lenition process affecting velar plosives (i.e., the chain /kk/>/k/>/g/>/Ø/) is exemplified (Penny 2002: 81). These natural, reorganizing processes – applying cross-linguistically as soon as something has been altered in any linguistic system – are what I call here *language restructuring*, which can be driven by both internal and external (contact) forces, with the latter usually being much more disruptive than the former.

Languages are highly complex in nature and organized into cooperating modules (i.e., syntax, morphology, phonology, etc.) consisting of hundreds of

Table 1.2 *Lenition of velar plosives*

Latin phoneme	Old Spanish phoneme	Example
/kk/	/k/	SICCU > *seco* 'dry'
/k/	/g/	SECURU > *seguro* 'sure'
/g/	/Ø/	LĒGĀLE > *leal* 'loyal'

sub-units (i.e., syntactic categories, morphemes, phonemes, etc.). In this sense, languages may be seen as *modular multibody systems*. The elements that make up languages coexist and influence each other. Each module interfaces with the others. Interfaces, therefore, can be conceived of as points of mapping between linguistic modules (Montrul 2011: 578).

Having acknowledged the complexity of language restructuring, it must be said that the mechanisms underlying the change are certainly not random; rather, they follow universal processes, which are constantly at work. As far as language contact is concerned, it will be shown how certain linguistic interfaces between grammatical modules tend to be highly vulnerable to the introduction of systemic changes (Lardiere 2000; Sorace 2003; White 2011). Such modifications, as expected, act as triggers; thus, they instantiate restructuring processes affecting a number of other aspects of the evolving linguistic systems. This book illustrates how such mechanisms – at the root of the aforementioned "creole-like" features – are responsible for having shaped what we know as the contemporary AHLA grammars.

My proposal on the evolution of the AHLAs, therefore, diverges quite significantly from the traditional creole life cycle adopted by some authors, according to whom pidgins become creoles and then eventually decreolize. Conversely, I am of the idea that such an evolutionary trajectory only represents one of the several potential paths of contact-driven restructuring. It is not applicable to a number of contemporary creoles, which appear to have become more "radical" only in a second phase of their development (see Lefebvre 1998 for Haitian French and Migge 2003 for Sranan Tongo), and, in my view, it does not apply to the AHLAs, since the available sociohistorical and linguistic evidence clearly suggests otherwise.

On the other hand, I posit that the AHLAs may be analyzed as the result of L1 acquisition (nativization) of advanced L2 grammars. This hypothesis is built on the notion that even though the acquisition of both L1 and L2 is subject to the same linguistic constraints imposed by UG, their evolutions significantly differ in that, as I have explained in Section 1.4, L1 development operates instinctively, while L2 acquisition progresses in a less natural way. L2 learners have access to UG, but a concomitance of biological and social factors hinders achievement of a full command of the TL (Herschensohn 2000).

Extending these concepts to the current study, my thought regarding YS, CVS and CS (and most other Afro-Latino varieties) is that African slaves in colonial times acquired relatively close approximations to Spanish (the TL). This means that each individual internalized an L2 grammar out of a set of possible grammars. Their linguistic output (x, y, z) represented the Primary

Language Data (PLD) for the following generations of speakers, who acquired such a vernacular as their L1 and *conventionalized it at the community level*. The aforementioned cross-generational language transmission is exemplified in (17), in which G1 and G2 represent two possible, acquirable grammars with divergent structural configurations (Sessarego 2013b, 2019b).

(17) a. Individual from Generation 1:
TLy ➔ UG driving L2 acquisition➔ G1 ➔ set of outputs X
b. Individual from Generation 2:
PLDx ➔ UG driving L1 acquisition ➔ G2 ➔ set of outputs Z

The scheme in (17b) depicts a case of nativization, consisting of Generation 2's L1 acquisition. This translates to an L1 grammar (G2) built on L2 inputs. Consequently, G2 shows crystallized aspects of an L2, which are acquired as an L1. This model is in line with the so-called "target shift" (Baker 1990), according to which, at some point in the evolution of certain creole languages, later generations of slaves no longer targeted the European lexifier, but rather they obtained most of their PLD from the means of interethnic communication that developed on plantations. Demographic figures play a fundamental role in this model. Indeed, Baker (1990) claims that a rapid increase in the enslaved population resulted in *very limited access* to the European language and this triggered the shift in language targets, which would be at the root of radical creole formation. As I have indicated elsewhere (Sessarego 2011a, 2013a, 2015, 2019a), the development of YS, CVS and CS departs from that of radical creoles. In fact, the scheme in (17) assumes that access to the European language in these Andean haciendas was *only partially constrained* by a combination of social and demographic factors and, consequently, these grammars more closely converged with Spanish from the early phases of their formation (Sessarego 2013b, 2019b).

1.6 Overview

Chapter 2 provides a sociohistorical analysis of the evolution of YS, CVS and CS. The chapter illustrates general aspects of the African Diaspora to the Americas and its specific linguistic consequences in Yungas (Bolivia), Chota Valley (Ecuador) and Chincha (Peru). Given the historical evidence available for these AHLAs, I propose that these contact varieties developed in isolated rural villages, not subject to the social pressures imposed by education, standardization and the linguistic norm. In such a context, advanced SLA processes could be nativized and conventionalized at the local level, thus crystallizing in the L1 varieties spoken by subsequent generations of these Afro-Andean communities.

Chapter 3 provides an overview of a number of theoretical proposals that have been put forward in the literature to account for language variation. It elaborates on models that combine formal generative theorizing and quantitative sociolinguistic methodology, in line with current minimalist analyses (Adger & Smith 2005; Sessarego & Gutiérrez-Rexach 2011; Sessarego 2014a). This chapter also stresses the importance of embracing a perspective of mutual complementation – rather than mutual exclusion – between these two fields, especially when the varieties under study consist of stigmatized vernaculars, for which it may be hard to obtain reliable grammaticality judgments and that may be characterized by high levels of inter- and intra-speaker speech variability (Cornips & Poletto 2005).

Chapter 4 analyzes gender and number agreement processes within the Determiner Phrase (DP) of YS, CVS and CS. The data presented there show a variety of reduced agreement configurations, which are rooted in L2 processing constraints applying at the *morphology–semantics interface*. A unified account of these phenomena is provided by adopting current formal proposals on the nature of feature valuation and checking (Frampton & Gutmann 2000; Pesetsky & Torrego 2007). In so doing, this chapter enhances a stronger dialogue between syntactic theory and variationist analysis, which is fundamental to account for the nature and evolution of the agreement domain across the DP of these Afro-Hispanic dialects.

Chapter 5 focuses on mechanisms that do not rely solely on the interaction between the morphological and semantic modules; rather, they are also significantly conditioned by the *syntax–pragmatics interface*. The chapter addresses the nature of certain pro-drop phenomena in these Afro-Andean vernaculars. In particular, it analyzes the presence in these dialects of three highly interrelated features and provides a model to explain this restructured configuration: (1) the use of non-emphatic, non-contrastive overt subjects; (2) the presence of non-inverted questions; (3) impoverished subject–verb agreement. The data presented there also serve as a testing ground for formal hypotheses on the nature of pronominal expressions across languages. In so doing, the chapter offers evidence for arguments questioning the validity of the Null Subject Parameter (Chomsky 1981; Rizzi 1982), or, more broadly, for recent proposals that revisit the concept of "parameter" in favor of new potential paths of analysis (Eguren, Fernández-Soriano & Mendikoetxea 2016).

Chapter 6 provides an overview of YS, CVS and CS declarative intonation in terms of the realization of pitch accents and phrase boundary tones. The inventory of these phonological targets in these vernaculars is much more reduced than what has been encountered in other native (non-contact) varieties of Spanish (Aguilar, De-la-Mota & Prieto 2009; Beckman et al. 2002; Prieto & Roseano 2010). The speakers of these dialects show evidence of duplicating nuclear and pre-nuclear pitch accents, as well as boundary configurations, at both levels of phrasing (i.e., intermediate and intonational phrases) (Sessarego & Rao 2016; Rao & Sessarego 2016, 2018; Sessarego, Butera & Rao 2019; Butera, Sessarego & Rao 2020). The nature of these phenomena is analyzed as pertaining to the *phonology–pragmatics interface*, since both phonological and discourse features are involved.

Finally, Chapter 7 concludes this book by summarizing its content and highlighting how the so-called "creole-like" features detected for the AHLAs can be better explained in terms of interface-constrained advanced SLA processes, which were subsequently nativized and conventionalized by following generations of speakers. Likewise, this chapter stresses the importance of these Afro-Hispanic vernaculars to linguistic theory by showing how these contact varieties can offer a window into possible L2 instantiations of UG as well as an ideal *testing ground* for formal hypotheses (Sessarego 2014a), which have primarily been built on standardized language data.

2 *The African Diaspora to the Andes and Its Linguistic Consequences*

This chapter provides a sociohistorical analysis of the African Diaspora to Spanish America with a focus on the linguistic consequences that such a phenomenon had on the formation of the Afro-Andean vernaculars here analyzed: Yungueño Spanish (YS) (Bolivia), Chota Valley Spanish (CVS) (Ecuador) and Chincha Spanish (CS) (Peru). Thus, the following sections will cast light on how certain social (external) factors might have shaped the linguistic (internal) evolution of these Afro-Hispanic grammars. Data indicate that, contrary to what has been suggested on different occasions by other authors (Lipski 2008 and Perez 2015 for YS; Schwegler 1999 for CVS; McWhorter 2000 for CVS and CS), the sociohistorical context in which these Afro-Hispanic varieties formed was not ideal for the development of Spanish-based creoles. On the contrary, as indicated elsewhere (Sessarego 2011a, 2011b, 2013a, 2013c, 2014a, 2014c, 2015), these varieties may be better depicted as the result of advanced SLA processes (not leading to the more intense grammatical restructuring often ascribed to creolization), which were conventionalized at the community level in rural villages, far away from the pressure exerted by schooling, standardization and the linguistic norm.

2.1 Divergent Views on the Origins of the Afro-Andean Spanish Varieties

As pointed out by Lipski (2005: 304), the debate on the origins of the Afro-Hispanic varieties of the Americas is far from being over, and the contrasting views on the development of the Afro-Andean dialects analyzed here illustrate the animated nature of this academic discussion. A number of authors have proposed divergent hypotheses to account for the evolution of these contact vernaculars. For example, by looking at the "radically simplified VP and DP of the basilectal Afro-Yungueño dialect," Lipski (2006a: 37) suggests a potential pidgin/creole root for this dialect, which would have gone through a subsequent phase of decreolization driven by contact with the more prestigious

Highland Bolivian Spanish. Perez (2015) also hypothesizes that YS derived from a restructured pidgin/creole, and claims that this vernacular would have originated from a Portuguese-based contact variety. This latter account is, therefore, in line with the long-lasting tradition that, at least since Granda (1968), links the development of the Afro-Hispanic varieties of the Americas to a preexisting Portuguese-creole root. This view on the origins of several Afro-Hispanic vernaculars has also been suggested on numerous occasions by Schwegler (1991a, 1991b, 1993, 1996, 1999), who, in a recent study (Schwegler 2014), has reproposed the same evolutionary path for a number of Afro-Latino varieties, among which he included YS (2014: 426–429) and CVS (2014: 420–426).

A Portuguese-creole origin for CVS has been envisioned by Schwegler since the late 1990s (Schwegler 1999). In that study, as in Schwegler (2014), the author states that the presence in this dialect of the apparently Portuguese third-person pronoun, *ele*, would represent evidence of an Afro-Lusophone creole substrate involved in the formation of this variety. Lipski (2009), however, appears to be less convinced of a potential decreolization process for this particular Afro-Andean vernacular. He provides a different account to explain the presence of *ele* in CVS by suggesting that this element should be seen as the result of a paragogical process of final *–e* insertion (i.e., *él + e*), quite widespread across the CVS lexicon (2009: 113).

Against the (de)creolization model for CVS is McWhorter (2000), who claimed that this Afro-Andean variety was never a creole, since, according to his Afrogenesis Hypothesis, Spanish never creolized in the Americas. In his much-debated book, *The Missing Spanish Creole*, McWhorter (2000) claims that creole languages developed out of pidgins, which originally formed in Africa in the castle factories where slaves were imprisoned before being shipped to the Americas. Given that Spain did not have slave castles along the western African coast, an Afro-Hispanic pidgin never formed in Africa. Consequently, a Spanish creole could not possibly develop on the other side of the Atlantic, in Spanish America, even though in certain Spanish colonies, such as Chota Valley (2000: 10–11), the sociodemographic conditions for creole formation would have been perfect: (a) thousands of African-born slaves speaking a variety of African languages; (b) minimal presence of white people speaking Spanish; (c) harsh working conditions in sugarcane plantations; and (d) a highly isolated region, far away from Spanish-speaking urban centers. The Afrogenesis Hypothesis has also been proposed by McWhorter to explain the lack of a Spanish creole in Chincha (2000: 12, 35, 37). He suggests that the local haciendas in the colonial period represented an ideal breeding ground for creole formation, but a Spanish creole could not possibly form, since an African-born Spanish pidgin was never introduced on these plantations in the first place.

All of these different accounts of the origins and evolutions of the Afro-Andean dialects have been formulated without paying too much attention to the available sociohistorical research on the Black Diaspora to the Andes. This chapter fills the gap with the purpose of showing that the conditions for (de)creolization were in all likelihood not in place in colonial Bolivia, Ecuador and Peru. In so doing, I argue that neither the Decreolization Hypothesis nor the Afrogenesis Hypothesis can account for the origin and evolution of these varieties.

In the following sections, I will first provide a general sketch of black slavery in the Andes, and then a more specific account of the living and working conditions of Afro-descendants in Yungas, Chota Valley and Chincha. The goal is, therefore, to understand how certain external social factors may have shaped these Afro-Andean grammars.

2.2   A Sociohistorical Sketch of Black Slavery in the Andes

Black slavery was introduced to the Andes from the very beginning of the Spanish colonization of the region (in the early decades of the sixteenth century) and lasted for more than 300 years, until the middle of the nineteenth century. Nevertheless, even after the abolition of slavery, Afro-Andeans did not obtain real freedom. On the contrary, in most cases, their living and working conditions did not improve, since – in practice – many of them did not find other occupations and had to keep working for their former masters as unpaid peons. They had to wait until the Land Reforms, which took place at different points during the second half of the twentieth century (1952 in Bolivia; 1964 in Ecuador; 1969–1975 in Peru), to see some improvements in their living and working conditions (de Janvry, Sadoulet & Wolford 1998). This meant becoming owners of small lots of land that belonged to the haciendas in which they had previously worked, obtaining access to education, and the possibility of moving without being bounded to the plantation. Even if over time the social conditions of Afro-Andeans have improved, their situation is far from optimal, since they still represent the most discriminated sector of Andean society (Hernández 2013).

This chapter has the purpose of casting light on the social dynamics that characterized the life of black communities in the Andes across the colonial phase up to the present day to better understand how certain external factors may have contributed to shaping the contact varieties they speak today. In order to achieve this goal, the black experience in the Andes is analyzed through three main chronological phases. The first phase concerns the early arrivals of black slaves and freedmen, who accompanied the Spanish *conquistadores* in the first expeditions of exploration and settlement during the sixteenth and seventeenth centuries (from 1530 to 1650). These people mainly came from already-settled colonies (mostly in the Caribbean) and from Spain. They were for the most part *ladinos*, and thus they were Christians who could speak the Spanish language and were familiar with Spanish culture. The second period (1650–1767) was characterized by an increase in the number of slaves taken to the region. This workforce was in part introduced to replace the by-then-decimated indigenous population. Nevertheless, in this phase, black workers were never exploited on a massive scale, since slave owners did not usually have enough capital to acquire large numbers of captives at a given time. The only organization that could systematically rely on an enslaved workforce was the Catholic Church, and in particular the Company of Jesus, which became the largest slave-owning organization in the region. The second phase ends with the expulsion of the Company of Jesus from the Spanish colonies in 1767 and the subsequent passage of its properties (including the slaves) to a state-run institution called the *Temporalidades*. The third and last phase (1767–present) is characterized by some initial social turmoil among the slaves working in the former Jesuit haciendas (due to the managerial shift brought about by the *Temporalidades*) and by a progressive acquisition of civil rights by the Afro-Andean communities, who obtained freedom during the nineteenth century but have been struggling against social injustice and discrimination up to the present day.

2.2.1 First Arrivals

The black presence in the Andes has been reported since the earliest Spanish colonial expeditions in the region, when Afro-descendants participated side-by-side with the Spaniards in the first exploring and conquering missions. The earliest chronicle of this type is probably the well-known case of a black soldier enlisted in the troupe of the *conquistador* Alonso de Molina during his arrival to Tumbes (northern coast of present-day Peru). Torres Saldamando (1900: 409) describes the event with the following words:

> El primer negro que pisó tierra peruana fue el que en 1526 desembarcó en Tumbes con Alonso de Molina cuando fue reconocido este puerto por los de Pizarro. (The first black person who entered Peru disembarked at Tumbes

with Alonso de Molina when that port was reconnoitered by Pizarro's men in 1526).

This episode is often mentioned in history books describing those early colonial encounters, since, apparently, the Indians who saw this black soldier could not believe the color of his skin and tried to wash away what they originally thought to be dye on his body (Helps 1900: 310; Bowser 1974: 4). The black presence in the region was not just sporadic at this point; rather, it is amply attested by colonial observers of the time. For example, Felipe Guamán Poma de Ayala (1615), in his well-known work *Nueva corónica y buen gobierno*, talks about several black people, either servants or freedmen, who worked as soldiers and assistants of various types in the first Spanish campaigns of conquest and settlement, as Figure 2.1 testifies.

Blacks played an active role in these early expeditions. Bryant (2005: 1), in his dissertation on the African Diaspora to Ecuador, points out how Afro-descendants were among the first founders of what would become Ecuador's capital city: Quito. He approaches the topic in this way:

> Inscribed on the outside walls of Quito's Cathedral is a list of the men who invaded, occupied and ultimately renamed the Inka city of Quito for Saint Francis on August 28, 1534. Listed among these individuals are two blacks – Juan (*de color negro*) and Antón (*negro*). Juan and Antón represented the hundreds (and perhaps thousands by this date) of black explorers, conquistadors, slaves and squires who had come to the Americas during the age of conquest (1492–1550). Although the biographical records for Juan and Antón are sketchy, sources indicate that they were freemen.

Brockington (2006: 130) concurs on the active involvement of several Afro-descendants in this early colonial phase. When describing the black presence in Bolivia, the author states what follows:

> The African slaves and people of African descent were active participants – voluntary or otherwise – in a militaristic, conquering/pacifying, horse-and-gun culture here, as elsewhere in the Spanish Americas at that time. I am convinced that some of them remained ... as, among other things, slave and free cowboys and ranch hands.

In order to understand what languages these people might have spoken, it is important to keep in mind that during this early colonial phase, the slaves entering the Andes did not usually proceed directly from Africa (Mellafe 1984; Bowser 1974). Rather, they came for the most part from already-settled colonies (in the Caribbean) or from Spain. On this point, Restall (2000: 190–219) reminds us how the Spanish Caribbean, and in particular

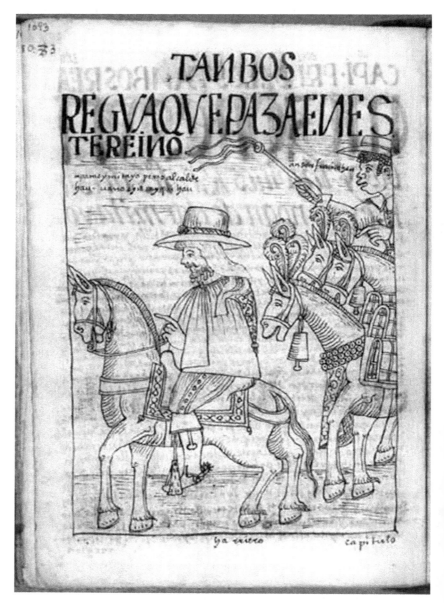

Figure 2.1 *A Spanish* conquistador *with his black servant*

Hispaniola, became a place where – as indicated by a local royal official at that time – slave traders could make "a living by buying Africans, teaching them some trade and then selling them at a profit on the mainland" (see Aguirre Beltrán 1946: 20). This implies that before being resold on the mainland, they often spent long periods of time (sometimes a number of years) acquiring job skills (along with the Spanish language) in the Caribbean.

This observation is backed by demographic records. Bowser (1974: 72–73), for example, shows how the majority of the slaves sold in Lima, Peru during this early phase (1560–1650) were not *bozales* (African-born slaves) proceeding directly from Africa. Rather, out of a total sample of 444 black captives, 369 individuals were brought from other Latin American colonies, where they had resided for some time (possibly several years), and thus had learned the Spanish ways before being sold in Peru.

Even though black people were present and visible in the Andes from the beginning of this early colonial phase, their introduction was not massive, since they were expensive to acquire. As Lockhart (1994) points out, big cargos of black slaves were not common. Single transactions concerning more than ten slaves were rare (1994: 177), captives were generally acquired one at a time, while sales of two or three captives were more sporadic (1994: 178). The reasons for these trading limitations in the region were multiple (Sessarego 2015: ch. 5). Three main factors may be seen as particularly crucial: logistic constraints, the Crown's monopoly over the slave trade, and the availability of an indigenous workforce.

As for the logistic constraints, it should be kept in mind that the countries now known as Ecuador, Bolivia and Peru do not have any direct access to the Atlantic Ocean. This means that taking African-born slaves to these lands implied a particularly strenuous trip, which systematically resulted in many casualties among the captives. As a consequence of such a geographical barrier, the price of a slave, who could be purchased for some 200–400 pesos in the ports of Cartagena (present-day Colombia) or Buenos Aires (present-day Argentina) during the sixteenth–seventeenth centuries, could easily reach 500–600 pesos in Lima, and the price would tend to increase in the Ecuadorian and Bolivian highlands, which were located further away from the major slave markets (Bowser 1974; Colmenares 1997; Brockington 2006).

An additional reason for the high price of slaves had to do with the fact that black captives were not traded on a free market; rather, this was a highly constrained business. The Spanish Crown held a monopoly on the introduction of slaves to its American colonies and granted only a limited number of *asientos* (licenses) to trading companies. In addition, on each slave transaction, the Crown charged *almojarifazgos* (import taxes) and *alcabalas* (sales taxes) (Bryant 2005). Such restrictions on the introduction of an African workforce to Spanish America resulted in the black population being a relatively small group in several colonies, especially when compared to the native population (Rosenblat 1954).

The relative availability of a native workforce, in fact, is certainly a factor that further determined the non-massive introduction of black captives to the Andes. Indeed, even though Indians could not technically be enslaved according to the Spanish legal system of the time (Sessarego 2018a), they were forced to work in precarious conditions for a minimal compensation. To achieve this, the Spaniards adopted a pre-Columbian working system implemented by the Incas, the *mit'a*. According to the *mit'a*, each man of a given Indian community had to carry out compulsory duties for a certain period of time. This system worked on a rotation basis according to which nobody would be required to work again until everyone had covered his own shift (Rostworowski Tovar de Díez Canseco 1999).

It has also to be pointed out that the Spanish Crown was not much interested in the development of a large-scale plantation business of the kind seen in the French and English colonies in the Caribbean. Rather, in the Andes – as in most of Spanish America – the main concern of the Spanish administration had to do with the extraction of precious metals, primarily silver and gold. The Andean region was particularly rich in this sense. In 1545, the biggest silver deposit of the Americas was discovered in the mountains of Potosí (current-day Bolivia). The high cost of black slaves (especially in the highlands), combined with their lack of fitness for the frigid temperatures of the region, induced the Spanish administration to largely rely on the native population to extract the precious metal. In 1578, under the administration of Viceroy Toledo, it was established that 14,248 native men would serve their *mit'a* shift in the silver deposit of Potosí, the *Cerro Rico* (Rich Mountain) (Bowser 1974: 40).

The reduced presence of an Afro-descendant group in the highlands is further supported by the available demographic information of the time. Crespo (1995: 26–29) reports data concerning the evolution of the black population for the city of Potosí for the seventeenth–nineteenth centuries (see Table 2.1). As the table shows, the Afro-descendant group never represented more than a small fraction of the total population. This trend is also reflected in the popular Peruvian saying *el gallinazo no canta en puna* 'the black buzzard does not sing in the mountains,'[1] indicating that black people were not fit for living and working in the highlands (Bowser 1974: 14).

---

[1] The black buzzard is a bird found in the coastal region of Peru.

Table 2.1 *Demographic figures for the city of Potosí (1611–1832)*

Year	Afro-descendant population	Total population	Afro-descendant population (%)
1611	6,000	160,000	3.75
1719	3,206	70,000	4.58
1832	1,142	224,000	0.51

While in the highland mining regions the presence of the black population was minimal during this first phase, in the main urban centers, and especially in the city of Lima, the Afro-descendant group was much more visible. Bowser (1974: 11) calculates that some 3,000 blacks were probably living in Peru by the 1550s, and that half of them resided in Lima. Rosenblat (1954: 88) provides approximate figures for the Ecuadorian population of the sixteenth century. He estimates that the blacks, mulattoes and *mestizos*[2] taken together would have been some 10,000, while whites were probably around 6,500. According to Tardieu (2006: 174, 231, 273), the majority of the Afro-descendants in Ecuador at that point resided in the cities of Guayaquil, Cuenca and Quito.

By relying on archival demographic data, Bowser (1974: 337–341) sketched the evolution of the Afro-descendant group in relation to the white and native populations in Lima up to 1636, and showed that the number of blacks/mulattoes was fairly comparable to the number of whites/*mestizos* during the period he analyzed (some 7,000 individuals in 1600, who almost doubled in number by 1636). He also argues that at that point Lima was in all likelihood the place with the highest Afro-descendant concentration in the entire Andean region, so that two-thirds of the total black/mulatto population of Peru lived in this city. These people were usually employed in a variety of urban jobs that required skilled workers: shoemakers, guardians, auctioneers, executioners, cooks, criers, constables, pipers, and masters of weights and measures, among many others (Lockhart 1994: 380).

The vast majority of these servants were in all likelihood Spanish-speakers, since many were *ladinos* and *criollos*, and only a smaller part were *bozales* (Bowser 1974). The increasing presence of locally born *criollos* is further attested by Bryant (2005: 78), who shows that between 1580 and 1600 only 25.8 percent of the slave transactions in Quito concerned African-born captives. He states that, given the geographical and financial constraints affecting the importation of slaves into the Andes, it was common practice

---

[2] Mestizos: offspring of white and indigenous parents.

among slave owners to incentivize local reproduction. Indirect evidence of this is also the fact that the prize of black women on recorded transactions was often established according to their potential capability of "producing a good number of Afro-Creole children" (2005: 79).

During this first phase of conquest and colonization, the agricultural sector, which was not based on large-scale plantations, relied primarily on the native workforce. However, over time, Afro-descendants came to populate the warmer regions of Ecuador, Bolivia and Peru, and to complement the indigenous population, which had been shrinking during the sixteenth and seventeenth centuries, due to wars, European diseases and the harsh working conditions imposed by the *mit'a* system (Bowser 1974; Brockington 2006). It has to be said that the first decades of the seventeenth century were characterized by a discrete increase of a black workforce in the agricultural sector, especially in the warmer coastal regions of Peru. However, even under those circumstances, the introduction of black slaves was never massive. On the contrary, after examining a sample of 41 coastal haciendas of the time, Bowser (1974: 94) concluded that even though in some coastal areas the Afro-descendants were becoming numerically significant, "the size of the slave population resident on most estates during this period was relatively modest and rarely exceeded forty slaves of all ages."

In summary, it was observed that during this early colonial phase, the enslaved population lived for the most part in urban centers, where they usually performed a variety of skilled jobs. The captives used in the highland mining centers were a very small minority, and the agricultural sector in the warmer regions was not characterized by a large-scale plantation economy, which would have required a substantial enslaved workforce. This scenario significantly reduced the probability of Spanish creolization in the countries analyzed here. This sociodemographic context is likely to have favored the acquisition of the colonial language by the black population. Moreover, in further support of this proposal, historical data indicate that the majority of the blacks in the Andes during this period did not arrive directly from Africa, and thus they were not always speakers of African languages. Conversely, they were for the most part either locally born *criollos* or they were brought from already-settled colonies (or from Spain), and thus they probably had a relatively good command of the Spanish language, as either an L1 or an L2.

2.2.2 The Second Wave

As indicated above, three main factors constrained the introduction of an Afro-descendant workforce in the Andean region: geographical barriers, the

Crown's monopoly over slave trafficking, and the relative availability of indigenous workers. Over time, the native population shrunk and the perceived need for black labor became more significant. Nevertheless, the logistic impediments and the financial restrictions related to the lack of a free market for slave trading did not change during this second phase (1650–1767), such that the introduction of a black workforce in the Andes never achieved massive dimensions.

Slave owners, in fact, usually did not have enough capital to acquire captives in large numbers. For this reason, the introduction of black workers to these territories happened gradually. The exploitation of black slaves during this phase mostly affected the warmer regions of these colonies, where agricultural activities could be carried out. While in the Peruvian coastal regions, such as Chincha, and in certain warmer highland valleys such as Yungas (Bolivia) and Chota (Ecuador), the enslaved population progressively grew during the seventeenth and eighteenth centuries, in the cities the number of black slaves systematically decreased. This demographic shrinkage affecting urban centers across the Andean region is best exemplified with data from Lima, which, as we have seen, was once the city with the highest percentage of blacks in the colony. MacLean y Estenós (1947: 30) and Centurión Vallejo (1954: 3) provide demographic data picturing this reduction in the Afro-descendant urban population for the capital of Peru. While in 1614 the black/mulatto group represented 40 percent of Lima's population, by 1720 it was just 17 percent. This decline continued throughout the eighteenth century. In fact, one hundred years later, in 1820, the Afro-descendant group in Lima made up only 13 percent of the total population.

The reason for this constant reduction in the percentage of blacks living in urban centers was in part due to the fact that during this phase many of them were transferred by their owners to rural areas to be employed in haciendas. This shift was based on economic reasoning. During the seventeenth and eighteenth centuries, in fact, the agricultural business grew and it made economic sense to employ this labor force in that sector, since it would provide a relatively good return on investment (Sessarego 2015: 98). Indeed, black slaves, unlike the natives, were conceived of as *piezas* (tokens) of "mobile capital" (Bryant 2005: 14) who could be transferred from one region to another quite easily. This piece of information is key to understanding what language varieties might have been brought to these early plantations. Since a good part of the rural enslaved workforce at this point consisted of *criollos* who had been transferred to these haciendas from urban centers, the chances are that they would have spoken vernacular varieties of Spanish rather than just African languages, and thus the likelihood of creole formation in these plantations was not high.

The majority of the haciendas during this phase were not large-scale plantations of the type encountered in the French and English Caribbean. On the contrary, as Aguirre (1997: 501) points out when he describes the agricultural system of colonial Peru, most estates consisted of "medium-sized plantations of 20–50 slaves." This being said, it has to be acknowledged that certain haciendas, especially during the second half of the eighteenth century, achieved considerable dimensions and ended up employing hundreds of black captives. This partial shift to larger agricultural facilities was primarily related to the development of the sugarcane industry. In fact, the nature of sugarcane growing implied bigger estates that allowed for a systematic rotation of the fields, distinctive of this type of cultivation (Flores Galindo 1984).

Sugarcane growing required skilled workers who could take good care of this high-maintenance crop. These people had to be properly trained and, for this reason, planters tended to prefer *ladinos* over *bozales*, since they could understand Spanish and thus learn the job more quickly. Flores Galindo (1984: 28) describes the development of this early sugarcane plantation business in the warmer coastal regions of the colony by using the following words:

> Ante la escasez de población indígena en la costa y ante la imposibilidad de sujetar a los mestizos, la caña exigió el recurso a la fuerza de trabajo que podían proporcionar los esclavos. Dado el aprendizaje que requería el cultivo, se prefirió a los negros que conocían el español y estaban habituados a las costumbres del país: los "ladinos" en lugar de los "bozales" (Confronted with the scarcity of an indigenous population along the coast and the impossibility of exploiting *mestizos*, sugarcane cultivation required an enslaved workforce. Given the training that farming sugarcane implied, planters preferred to rely on the blacks who could speak Spanish and knew the Spanish ways: they preferred *ladino* slaves over *bozales*).

Even though the sugarcane industry gradually developed and some plantations achieved large-scale dimensions, for the most part the agricultural economy of the territories now known as Peru, Ecuador and Bolivia was based on small and middle-sized haciendas, which did not rely on the massive exploitation of enslaved black workforce. The reasons behind the limited use of black captives had to do, once again, with their high cost. In fact, laymen did not usually have access to enough capital to purchase slaves in large numbers; the only institution that disposed of such financial resources at that time was the Catholic Church, and in particular the Company of Jesus.

By 1767, when the Jesuits were expelled from Spanish America, the Company of Jesus owned 5,224 slaves in Peru. Most of them were used on coastal sugarcane plantations (62.3 percent), 29.8 percent were employed in vineyards, and the remaining captives worked on highland farms (Macera 1966: 36). A close analysis of the local demographic figures (Cushner 1980: 89–110) reveals that, during the peak of the Jesuit sugarcane business (the years 1730–1767), the purchase of new captives was quite constrained (Sessarego 2015: 107), and that even the largest plantations had relatively few enslaved laborers.

Macera (1966) provides a detailed analysis of how Jesuit haciendas were run. He shows that the Jesuits were able to obtain high production rates from the enslaved workforce, while creating a working and living environment that would minimize the risks of revolt by generating a feeling of community among the captives. They supported the creation of nuclear families and incentivized local births by favoring marriages through keeping an almost equal number of men and women in each plantation. Slaves were provided with high-calorie foods so that they could tolerate the intense workload typically related with sugarcane harvesting. Each family was also assigned a small piece of land, called *chacra*, on which they could grow their own crops and raise animals. This custom, besides providing enslaved families with extra food, created a sense of ownership and belonging to the local community.

Captives were also systematically Christianized. The Jesuits devoted much energy to this task. Macera (1966: 30) describes several activities that had this purpose: *bozales* were methodically catechized, children had to attend daily religion classes, everybody was required to go to Mass on Sundays and during holy days (i.e., Christmas, Easter etc.), and religious ceremonies (i.e., baptisms, weddings, funerals, etc.) were regularly celebrated. All in all, it appears that the emphasis placed on Christian indoctrination also served as a means by which captives had significant exposure to the Spanish language. As a result, it may be inferred that language acquisition was facilitated.

In summary, it appears that a concomitance of several sociodemographic factors significantly reduced the possibility of a Spanish creole forming or being preserved in the Andes through this second phase. The agricultural sector consisted for the most part of small and middle-sized estates, since geographical and economic constraints did not favor the introduction of a large black workforce in these territories. Even when larger agricultural complexes existed, landlords preferred to rely on *ladino* and *criollo* captives, since they spoke Spanish and thus could learn the job more quickly. Most of the slaves who ended up in these haciendas, in fact, were not brought directly from

Africa; a good proportion were transferred to these rural areas from urban centers within the colony. The largest slave-owner institution, which could actually rely more systematically on an enslaved workforce, was the Company of Jesus. The Jesuits, in fact, used black captives in several agricultural enterprises across Bolivia, Ecuador and Peru. Nevertheless, due to forced participation in social and religious practices, the acquisition of Spanish by the captives was favored over the development of a creole language in the community.

2.2.3 The Gradual Path to Social Emancipation

Even though the Jesuit management was family-oriented and tried to create a sense of community among the captives as a way of reducing the potential risk of rebellions, it has to be said that the working conditions in these plantations could be harsh and that corporal punishment was often applied to slaves who did not follow the rules (Cushner 1980: 89–90). Unfortunately, after the expulsion of the Company of Jesus from Spanish America in 1767, the lives of Afro-descendants working on those plantations did not improve. At that point, in fact, the Jesuit haciendas (and the captives working on them) passed under the control of the *Temporalidades* council, a public institution in charge of selling the properties confiscated from the Company of Jesus to private buyers.

Historical records show that the new administration did not care much about the well-being of the slaves and the preservation of the traditional community norms implemented by the Jesuits. On many occasions the *Temporalidades* attempted to take away the *chacras* from the captives, and in some cases even the integrity of slave families was put at serious risk, since the new administration tried to sell family members individually, as single tokens. The new management under the *Temporalidades* led to a series of revolts across the former Jesuit plantations. These violent episodes, combined with the *Temporalidades*' general lack of business skills, resulted in a disastrous effect on the agricultural sector of the colonies. The Jesuits had built a well-administrated economic empire, which fell apart as soon as the *Temporalidades* started to manage it (Andrien 1995).

The following decades were characterized by tensions between Spain and its Latin American colonies, which entered into a series of independence wars. After years of conflicts between different Latin American armies and the Spanish forces, the territories now known as Ecuador, Peru and Bolivia managed to become independent, in 1822, 1824 and 1825, respectively

(Luna Desola 1978: 88–89). Subsequently, these new countries went through convoluted phases of slavery abolition (Clementi 1974). In principle, slavery was abolished in Bolivia in 1826, in Ecuador in 1851 and in Peru in 1854; however, in practice, for more than a century the Afro-descendant population of the Andes did not enjoy the same rights and freedoms as the white and mestizo citizens living in those regions (Hernández 2013).

This situation is well explained by Hassaurek (1867: 328–329), who visited Ecuador from 1861 to 1865 and used the following words to describe the living conditions of the Afro-descendants of Chota Valley:

> The Indians have entirely disappeared from the valley. The Negroes, who have taken their places, are *concertados* ... They are slaves in fact, although not slaves in name. Their services are secured by a purchase of the debts which they owe. As long as they remain in debt, which state, thanks to the skillful management of their masters, almost always lasts till they discharge the great debt of nature, they must either work or go to prison. Like the Indians, they are ignorant of their legal rights. They are hardly ever able to pay their debts, which, on the contrary, continue to increase, as their wages of one half real to one real are insufficient to satisfy their wants. When slavery was abolished in Ecuador, the owners of the Negroes in the sugar district immediately employed them to work for wages and managing to get them into debt, secured their services as debtors. Thus it may almost be said that they profited, instead of losing by, the abolition of slavery. They pocketed the compensation which the law provided for the slave owners and at the same time retained the slaves. It is true that the blacks do not work so much now as when they were bondmen, nor can their masters beat them as unmercifully as they did before; but, on the other hand, it must be considered that it is much cheaper now to purchase a Negro than it was then. Now, by paying a debt of fifty or seventy dollars which the poor fellow owes to somebody, his services may be secured, while formerly it took, perhaps, ten times that amount to purchase a slave.

This passage offers a good description of the living conditions of most Afro-descendants after the abolition of slavery, not only in Ecuador, but also in Bolivia and Peru. In Peru, in particular, soon after the declaration of abolition in 1854, in a law of January 1855 it was established that former slaves had to keep working on the same haciendas for a minimal wage. A few months later, the Government gathered a group of planters and assigned them the task of redesigning the rights and duties of the black workforce used in the fields. A politician of the time, Member of the Parliament Santiago Távara (1855: 34), classified such a regulatory plan as "worse than the recently abolished slavery system."

Unfortunately, until the advent of the Land Reforms, which took place in the second half of the twentieth century, the vast majority of the blacks living in rural areas continued to work on haciendas as peons receiving wages under the level of basic sustentation. Legally, they were not slaves, but in practice they still had to work almost for free and were not allowed to leave the hacienda without the owner's permission.

The Land Reforms of 1952 in Bolivia, 1964 in Ecuador and 1969–1975 in Peru assigned to local families a piece of land that had previously belonged to the hacienda on which they had been working as peons until that point. That provided them with a basic foundation on which to build a better life. Over the past few decades, these communities have gained access to education and mobility, so that many younger black Bolivians, Peruvians and Ecuadorians have left these rural villages in order to move to bigger cities, to study and obtain better-paid jobs. Even though the living and working conditions of Afro-Andeans have significantly improved over the past century, their situation is far from being favorable, since they still represent the most discriminated segment of Andean society (Hernández 2013).

Given the relative isolation that these rural communities traditionally experienced up to the Land Reforms, they managed to preserve vernacular varieties that present some significantly divergent features from standard Latin American Spanish. Nevertheless, due to this more recent access to education and mobility, the younger speakers of these communities tend to substitute some of the traditional Afro-Andean features with more prestigious standard Spanish ones (Sessarego & Gutiérrez-Rexach 2011, 2012; Sessarego 2011a, 2012a, 2012b, 2013d, 2017c; Sessarego & Rodríguez-Riccelli 2018). This cross-generational language shift is what some scholars may classify as "decreolization." However, I would be cautious with using this term in this specific case, since it would imply that these dialects were creoles at some point. On the contrary, I suggest that neither the sociohistorical, nor the linguistic evidence that we have indicates that these vernaculars went through such an intense process of grammatical restructuring. In fact, even the varieties spoken by the oldest Afro-Andean informants – who spent their entire lives in these rural villages – are not that radically divergent from standard Latin American Spanish. In the following sections, we will take a closer look at these three specific Afro-Andean communities to cast further light on the issue.

2.3 A Closer Look at Three Afro-Andean Communities

Having provided the general sociohistorical background that characterized the African Diaspora to the Andes, we will now pay attention to three specific Afro-Andean communities: Yungas (Bolivia), Chota Valley (Ecuador) and

A Closer Look at Three Afro-Andean Communities   51

Map 2.1 *Three Afro-Andean communities: Yungas, Chota Valley, Chincha*

Chincha (Peru). These focused analyses will offer a view of three different, but to a good extent parallel, rural settings, and thus help us cast light on the potential origin of the Afro-Hispanic vernaculars spoken in these regions (see Map 2.1, adapted from Klee & Lynch 2009: 6).

2.3.1   Yungas, Bolivia

The Yungas are tropical valleys located in the Department of La Paz, Bolivia. It is still not completely clear when the first black people arrived in this region; however, in a report of 1805, the overseer of the local Mururata hacienda, Mr. Francisco Xavier de Bergara, mentions that the owner, the Marquesa de Haro, was the first landlord in the area to rely on a black workforce (Crespo 1995: 105). This note, therefore, may be taken as a clue suggesting that the first significant presence of an enslaved black population in these valleys might date to the end of the eighteenth or the beginning of the nineteenth century.

This hypothesis appears to also be indirectly supported by the existence of several documents of that period concerning purchase transactions of just a few slaves at a time. For example, Portugal Ortiz (1977: 78) reports the sale of a married couple from Angola, who were purchased by a priest living in Chulumani in 1761, as well as the purchase of a young girl who was employed by a Yungan landowner in 1773 to carry out agricultural work in a local hacienda. These small sales, concerning only a few captives in each transaction, are perfectly in line with the overall historical records concerning the Black Diaspora to Bolivia. Several historians, in fact, as we saw, concur on saying that the logistic and financial constraints on slave trading did not allow for a large-scale introduction of a black workforce to the agricultural sector of the colony. Rather, slave transactions usually concerned no more than one or two slaves at a time (Lockhart 1994; Bridikhina 1995). In line with this constrained black presence in the region are the data provided by Crespo (1995: 96), who reports the information contained in a document written by a local priest working in the village of Chirca in 1802. He provides the number of Afro-descendants and natives living in the local haciendas. Of these small plantations, only four used a black workforce. They were Guayraoata, with 15 Afro-descendants (blacks and mulattoes) and 50 Indians, San Agustín (17 Afro-descendants and 28 Indians), Yacata (23 Afro-descendants and 128 Indians), and Collpar (28 Afro-descendants and 142 Indians).

Little demographic information is available for the Yungan haciendas until 1883. For that period, Portugal Ortiz (1977: 87–91) provides a more detailed picture of two local villages: Pacallo and Mururata. In Pacallo there were 67 whites, 63 *mestizos*, 340 Indians and 56 Afro-descendants; Mururata counted 55 whites, 183 *mestizos*, 236 Indians and 324 Afro-descendants. He also reports, without categorizing the inhabitants into specific ethnic groups, the villages of Chulumani, with 14 Afro-descendants out of a total population of 220; Tajmo, Calupre, Chigno, Chimasi, Tolopala and Suquillo, with 49 out of 902; Coroico, with 113 out of 5,335; Impata, with 252 out of 2,465; Coripata, with 315 out of 3,867; Chupe, with 240 out of 1212; and Lanza, with 102 out of 8,255.

When we analyze this demographic information for the eighteenth and nineteenth centuries, what emerges is certainly not a large-scale plantation society that heavily relied on a black labor force. On the contrary, the Afro-descendant group appears to be a significantly constrained minority. Even in Pacallo and Mururata, the haciendas with the highest percentages of blacks and mulattoes, there are no huge disproportions between the Afro-descendants and the white/*mestizo* group (Pacallo: 56 blacks/mulattoes vs. 130 whites/mestizos; Mururata: 324 blacks/mulattoes vs. 233 whites/mestizos). Data indicate that only in Mururata did the black/mulatto group outnumber the whites and *mestizos*. If we consider that the mulattoes were probably Spanish speakers (since, by definition, one of their parents was white) and that even the blacks at this point had probably not arrived to the Yungas directly from Africa, the chances of language creolization in such a context are quite slim.

The analysis of nineteenth-century Yungas provided by Busdiecker (2006: 38) is consistent with the aforementioned demographic data. She describes a system of small and medium-sized haciendas, where slaves were not the only source of labor, but rather they were complemented by both Indians and freed blacks, who received different forms of compensation for their work. In addition, data indicate that manumission was not rare. In fact, even though the working conditions were harsh, some slaves managed to save enough money over time to buy their own freedom (Portugal Ortiz 1977: 69). The most famous case of self-manumission is the story of King Bonifaz, who became well known for helping other captives buy their own freedom. For this reason, in the nineteenth century, he was symbolically proclaimed King of the Afro-Bolivian population by the members of the local community. This symbolic monarchy is still in place today, and the current King, Julio Pinedo, is an inhabitant of the local Mururata village (Sessarego 2011a: 41).

In summary, the available information we have on black slavery in the Yungas appears to indicate that Afro-descendants came to populate these valleys gradually, in all likelihood beginning in the eighteenth century. In particular, we observed that a large-scale plantation society was never in place in this region: the black/mulatto group never represented the majority of the population and the workers on these farms were not just slaves; rather, the enslaved workforce was systematically complemented by paid workers. Working conditions were probably not as harsh as in other American colonies. In fact, it appears that black captives had chances to accumulate some capital and eventually buy their own freedom. All in all, this scenario suggests that Afro-descendants probably had relatively good access to the Spanish spoken by the white/*mestizo* population. Moreover, given the geographical and financial constraints that characterized slave trafficking in the Andes, in all likelihood a good percentage of Yungan slaves were *criollos*, rather than African-born *bozales*. All of these factors significantly reduce the possibility of a creole language forming in colonial Yungas and therefore decrease the likelihood of contemporary YS being the result of a (de)creolization process.

2.3.2 Chota Valley, Ecuador

Chota Valley is a tropical region located on the border between the Provinces of Imbabura and Carchi, in the northern Ecuadorian Andes. The first record of an Afro-descendant presence in this area dates to a letter written in 1582 by a local priest, Antonio de Borja. In this document, he stated that in the valley, which by that time was inhabited for the most part by native people, there were six Spaniards, who owned a few slaves working on vineyards (Coronel Feijóo 1991: ch. 1).

As for this initial phase, historical data appear to suggest that blacks occupied an intermediate position between the Spaniards and the natives, and thus they might have had relatively good access to the Spanish language. They were a minority group, often employed by the settlers to exert violence against the local native populations, as indicated in a report of the time quoted by historian Coronel Feijóo (1991: 69):

> Mayordomos, esclavos negros y propietarios a punta de piedras, látigo, rejo y palo, comienzan a imponer nuevas normas de distribución del agua sobre las antiguas reglas indígenas ... andan con palos, rejones, perros, rodando y aguardando el agua (Supervisors, black slaves, and owners impose new water distribution rules on old Indian norms; they use stones, whips, spikes, and sticks ... they walk around with sticks, big spikes, and dogs to control water resources).

Coronel Feijóo (1991) has also shown how by the beginning of the seventeenth century the Company of Jesus managed to acquire properties across the valley and to gradually implement a shift in the labor force, from native workers to Afro-descendants. Such a shift was primarily driven by the fact that Indians systematically ran away. This progressive introduction of black workers, nevertheless, was not extensive, due to the financial constraints that affected the slave trade, as Coronel Feijóo (1991: 81) clearly points out:

> Hablar de importación masiva de negros, para la época, parece sobredimensionado; difícil resulta atribuir a los estancieros de la zona un negocio de tal magnitud (To talk about massive black importation, at that time, seems to be an overstatement; it is difficult to ascribe such a large-scale business to local settlers).

By the end of the seventeenth century, the Jesuit agricultural enterprise expanded and, as a result, began to rely more significantly on an enslaved workforce. Historical analyses of the Jesuit haciendas suggest that the majority of the captives used on these farms were locally born *criollos* (Peñaherrera de Costales & Costales Samaniego 1959: 215; Coronel Feijóo 1991: 93). This statement may be further supported by the data provided by Colmenares (1997) on the number and origins of the captives sold during the same period in Popayán (current-day Colombia), the most important slave market of the northern Andes (Bryant 2005). Colmenares (1997: 35) shows that, even during the peak of the slave trade in the 1730s, 60 percent of slave transactions concerned captives who were born in Spanish America.

According to the data reported by Cushner (1982: 136), by 1767 – the year in which the Jesuits were expelled from the colony – in their Chota Valley haciendas there were a total of 1,364 slaves, of whom 488 were children under the age of ten and 94 were classified as "too old to work." This demographic picture suggests, on the one hand, that birth rates were probably high (since small children were in all likelihood locally born and not shipped directly from Africa) and, on the other hand, that life expectancy was probably quite high (given that many slaves achieved an elderly age).

As was the case in many other Jesuit haciendas across Latin America, in Chota Valley the Company of Jesus also incentivized local slave reproduction and self-maintenance (Bouisson 1997: 48–51): an equal number of men and women in each plantation, support for nuclear families through marriage, each family had an independent house and a *chacra*, slaves could grow their own products during their time off and sell them at the local market, and they could accumulate capital and thus purchase their own freedom over time. Coronel Feijóo (1991: 110) even suggests that by the end of the eighteenth century there is evidence of black people renting out their *chacras* to white and *mestizo* workers.

All of this information certainly diverges significantly from the typical plantation societies documented for the English and French Caribbean (Klein & Vinson 2007; Browne 2017; Burnard & Garrigus 2018). Rather, Chota Valley haciendas appear to have been small farms in which a certain degree of social flexibility and chances to improve one's living conditions were provided to the members of the Afro-descendant group. These elements, in addition to the fact that most of the captives were in all likelihood *criollos*, suggest that the (de)creolization hypothesis is not the most feasible explanation for the nature of CVS grammar.

2.3.3 Chincha, Peru

The earliest document attesting black presence in the region analyzed for the study of CS (i.e., the haciendas of San José, San Regis, El Carmen and El Guayabo) dates to 1688. This record is a wedding agreement describing the dowry that Rosa Josepha de Muñatones y Aguado would bring to her marriage with Don Andrés de Salazar. The dowry consisted of the San José hacienda, which included, among other property "goods," 87 slaves (CHSJ 2012: 4). Historical data also confirm the existence in that period of the San Regis hacienda, which bordered San José and was purchased by the Jesuits in 1692 (Macera 1966: 22).

During the 1730s the San José hacienda was sold to Don Agustín de Salazar y Muñatones, who in the 1760s also bought San Regis, right after it had been expropriated from the Jesuits by the *Temporalidades* (CHSJ 2012: 4). Macera (1966: 43) reports the inventory of San Regis at the time of the expropriation. It included 302 slaves, of whom 166 were classified as fit to work, 77 were too young to carry out most of the heavy tasks, and 59 were too old. The existence of a significant number of young captives also indicates that they were probably born locally, while the presence of a number of elderly slaves suggests that life expectancy was relatively high.

Flores Galindo (1984: 108) also provides a description of the San Regis hacienda during this period. The number of slaves he counted matches the one provided by Macera (1966): 302 *piezas*. In addition, when analyzing the labor dynamics of the region, Flores Galindo (1984: 109) stresses one more time how most of the black workers used in these coastal haciendas must have been *criollos*, rather than *bozales*, since that was the option preferred by the landlords for that kind of job:

> Los grandes propietarios de la costa ... preferían a los negros criollos: con ellos era más factible desarrollar los lazos paternales y, además, se podía esperar que estuvieran entrenados en cultivos tan laboriosos como la caña o tan delicados como la vid (The most important coastal landlords ... preferred locally born blacks: with them it was easier to develop paternal connections and, moreover, one would expect them to be more familiar with sugarcane and winery cultivations, which required highly skilled labor).

This information, when combined with the data provided by Macera (1966) on the systematic indoctrination carried out in the Jesuit plantations (which also implied significant exposure to the Spanish language), further decreases the possibilities of a creole variety forming or being preserved in colonial Chincha.

The sociodemographic figures reported for these Peruvian haciendas appear to align quite closely with the data collected for Bolivian Yungas and Ecuadorian Chota Valley. In all of these cases, decreolization does not seem likely, since the historical conditions for a creole language to form in these regions were not present to begin with. Rather, it appears more feasible to envision a context leading to the development of contact varieties much closer to Spanish (see Figure 1.3). Given the relative isolation of these Afro-Andean villages until the Land Reforms, it is not difficult to imagine how a set of non-standard linguistic phenomena (i.e., the so-called "creole-like" features) could have been nativized and conventionalized at the community level and consequently preserved in these rural dialects up to the present day.

3 *Reconciling Formalism and Language Variation*

When analyzing non-standard varieties characterized by high levels of inter- and intra-speaker speech variability, it is of fundamental importance to understand both the linguistic and the social dimensions in which these vernaculars are spoken. To do so, and to collect and elaborate the data, I find it of particular use to combine formal generative theorizing and quantitative sociolinguistic methodology, two fields which, unfortunately, have usually faced a relationship of mutual exclusion, rather than collaboration. This chapter shows how formalism and language variation can and must be reconciled if the goal is to offer a more fine-grained analysis of the phenomena found in non-standard varieties such as the AHLAs.

The study of intra- and inter-speaker language variation has never been a hot topic in generative linguistics, whose object of investigation has traditionally been concerned with "an ideal speaker-listener, *in a completely homogeneous speech-community*, who knows their language perfectly and is unaffected by such grammatically irrelevant conditions as memory limitations, distractions, ... in applying his knowledge of the language in actual performance" (Chomsky 1965: 3). Indeed, building on the competence/performance dichotomy (Chomsky 1965: 10–15), the goal of formal linguistic theory has always been to understand the nature of the I(nternal)-language, which has been systematically approached by relying on the grammaticality judgments of a limited set of native informants (often educated speakers of standardized languages).

This methodology has led to highly sophisticated grammatical generalizations, exactly because it managed to put aside all the "noisy" complexities associated with performance (Barbiers 2009: 1608). For that same reason, however, the generative approach has often been criticized by sociolinguists, who have traditionally paid closer attention to the E(xternal)-language, by relying on bigger corpora of naturalistic speech samples (Newmeyer 2003; Guy 2005), often obtained by means of sociolinguistic interviews (Labov

1966, 1972a, 1972b), and analyzed with different sets of quantitative tools (Tagliamonte 2006, 2012, 2016).

During the past 30 years, generative scholars have gradually begun to pay closer attention to non-standard dialects and less prestigious vernaculars (Kayne 1996, 2000; Adger & Smith 2005). In this manner, with the goal of developing more fine-grained generalizations, the field has progressively shifted toward combining methodological approaches that originally appeared to be unreconcilable (Cornips & Poletto 2005). In the following sections, an overview of the main proposals dealing with inter- and intra-speaker variation will be offered. In so doing, this chapter highlights the importance of reconciling formal and variationist methodologies to obtain more comprehensive and reliable datasets, which are fundamental for the study of the non-standard linguistic phenomena encountered in the AHLAs. This is meant, therefore, to pave the way for the linguistic research that will be developed in the rest of this study.

3.1   Synchronic Variation in Traditional Generative Grammar

Inter- and intra-speakers' speech variability has always been excluded from mainstream generative theories of grammar (Chomsky 1957 et seq.), and even typological studies, often dismissed as "descriptive" and "surface-oriented," were not a matter of primary concern. In a recent review on the evolution of generative theorizing, Newmeyer (2017: 549) highlights the early skeptical words Chomsky (1965: 188) had for Greenberg's typological work:

> Insofar as attention is restricted to surface structures, the most that can be expected is the discovery of statistical tendencies, such as those presented by Greenberg (1963).

With the advent of the Principles & Parameters (P&P) program (Chomsky 1976, 1981, 1986), more and more attention started being paid to typological diversity, and Chomsky's attitudes toward Greenberg's universals gradually changed (see Newmeyer 2017: 549–550), to the point of classifying them as "of obvious relevance" (Chomsky 1981: 95), "very rich ... and ... very suggestive" (1982: 111) and "important, ... yielding many generalizations that require explanation" (Chomsky 1986: 21).

The P&P framework, in fact, pays close attention to cross-linguistic variation and proposes that languages can essentially be conceived of as combinations of a limited number of universal principles and a set of binary parameters, which are acquired through exposure to the linguistic environment and which would be responsible for the attested variation across languages. Therefore, principles would be innate and, consequently, shared by all languages (thus, they do not need to be acquired), while parameters would be triggered either one way or the other (+ or − value) by exposure to language. Chomsky (1988: 63) uses the following words to describe how children acquire a language:

> Acquisition of language is in part a process of setting the switches one way or another on the basis of the presented data, a process of fixing the values of the parameters.

Chomsky's more recent positive attitudes toward typological studies and cross-linguistic variation, however, have never been coupled with a similar enthusiasm for inter- and intra-speakers' speech variability. Indeed, cases of language-internal variation have usually been dismissed as instances of E-language, not relevant to the study of the I-language. According to the P&P model, in fact, once a parameter is set, that would be for good; thus, this framework does not envision that grammars could change during the lifespan of a speaker. This theory of grammar does acknowledge that languages change, but only diachronically, as the result of a cross-generational transmission mismatch, since each new generation of children would acquire and adopt a grammar that slightly differs from the systems internalized by their parents.

As a consequence of these theoretical assumptions, the study of formal syntax has traditionally been built on the grammaticality judgments of a reduced number of speakers, who were not asked to speak freely, but rather to rely on their metalinguistic intuitions (Chomsky 1966). Conversely, linguistic corpora, probabilistic modeling, and analysis of how people actually speak in society have never been popular research tools among generative scholars, to the extent that Chomsky (1965: 4) once even stated that the "observed use of language ..., habits, and so on, ... surely cannot constitute the actual subject matter of linguistics, if this is to be a serious discipline."

3.2 The Sociolinguistic View on the Matter

Chomsky's emphasis on the competence vs. performance contrast (and on how the systematicity of language could only be understood by studying the former aspect of such a dichotomy) paradoxically triggered a renewed interest in the study of language from a social perspective (Lavandera 1988: 1), which indirectly opened the doors to the development of what is known today as quantitative sociolinguistics (Labov 1966, 1972a, 1972b, 1984), a field whose main goal is the synchronic analysis of language variation and change in society. Sociolinguists, in diametrical opposition to generative scholars, build their hypotheses on big corpora of naturalistically occurring speech and have developed a number of techniques to study the "real vernacular" or the form of speech used by regular people when paying no metalinguistic attention to the way they talk (Labov 1972b).

Labov (1969) applied Chomsky's notion of language systematicity beyond the realm of competence to show that naturally produced speech is also rule-governed, in line with the concept of "orderly heterogeneity" (Weinreich, Labov & Herzog 1968: 100). In particular, Labov (1969) borrowed the idea of "optional rule" from Chomsky's (1957: 45) early transformational models, and adapted it to performance data to argue that the variable application of grammatical rules depends on both internal (linguistics) and external (social) factors and that, consequently, it can be modeled in a probabilistic fashion (Tagliamonte 2006: 129).

According to this theoretical approach, therefore, language has a probabilistic component; people make choices when they speak and, thus, in each speech community (Labov 1972b: 120–121), *there exist more ways of saying the same thing*. This observation lies at the roots of the "principle of sameness," implying the existence of more variants of the same linguistic variable (Labov 1972a). Over the years, sociolinguists have built several statistical tools to account for variation. One of the most well-known computer software programs that was specifically created to account for variable linguistic data is Varbrul, which was subsequently further developed into more powerful computer programs (i.e., GoldVarb, GoldVarb X, Rbrul etc.; see Tagliamonte 2016 for a review).

3.3 Synchronic and Diachronic Attempts to Reconcile Variation and Formalism

While within the sociolinguistic tradition, the study of individuals' language variation and non-standard vernaculars has been the main research engine for the past 50 years, within the generative enterprise, these topics have not received much consideration, and thus they have – for the most part – been excluded from the research agenda. However, during the past few decades, some attempts to reconcile these two research areas have been made. I find particularly worthy of mention the proposal by Kroch (1989, 1994) in relation to diachronic language variation, and the one by Kayne (1996 et seq.), who addressed synchronic variation across non-standard dialects, leading the way to studies in microparametric syntax (Black & Motapanyane 1996; Benincà

1989, 1994; Poletto 2000; Barbiers & Cornips 2001; Cornips & Poletto 2005; Kato & Ordóñez 2016).

Kroch's (1989, 1994) proposal to combine formal insights and quantitative methodologies was partially driven by the necessity of relying on performance data to study diachronic language variation and change, since it is materially impossible to have access to the grammatical intuitions of speakers who are no longer alive. The analysis of historical linguistic corpora – and the consequent detection of numerous patterns of variation – made it desirable for the field to formalize a theory of variation and change that could go beyond the very rigid postulation of the original P&P model, which conceived of parameters as permanently fixed during the lifespan of speakers (Chomsky 1981). For this reason, to account for the evolution of syntactic variants diachronically, Kroch suggests that different syntactic forms (associated with the same meaning) may coexist in the speech community and, therefore, in the minds of speakers. Those forms constantly compete, until change takes place and "one form tends to drive the other out of use and thus out of the language" (Kroch 1994: 187).

Kroch (1989, 2000), therefore, embraces the use of E-language data to unveil the nature of I-language structures and claims that the statistical tendencies detected in linguistic corpora reflect the grammatical evolution of parameters that belong to individuals' competence. Kroch's proposal, in this sense, may represent the first significant step toward the convergence of formal theorizing and performance data. He accounts for variation by suggesting that speakers may alternate between competing grammars with divergent parametric configurations, a proposal that has subsequently inspired a number of authors working on synchronic instances of language variation (Toribio 2000; Henry 2005; King 2005).

In the 1990s a new attempt to refine the P&P model was put forward. It concerned the analysis of non-standard varieties, this time from a synchronic perspective, to cast light on dialectal differences, with the goal of uncovering "microparametric correlations." Kayne (1996), in fact, was the first scholar to propose the notion of "microparameters," or the "switches" responsible for the linguistic differences found across closely related varieties. This led to the development of the research field known as "microvariation." The main objective of microvariationist studies is to test syntactic hypotheses and potential grammatical correlations across closely related languages. In fact, Kayne (1996: xii) conceives of microvariationist syntax as a "testing lab" for grammatical theories. He states:

> Comparative work on the syntax of a large number of closely related languages can be thought of as a new research tool, one that is capable of providing results of an unusually fine-grained and particularly solid character.

If it were possible to experiment in languages, a syntactician would construct an experiment of the following type: take a language, alter a single one of its observable syntactic properties, examine the result to see what, if any, other property has changed as a consequence of the original manipulation. If one has, interpret that result as indicating that it and the original property that was altered are linked to one another by some abstract parameter.

Experiments of the type described by Kayne are for obvious reasons impossible to run; nevertheless, by studying and comparing closely related dialects one may approximate similar findings. Three examples of research projects aimed at analyzing microvariation are the Italian Syntactic Dialect Atlas (ASIt), the Syntactic Atlas of Dutch Dialects (SAND) and the Syntactic Atlas of Spanish (AsinEs).[1] These projects have a number of goals. Not only do they document and describe linguistic variables across dialects, but they also relate them to aspects of language variation and change to better understand potential correlations among variables and thus test – and possibly refine – formal theories, which were originally developed based on standardized language data.

Researchers working on microvariation are well aware of the fact that the "ideal speaker-listener, in a completely homogeneous speech-community" (Chomsky 1965: 3) is just a theoretical abstraction not found in real practice. They are also conscious of the fact that dialects do not exist in isolation; rather, they are often in contact with other dialects and with standard varieties. Each speaker is in some sense linguistically unique, and thus each grammar may be said to present individual microparameters (Barbiers & Cornips 2001: 2).

3.4 Variation and Minimalism

The microparametric move toward a more empirical approach to the study of inter- and intra-speaker variation has been accompanied by recent proposals within the Minimalist Program (Adger 2006, 2007; Adger & Trousdale 2007), and even Chomsky's attitudes, which were originally rather skeptical toward the use of E-language data (Chomsky 1957 et seq.), appear less critical today, acknowledging that sociolinguistic research may be complementary to formal analysis. Thus, as recently highlighted by D'Alessandro and van Oostendorp (2017: 23) in a paper on the diversity of linguistic data, Chomsky (2001: 34) states:

---

[1] Additional information concerning these Atlases may be found at the following websites: http:// asit.maldura.unipd.it/, www.meertens.knaw.nl/projecten/sand/sandeng.html and http://asines .org/.

Internalist biolinguistic inquiry [Chomsky's term for what we call Chomskyan linguistics here] does not, of course, question the legitimacy of other approaches to language, any more than internalist inquiry into bee communication invalidates the study of how the relevant internal organization of bees enters into their social structure. The investigations do not conflict; they are mutually supportive.

Along the lines of this more cooperative approach, some authors have begun to combine aspects of generative syntax and sociolinguistics by enhancing academic dialogue and integrating theoretical and methodological aspects of these two historically divergent research tracks (Parrott 2007, 2009; Sessarego 2013d, 2014a). With the extension of theoretical analyses beyond the parametric interlanguage domain (Adger & Smith 2005, 2010), individual variation has become a significant aspect of formal research, thus bringing to the attention of the generative community naturalistic speech samples and linguistic phenomena that in the past have been – for the most part – neglected for being perceived as uninteresting performance errors.

This step toward a more empirical methodology has been favored, to some extent, by the derivational approach entailed by the Minimalist Program (Chomsky 1995). As detailed in Chapter 1, syntactic derivations are no longer conceived of as a rule-based process on string sequences. Rather, syntactic objects are understood as bundles of features whose computation is strictly dependent on valuation and checking mechanisms. Of relevance is also the distinction between interpretable and uninterpretable features. Interpretable features can be read at Logical Form (LF), and thus they contribute to the semantic interpretation of the syntactic object, while uninterpretable features lack such a semantic contribution; they are present in the derivation only to trigger the necessary syntactic operations. Such uninterpretable features have to be matched via *Agree* and are finally erased before Spell Out.

Given these assumptions, the Minimalist Program is endowed with a computational machinery that can account for important aspects of variation, since it admits several phonological outputs for a single semantic interpretation. Adger and Smith (2005) and Adger and Svenonius (2011) think of variation in terms of (un)interpretable features. In their view, the items entering the derivation may, or may not, be specified for certain uninterpretable features. Since these features are not readable at LF, their presence or absence will not have any effect on the interpretation of the operationalized structures. Thus, from a semantic standpoint, constructions either presenting or lacking uninterpretable features will be equivalent and equally legitimate for a convergent derivation. Notice that this postulation is perfectly in line with the fundamental sociolinguistic *principle of sameness* (Labov 1972b: 323). In fact, since certain features have no interpretation at LF, this implies that the speaker is alternating between different ways of saying the same thing (Sessarego & Gutiérrez-Rexach 2011).

In line with this theoretical architecture, variation can now be reduced to the specification of uninterpretable features in a derivation. The syntactic module and its operations (*Merge, Move, Agree*) remains invariable or "perfect" (Brody 2003), since variation is limited to the lexical component (Borer 1984). Variation occurs when one item or the other enters the numeration and participates in the syntactic derivation. Overt variation is, therefore, conceived of as the result of covert lexical selection. External and internal factors – in line with the sociolinguistic tradition – play a key role in conditioning such a variation; however, unlike the traditional Labovian model, they are not built into the notion of grammar. In other words, what is variable is not the syntactic operation, but rather the lexical selection (Adger & Smith 2005: 164).

This model also differs from Kroch's (1989, 1994) proposal of competing grammars displaying diverging parametric settings. On the other hand, Adger and Smith (2005) conceive of a system in which there is only one grammar, with invariable and universal syntactic operations, and a numeration of lexical items, which may or may not be endowed with specific sets of uninterpretable features. To quote their words, "this is a very minimal theory, since the idea that speakers have to choose lexical items is one which we simply cannot do without" (2005: 164).

Adger and Smith (2005: 154) show how this covert lexical selection leading to overt variation would take place with an example proceeding from Buckie English, the vernacular dialect spoken by a community of fishermen located on the Moray Firth in Scotland, in which it is possible to hear sentences presenting variable subject–verb agreement, as in (18).

(18) Buckie English
    a. He says 'I thocht **you were** a diver or somethin'.
       'He said "I thought you were a diver or something."'
    b. Aye, I thocht **you was** a scuba diver.
       'Yes, I thought you were a scuba diver.'

Adger and Smith (2005: 165–167) account for cases like (18a) by assuming that pronouns carry interpretable and valued person and number features, while tense (T) bears unvalued and uninterpretable specifications. Thus, when the operation *Agree* applies between T and the pronoun, these specifications will be checked and valued, as in (19), resulting in a standard subject–verb agreement configuration at Spell Out (20).

(19) T [*i*tense:PAST, *u*case:NOM, *u*num:, *u*pers:] ... pronoun [*i*num:SG, *i*pers:2, *u*case:]

→T [*i*tense:PAST, *u*case:NOM, ~~*u*num:SG~~, ~~*u*pers:2~~] ... pronoun [*i*num:SG, *i*pers:2, ~~*u*case:NOM~~]

(20) Spell Out: you were
you.NOM be.PAST.2.SG

To account for cases like (18b), on the other hand, the authors suggest that in the lexicon of Buckie English, besides the standard-like T head represented in (19), there is also another tense entry, T2, which presents the same interpretable features as T, but bears different uninterpretable features, and thus lacks [*u*pers] (21). Given these assumptions, the application of *Agree* between T2 and the pronoun will yield a different result, as indicated in (22), in which the person feature will not be computed, and thus the verb form will surface with the third-person default value (see Harley & Ritter 2002 and Corbett 2006, 2012 on the nature of feature complexity and default values).

(21) T2 [*i*tense:PAST, *u*case:NOM, *u*num:]... pronoun [*i*num:SG, *i*pers:2, *u*case:]

→T2 [*i*tense:PAST, *u*case:NOM, ~~*u*num:SG~~] ... pronoun [*i*num:SG, *i*pers:2, ~~*u*case:NOM~~]

(22) Spell Out: you was
you.NOM be.PAST.3.SG

Adger and Smith's (2005) proposal accounts for the type of variability attested in Buckie English and, for this reason, it has recently been borrowed and adapted by some authors to explain similar cases of morphosyntactic variation encountered in other languages. (See Parrott 2007 for American English; Parrott 2009 for Danish; Sessarego 2013d, 2014a, 2019b for the AHLAs; Sessarego & Ferreira 2016 for Popular Brazilian Portuguese; and Romero & Sessarego 2018 for Istanbul Judeo-Spanish.) This model represents, in my view, a significant step forward in the integration of formal theorizing and sociolinguistic methodologies. Thus, it is adopted in this book to formalize certain aspects of morphosyntactic variation characterizing YS, CVS and CS. Specifically, as will be shown in Chapters 4 and 5, postulating the existence of competing lexical entries endowed with divergent feature specifications appears to be particularly suitable for the analysis of the variable agreement phenomena found in these Afro-Hispanic vernaculars.

4 Variable Phi-Agreement across the Determiner Phrase

One of the morphosyntactic features most commonly associated with a potential creole origin for the Afro-Hispanic and Afro-Lusophone vernaculars spoken in the Americas is variable gender and number agreement across the Determiner Phrase (DP) (Granda 1968; Otheguy 1973; Lipski 2006a, 2006b; Perez 2015; Guy 1981, 2004, 2017; Baxter, Lucchesi & Guimarães 1997). My opinion on this matter is quite divergent from the claims proposed in several of these studies. While I certainly acknowledge that variable agreement is a clear indicator of contact-driven language restructuring, at the same time I struggle with the idea that the contemporary Afro-Latino varieties spoken in the Americas should be conceived of as the result of a (de)creolization process.

The reason behind my concern is not only rooted in the available sociohistorical evidence, which has shown on a number of occasions that the conditions for creole formation were not ideal in colonial Latin America (Sessarego 2017a; Díaz-Campos & Clements 2005, 2008; Clements 2009; Mintz 1971; Laurence 1974); it is also based on contemporary second-language acquisition (SLA) research. In fact, it is well known that variable agreement is a persistent property of second-language (L2) varieties, which may lead to fossilization phenomena even in the speech of advanced L2 and heritage speakers (Franceschina 2005; Lardiere 2007; Alarcón 2011; Cuza & Pérez-Tattam 2016). For this reason, the mastering of the inflectional morphemes associated with phi-features has often been classified as the "bottleneck of acquisition" (Slabakova 2008, 2009).

In this chapter, agreement data for Yungueño Spanish (YS), Chota Valley Spanish (CVS) and Chincha Spanish (CS) (Sessarego 2011a, 2013a, 2014a, 2015) will be provided. I will propose an SLA-based analysis that conceives variable gender and number agreement as the by-product of processing constraints applying at the morphology–syntax/semantics interface. Given that these phenomena are also common in *advanced* L2 varieties of Spanish, it is argued that they should not be necessarily understood as the result of a (de)creolization phase.

The agreement variability under analysis is ascribed to a cross-generational change, consisting of the systematic substitution of stigmatized basilectal Afro-Andean features with more prestigious Andean Spanish ones. Statistical results point in the direction of a gradual shift toward the formal register/ standard norm, which has been favored by the increasing social pressure exerted on these speech communities after the end of the hacienda system (Sessarego 2011b, 2014a). In fact, thanks to the Land Reforms that took place in these countries during the 1950s–1970s, the hacienda system fell apart, and Afro-descendants, who until that point had been forced to work on plantations as unpaid peons, obtained access to education and mobility. These social changes significantly increased the exposure of the members of these communities to standard Spanish (stSp), which triggered a gradual and systematic language shift from the traditional Afro-vernaculars toward the local standard Spanish varieties (Sessarego & Gutiérrez-Rexach 2011; Gutiérrez-Rexach & Sessarego 2014).

4.1   Fieldwork and Data Collection

As indicated in Chapter 3, due to the increasing attention paid to non-standard varieties of certain European languages (e.g., Italian, Dutch and Spanish) in recent years, some researchers have begun to combine formal theorizing and sociolinguistic methodologies with the objective of obtaining more reliable linguistic data from informants who may be metalinguistically aware of the stigma attached to the dialects they speak (Poletto 2000; De Vogelaer 2006; Seiler 2004; Henry 2005; Sessarego 2014a). In fact, as Cornips and Poletto (2005: 944) correctly point out, "adult responses on acceptability-judgment tasks rely at least in part also on explicit, prescriptive notions held by speakers." For this reason, it is not uncommon for informants of non-standard dialects to reject certain constructions presented to them during a grammaticality task not because they perceive them as ungrammatical, but rather because they associate such examples with non-prescriptive speech. This phenomenon can make the study of stigmatized varieties particularly challenging.

As for the Afro-Hispanic vernaculars, the high level of stigma and racial discrimination usually associated with these dialects and their speakers can significantly interfere with the reliability of data collection (Sessarego & Gutiérrez-Rexach 2011). While conducting fieldwork in certain Afro-Hispanic communities, it is not uncommon to perceive the feeling of unease certain speakers have when speaking about their native variety. Several members of these societies grew up believing that their language is in some sense "uncivilized" and "inferior to the standard." This belief has been documented for a number of Afro-Latino groups (Sessarego 2011a, 2013a, 2015; Lipski 2006a, 2006b) and may be best exemplified with Lipski's (2008: 23) words, when he describes the attitudes of some Afro-Bolivians toward their own traditional language:

> Many Afro-Bolivians refuse to speak the traditional dialect and even claim not to know it, with the excuse that "we are already civilized." In other words, the same Afro-Bolivians do not recognize the restructured character of their traditional dialect; some think it is "poor speech" or not being "civilized," while others think that it is only a few idioms implanted into a neutral Castilian.[1]

There are several ways of diminishing the effects of the prescriptive norm on the non-standard variety while collecting data. Sociolinguists have developed a number of techniques to do so (Labov 1984). In more recent studies, several generative researchers have also recognized the importance of the need for multifaceted methodologies to test the validity of grammaticality judgments (Tremblay 2005), especially because, in some cases, such judgments may be gradient rather than dichotomous (Sorace & Keller 2005).

The study of variable gender and number agreement across the DP in Yungas, Chota Valley and Chincha has proven to be highly sensitive to matters of stigma and prescriptive attitudes (Sessarego & Gutiérrez-Rexach 2011, 2012; Gutiérrez-Rexach & Sessarego 2014). In order to mitigate some of the aforementioned problems, a hybrid methodology was adopted during the data collection. For this reason, sociolinguistic interviews and grammaticality judgments were combined. Thirty-six informants participated in this study on phi-agreement (out of a total of some 150 speakers who, between 2008 and 2013, took part in a broader project investigating Afro-Andean grammars). Twelve members of each community were individually recorded during an hour-long sociolinguistic interview. In order to obtain a cross-generational trajectory of the evolution of these agreement systems, informants were divided into three age groups (80+, 51–80 and 21–50).

All of the participants were native speakers of their Afro-Andean variety and did not speak any other language common to the region (Quechua/Quichua,

---

[1] Original Spanish version: Muchos afrobolivianos se niegan a hablar el dialecto tradicional y aun afirman desconocerlo, con la excusa de que "ya somos civilizaos." En otras palabras, los mismos afrobolivianos no reconocen el carácter reestructurado de su dialecto tradicional; algunos piensan que es "hablar mal" o no ser "civilizado," mientras que otros estiman que se trata sólo de unos modismos injertados en un castellano neutral.

Aymara, etc.). These recorded conversations were carried out according to traditional sociolinguistic methodology: speakers were asked general/open questions and were invited to talk about topics they found interesting. This was done to put them at ease. The goal was, therefore, to reduce as much as possible their level of metalinguistic awareness to obtain more colloquial/ vernacular data by limiting potential effects related to the Observer's Paradox (Labov 1972a). Only in a second phase, usually a few days after the sociolinguistic interview, was the same informant asked for grammaticality judgments. These specific steps in the elicitation process were followed in order to avoid influencing the results of the interviews by telling the speaker the nature of the phenomena under investigation in advance (Sessarego 2014a).

In order to understand whether a certain pattern existed in a given community, in line with Cornips and Poletto's (2005: 944) methodology, I relied on both direct and indirect grammaticality judgments. For this reason, the participants were not only asked direct questions, such as 'Do you judge X correct in your dialect?', 'Can you say X?' and 'Does X sound right to you?', but also indirect questions, such as 'Have you ever heard anybody say X?', 'Is X present in this community?', 'Do you think that somebody could say X?' and so on. A comparison between the data collected through grammaticality judgments and the more natural speech proceeding form the sociolinguistic interviews showed that several of the speakers who claimed not to use a certain construction, but to know people who may employ it sometimes, were actually found producing it themselves on several occasions during the unmonitored sociolinguistic conversation. These results suggested that such structures were indeed possible patterns in their grammar and further highlighted the importance of relying on a number of data collection techniques when investigating stigmatized varieties.

4.2 Agreement Configurations Based on Both Grammaticality Judgments and Sociolinguistic Interviews

The data presented in this section represent a systematized overview of the results obtained from previous studies on YS (Sessarego 2011a, 2013d, 2014a; Sessarego & Gutiérrez-Rexach 2011; Sessarego & Ferreira 2016), CVS (Sessarego & Gutiérrez-Rexach 2012; Sessarego 2013a) and CS (Gutiérrez-Rexach & Sessarego 2014; Sessarego 2015). As indicated in Section 4.1, these data were collected by relying on both formal and sociolinguistic methodologies and reflected much grammatical variation. In particular, while speakers' intuitions on number agreement tended to be quite homogeneous, grammaticality judgments on gender patterns led to a high degree of heterogeneity among the members of these communities. Here, I will first summarize my findings for the aforementioned gender agreement configurations, and then I will elaborate on the nature of number agreement.

The results of the YS grammaticality judgments on gender agreement present the highest degree of variation. In fact, the grammatical intuitions of certain members of this community, usually the most elderly ones, tend to significantly diverge from the patterns reported by the youngest participants, which are more aligned with the standard Spanish (stSp) norm. Indeed, as is well known, stSp is characterized by a rich gender agreement system, in which all the grammatical categories within the DP (weak/strong quantifiers, prenominal/postnominal adjectives, articles and demonstratives) agree with the value (masculine or feminine) introduced in the derivation by the noun (N), as shown in (23).

(23) a. Toda la cerveza fría.
all-F. the-F. beer-F. cold-F.
'All the cold beer.'
b. Mucha/esta/una cerveza fría.
much-F./this-F./a-F. beer-F. cold-F.
'Much/this/a cold beer.'

The grammatical intuitions reported by my YS informants indicated the presence of at least three different gender agreement systems in the Afro-Yungan villages I surveyed (Tocaña, Mururata and Chijchipa). I labeled these grammatical configurations as groups A, B and C. Group A, consisting of one elderly speaker, shows gender agreement on definite articles and demonstratives, while presenting default masculine gender specifications on the remaining DP categories, as exemplified in (24).

(24) a. Todo la cerveza frío.
all-M. the-F. beer-F. cold-F.
'All the cold beer.'
b. Mucho/esta/un cerveza frío.
much-M./this-F./a-M. cold-M. beer-F.
'Much/this/a cold beer.'

In Group B (seven participants from the elderly and middle-age groups) a slightly more developed agreement domain is found, which is not only limited to articles and demonstratives but also extends to prenominal adjectives and weak quantifiers, as in (25). Agreement patterns are even more robust in Group

C (four young informants), where all DP elements agree in gender with the noun, as in stSp (23).

(25) a. Todo la cerveza frío.
   all-M. the-F. beer-F. cold-M.
   'All the cold beer.'
   b. Mucha/esta/una buena cerveza frío.
   much-F./this-F./a-F. good-F. beer-F. cold-M.
   'Much/this/a good cold beer.'

An analysis of the grammatical survey carried out in the Afro-Ecuadorian communities of Chota Valley (Tumbabiro, Carpuela, El Juncal, Cuajara and Concepción) led to similar results. This time, only two different configurations could be detected (Groups D and E). The participants belonging to Group D (three elder informants) showed the grammatical patters illustrated in (26), in which all DP categories except for strong quantifiers show gender agreement. As for Group E, the judgments of the remaining nine speakers converged toward the standard pattern (23), in line with the configuration reported for YS Group C.

(26) a. Todo la cerveza fría.
   all-M. the-F. beer-F. cold-F.
   'All the cold beer.'
   b. Mucha/esta/una cerveza fría.
   much-F./this-F./a-F. beer-F. cold-F.
   'Much/this/a cold beer.'

The grammatical findings proceeding from the investigation on Afro-Peruvian Spanish, which took place in the Chincha villages of El Carmen, El Guayabo, San José and San Regis, led to three different agreement patterns (Groups F, G and H). Afro-Peruvian Group F (two elderly informants) corresponds to Afro-Ecuadorian Group D, in which strong quantifiers are the only DP categories that do not agree with the noun, as in (26). Group G, which is composed of two elderly members of the community, presents an agreement system in which all elements but postnominal adjectives are morphologically marked for gender, as in (27). Group H (eight speakers) presents the standard agreement system, exemplified in (23) and already detected for YS Group C and CVS Group E.

(27) a. Toda la cerveza frío.
   all-F. the-F. beer-F. cold-M.
   'All the cold beer.'

72 *Variable Phi-Agreement across the Determiner Phrase*

    b. Mucha/esta/una   cerveza frío.
       much-F./this-F./a-F beer-F. cold-M.
       'Much/this/a cold beer.'

The grammatical configurations encountered in these Afro-Andean communities are summarized in Table 4.1, where the different groups, their (non)-agreeing categories and examples are reported.

Table 4.1 *Gender agreement configurations found in in Yungueño Spanish, Chota Valley Spanish and Chincha Spanish*

Grammars	Groups	Agreeing categories	Non-agreeing categories	Example
G1	A	Definite articles, demonstratives	Strong quantifiers, weak quantifiers, prenominal adjectives, postnominal adjectives	(24)
G2	B	Definite articles, demonstratives, weak quantifiers, prenominal adjectives	Strong quantifiers, postnominal adjectives	(25)
G3	C, E, H	Definite articles, demonstratives, strong quantifiers, weak quantifiers, prenominal adjectives, postnominal adjectives	—	(23)
G4	D, F	Definite articles, demonstratives, weak quantifiers, prenominal adjectives, postnominal adjectives	Strong quantifiers	(26)
G5	G	Definite articles, demonstratives, strong quantifiers, weak quantifiers, prenominal adjectives	Postnominal adjectives	(27)

As we can observe by looking at Table 4.1, the grammaticality judgments of the Afro-Andean informants interviewed yielded five different gender agreement configurations (G1–G5). When these results are analyzed in light of the variationist data proceeding from their sociolinguistic interviews, the picture gets even more complex. Indeed, when comparing the findings of the grammatical intuitions with the free-speech conversations, it became clear that several informants, who claimed during the grammatical task not to use a certain pattern, were found using it on multiple occasions when paying no metalinguistic attention to their speech. Sometimes speakers would variably alternate between different forms within the same utterance, as in example (28), which was extracted from a CS interview. In this example, it is possible to observe how, in the very same sentence, two instances of the strong quantifier *todo* 'all' present different gender agreement patterns, even though both appear with feminine nouns (Gutiérrez-Rexach & Sessarego 2014: 149). For some of the members of the Afro-Andean communities I interviewed, the lack of gender agreement on strong quantifiers was in the range of 50–60 percent. This suggests that cases of agreement variability are highly common in these varieties; thus, they could hardly be regarded as performance errors or "noise" (Sessarego 2014a: 127).

(28) Había   todo   una   plantación   de   algodón
     had   all-M.SG. a-M.SG.   plantation-F.SG. of   cotton-M.SG.
     y   toda   la   gente,   los   antiguos,   tenía
     and   all-F.SG. the-F.SG. people-F.SG.   the-M.PL. old-M.PL.   had
     que   trabajar   bajo   el   patrón.
     that   work-INF. under   the-M.SG.   owner-M.SG.
     'There was an entire cotton plantation and all the people, the previous generations, had to work for the owner.'

Findings from grammaticality judgment tasks on number agreement led to a less heterogeneous picture. In fact, while for gender agreement five different configurations were detected (see Table 4.1), in the case of number concord all of the interviewed speakers seemed to be well aware of a clear-cut binary distinction, which would yield to only two possible grammatical systems: in the traditional vernacular, number is marked non-redundantly across the DP, as in (29), while in stSp, morphological redundancy is the rule (30) (Sessarego 2014a: 128).

(29) YS[a]
     Mis/ejes/lu/mucho   buen   plato   tradicional.
     my-PL./this-PL./the-PL./much-SG.   good-SG. dish-SG.   traditional-SG.
     'My/these/the/many/four good traditional dishes.'

     [a]In traditional YS, *ejes* corresponds to stSp *esos/esas* 'these' (plural M/F), while YS *lu* corresponds to stSp *los/las* 'the' (plural M/F).

(30) stSp
Mis/esos/los/muchos buenos platos tradicionales.
My-PL./this-PL./the-PL./much-SG. good-PL. dish-PL. traditional-PL.
'My/these/the/many/four good traditional dishes.'

Nevertheless, even though the grammatical intuitions for number agreement of all of my informants converged, a comparison with the data proceeding from the sociolinguistic interviews revealed that much variation was still present, so that morphological number was realized quite variably across the different DP grammatical categories. Example (31) is taken from a YS speaker, who had a 40 percent rate of number agreement alternation, a level that, again, is difficult to reconcile with a simple matter of E-language performance errors.

(31) YS
Lu pequeño se ha muerto, mis hijas
the-M.PL. small-M.SG. REFLEX AUX died-SG. my-PL. daughter-F.PL.
jovena también se ha muerto. Mis hijo se ha muerto.
young-F.SG. too REFLEX AUX died my-PL. son-M.SG. REFLEX AUX died-SG.
Uno vivía aquí, uno a la Argentina.
one-M.SG. lived here one-M.SG. to the-F.SG. Argentina-F.SG.
'The kids died, my daughters died too. My sons died. One of them lived here, the other in Argentina.'

The collected data clearly indicate that variation is a natural component of human languages. This is an empirical fact, which appears to be particularly true for varieties – like these Afro-Andean dialects – that have not undergone intense processes of standardization (Kroch 1978; Weiss 2001; Gadet & Pagel 2019). This being said, however, it is also important to acknowledge that the attested variability is not random but rather highly structured. As will be shown in the following section, these data reflect the "orderly heterogeneity" of language (Weinreich, Labov & Herzog 1968: 100), and thus pattern according to precise linguistic and social factors.

4.3 Quantifying Variation

Besides exploring the possible configurations that emerged from speakers' intuitions on grammaticality judgments, my study of Afro-Andean grammars has been oriented toward the much more variable scenario emerging from the analysis of sociolinguistic interviews. For this reason, during the past few years several quantitative investigations have been carried out to cast light on the internal (linguistic) and external (social) factors influencing phi-agreement

Table 4.2 *Cross-generational variable rule analysis of the contribution of Grammatical Category and Generation to the probability of lack of gender agreement in the Yungueño Spanish DP*

(Total = 2,604; significance = 0.001)

	Factor weight	Lack of agreement %	N	Data %
Grammatical category				
Postnom. Adj.	.95	53	272	10
Strong. Q.	.66	35	275	11
Prenom. Adj.	.64	14	220	8
Indef. Art.	.62	12	280	11
Weak Q.	.60	10	102	4
Dem.	.24	3	84	3
Def. Art.	.23	2	1,371	53
	Range 72			
Generation				
81+	.67	21	651	25
51–80	.56	11	927	36
21–50	.35	1	1,026	39
	Range 39			

variability in these dialects (Sessarego 2013d; Sessarego & Gutiérrez-Rexach 2011; Sessarego & Ferreira 2016; Gutiérrez-Rexach & Sessarego 2014; Sessarego & Rodríguez-Riccelli 2018). As for instances of gender and number agreement in the DP, the data extracted from the sociolinguistic corpus of natural speech were run using GoldVarb X, a software program that requires the establishment of a basic variant and directionality between variants in order to perform analyses. GoldVarb X calculates the degree to which a given independent factor favors (> .50) or disfavors (< .50) the process in question, thus yielding or not to a certain variant realization for the linguistic variable under analysis (Tagliamonte 2006: 128–129).

The results obtained by using GoldVarb X to analyze variable gender agreement in the Afro-Andean datasets indicate that two main factor groups have a significant effect on this phenomenon: Generation and Grammatical Category (see Tables 4.2–4.4). In fact, for YS, CVS and CS, older speakers tend to present less agreement than younger informants, and a clear hierarchy

Table 4.3 *Cross-generational variable rule analysis of the contribution of Grammatical Category and Generation to the probability of lack of gender agreement in the Chota Valley Spanish DP*

(Total = 2,082; significance = 0.000)

	Factor weight	Lack of agreement %	N	Data %
Grammatical category				
Postnom. Adj.	.95	43	283	14
Strong. Q.	.87	24	240	12
Prenom. Adj.	.76	15	160	8
Indef. Art.	.70	11	185	9
Weak Q.	.66	8	73	3
Dem./Def. Art.	.19	1	1,141	54
	Range 76			
Generation				
81+	.78	21	678	33
51–80	.55	11	840	40
21–50	.13	2	564	27
	Range 65			

of agreeing categories can be identified across each generation (Gutiérrez-Rexach & Sessarego 2014).

While Generation and Grammatical Category are significant for each of the three dialects analyzed, findings also indicate that the effects of the linguistic and social factors are not homogeneous across YS, CVS and CS. Indeed, CS presents fewer instances of gender variation and, consequently, it also shows lack of alternation for certain factors. For this reason, the first GoldVarb X run I performed on this dialect provided several "knock-outs." GoldVarb X knock-outs indicate that variation is not present for certain factors, and thus the program cannot run a variable rule analysis on the data (Tagliamonte 2006: 152). In order to overcome this problem, some grammatical categories and generations had to be collapsed, and a new run had to be carried out on the recoded tokens. The statistical results for this and the other Afro-Andean vernaculars are reported in Tables 4.2–4.4 (Gutiérrez-Rexach & Sessarego 2014: 146–148).

As the tables show, in each dialect, Grammatical Category is the most significant factor group. In YS and CVS all DP categories favor lack of

Table 4.4 *Cross-generational variable rule analysis of the contribution of Grammatical Category and Generation to the probability of lack of gender agreement in the Chincha Spanish DP*

(Total = 2,455; significance = 0.000)

	Factor weight	Lack of agreement %	N	Data %
Grammatical category				
Postnom. Adj.	.94	11	261	11
Strong. Q.	.92	9	249	10
Other Ds.	.34	1	1,945	79
	Range			
	60			
Generation				
81+	.76	6	781	32
51–80	.37	1	1,674	68
	Range			
	39			

agreement with the exception of demonstratives/definite articles. Conversely, in CS only postnominal adjectives and strong quantifiers favor this phenomenon. In fact, as indicated before, due to the lack of agreement variation for certain Ds in this Peruvian dialect, in order to avoid knock-outs, several categories had to be merged under the label Other Ds (see Table 4.4).

As for the Generation factor group, again, we can observe how YS and CVS behave similarly, with speakers in the 81+ and 51–80 groups favoring lack of agreement. On the other hand, in CS the age groups 21–50 and 51–80 had to be collapsed and, for this reason, the only generation favoring this phenomenon is 81+. Overall, by looking at the percentages of lack of agreement in each table, it is possible to conclude that, of the three, YS is the most divergent vernacular from stSp, followed by CVS and CS, in that order.

Figures 4.1–4.3 graphically show the evolution of the agreement domain across generations and grammatical categories in these Afro-Andean dialects. By looking at these graphs, we can see even clearer how – over three generations of speakers – gender agreement has experienced an incremental expansion along the same path of DP categories (from definite articles/demonstratives to postnominal adjectives). This suggests that the evolution of agreement is certainly not random. Rather, it is constrained by a specific syntactic hierarchy, as shown in (32) (Sessarego & Gutiérrez-Rexach 2011; Sessarego 2014a).

78 Variable Phi-Agreement across the Determiner Phrase

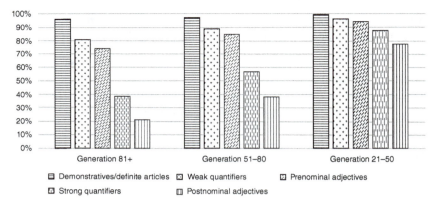

Figure 4.1 *Gender agreement evolution across the Yungueño Spanish DP*

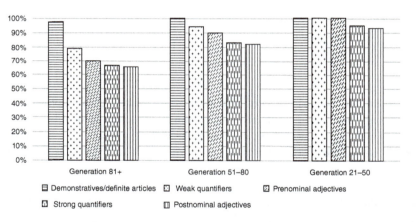

Figure 4.2 *Gender agreement evolution across the Chota Valley Spanish DP*

(32) Definite articles/Demonstratives > Weak quantifiers > Prenominal adjectives > Strong quantifiers > Postnominal adjectives

This phenomenon is, nevertheless, driven by social factors. As indicated in previous studies (Sessarego 2014a; Gutiérrez-Rexach & Sessarego 2014), with the Land Reforms (1950s–1980s) the hacienda system ended and, consequently, the members of these Afro-Andean communities had access to education and mobility. Exposure to the standard norm has been higher for younger generations and, as expected, this is reflected in the way they speak.

In the literature on vernacular speech, similar cases of variation have often been analyzed as the result of alternation between speech styles (i.e., formal vs.

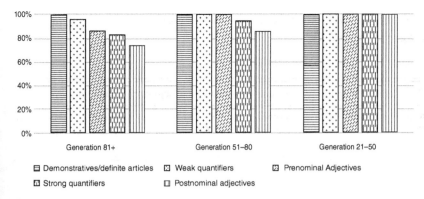

Figure 4.3 *Gender agreement evolution across the Chincha Spanish DP*

informal). For example, in DeCamp's (1971: 353) generative analysis of post-creole speech continua, the author envisions the existence of a [+/− oratorical] stylistic feature, which would be at the root of the attested variability. Another model that tries to formalize variation by relying on speech style alternation is the proposal offered by Henry (2005) to account for the variation between *there are* and *there's* in Belfast English. In this case, according to the author, speakers would switch between a formal and an informal grammar. The formal grammar, in contrast with the informal one, would require the verb to agree with the subject, while, in informal contexts, default singular verb forms would appear even with plural subjects (i.e., *there's cats*).

The aforementioned proposals are certainly of interest but, unfortunately, they appear to be of little help for the gender agreement data so far considered. This is because, in just an hour of recorded interview time, the switches between potential grammars and styles were so many that the attested variation could not possibly be conceived of as a matter of formal vs. informal speech (see example (28) and Tables 4.2–4.4). A systematic formalization of variation becomes even more complex if we add to the picture the data concerning variable plural marking, since the number of potentially competing grammars would increase exponentially (see example (31) and Table 4.5 for number agreement variation in the speech of elder YS informants, Sessarego 2014a: 131), thus further reducing the feasibility of such an account (Delicado-Cantero & Sessarego 2011; Sessarego & Ferreira 2016).

In recent works, models have been offered to explain the attested phi-agreement variability without reducing it to a mere matter of style (Sessarego & Gutiérrez-Rexach 2011; Sessarego 2013d). The proposal builds

Table 4.5 *Variable rule analysis of number agreement variation in the Yungueño Spanish DP*

(Total = 532; significance = 0.007)

Grammatical category	Following phonological segment	Following stress
Adjective .65 (N = 47)	Vowel [.53] (N = 121)	Weak [.51] (N = 230)
Noun .55 (N = 313)	Pause [.49] (N = 61)	Heavy [.50] (N = 302)
Determiner .38 (N = 172)	Consonant [.47] (N = 350)	

on current minimalist ideas on feature valuation and checking (Pesetsky & Torrego 2007), which partially contrast with previous assumptions on the nature of syntactic agreement (Chomsky 2001). By elaborating on Adger and Smith's (2005) proposal, which has already been laid out in Section 3.4, in the following section I will present an account that does not conceive of inter-speaker variation as code-switching between styles and/or grammars. Rather, the attested morphosyntactic phenomena are here analyzed as the result of a variable lexical selection within a single grammatical system, which is characterized by invariable and universal syntactic operations (Brody 2003).

4.4 Reconciling Variable Outputs with Invariable Syntax

The analysis of free-speech data appears – at first – not to be strictly relevant for formal linguistic theory, which has been primarily concerned with the study of I-language to cast light on the nature of UG. This being said, it has also to be mentioned that, within the Principles and Parameters (P&P) framework, a number of efforts were made to explore aspects of dialectal variability to the point of postulating the existence of microparameters (Kayne 1996; Black & Motapanyane 1996). If, on the one hand, it is true that more investigations have been carried out across closely related language varieties, on the other hand, language-internal variation has traditionally been out of the reach of formal proposals. Nevertheless, during the past few years, several researchers have begun to devote more attention to this issue (Adger & Smith 2005; Adger 2006; Parrott 2007; Sessarego 2013d).

The study carried out by Adger and Smith (2005) to cast light on Buckie English variability represents a clear step forward in this direction. It proposes a model that, while reconciling the social and the formal aspects of this speech community (Cornips & Corrigan 2005), also accounts for its variable patterns. As illustrated in Section 3.4, Adger and Smith's analysis assumes that the syntactic module of the language faculty remains invariable or "perfect" (Brody 2003), since variation is limited to the lexical component. Thus, variation occurs when one item or another is selected from the numeration and participates in the syntactic derivation. This proposal, then, is in line with minimalist assumptions on the nature of language computation (Chomsky 1995, 2001) and, at the same time, builds on the sociolinguistic principle of sameness (Labov 1972a). Indeed, by ascribing variation to the specification of uninterpretable features (which cannot be read at LF), it implies that all of the potentially alternating structures consist of different ways of saying the same thing (Labov 1972b: 120–121).

A number of internal (linguistic) and external (social) factors may affect the item selection: level of activation in the mental lexicon, frequency, speaker's education, age, etc. (Adger & Smith 2005: 164). Such a variable choice is exactly what can be observed when the Afro-Andean data on variable phi-agreement are approached quantitatively (see Tables 4.1–4.4). This model, therefore, goes well beyond the notion of (micro)parameters; it also accounts for idiolectal and language-internal variability without conceiving of the presence/absence of a given set of features as an on/off "switch" that applies across the board to all the speakers of a certain dialect.

The overt agreement phenomena detected in the Afro-Andean vernaculars under analysis are here analyzed as the result of a covert syntactic operation called *Agree*. *Agree* is depicted as a relation between two objects within a syntactic domain: a probe and a goal (Chomsky 1995). The probe consists of an unvalued set of phi-features, which have to receive a value from some other syntactic constituent during the derivation (Béjar 2008: 133–134). In order for *Agree* to apply, several formal requirements have to be met (Preminger 2014): (a) there must be a configuration in which an unvalued instance of a feature F (probe) c-commands another instance of F (goal); (b) these two features have to be sufficiently close to each other (Locality Condition); (c) a probe can agree with a goal if there is no other instance of the same probe in between the two (Minimality Condition); and (d) at least one of the relevant syntactic objects must bear an unvalued feature (Activity Condition).[2]

---

[2] I adopt here Adger's (2010) version of the Activity Condition, which prescribes that the probe should bear an unvalued feature. It does not align completely with the original postulation of the Activity Condition (Chomsky 2000, 2001), which indicates that both the probe and the goal should carry an unvalued instance of F (see also Pesetsky & Torrego 2001; Svenonius 2002; Bežač 2004).

Recent proposals on the nature of *Agree* suggest an analysis that partially diverges from the original account of this operation, which conceived of it as a "feature assignment" mechanism (Chomsky 1995, 2000). Conversely, this operation is now understood as a matter of "feature sharing" (Frampton & Gutmann 2000), a concept that converges with the idea of agreement as an instance of "feature unification," common to head-driven phrase structure grammar (HPSG) (Pollard & Sag 1994). Pesetsky and Torrego (2007: 4), who embrace this novel perspective, formalize *Agree* as follows:

(33) *Agree*
   a. An unvalued feature F (a probe) on a head H at syntactic location α (Fα) scans its c-command domain for another instance of F (a goal) at location β (Fβ) with which to agree.
   b. Replace Fα with Fβ, so that the same feature is present in both locations.

From (33) it follows that the application of *Agree* will imply that a feature value, once introduced into the derivation, will be cyclically probed by all unvalued items c-commanding it, resulting in the sharing of such a value across probes. Pesetsky and Torrego's (2007) proposal deviates from Chomsky's (2001: 5) Valuation/Interpretability Biconditional statement, summarized in (34).

(34) Valuation/Interpretability Biconditional
      A feature F is uninterpretable if F is unvalued.

Pesetsky and Torrego, in fact, opt for a system in which the requirement stated in (34) is removed. For this reason, lexical items can now enter the derivation with two combinations of properties that were not contemplated in the original model proposed by Chomsky: (a) uninterpretable but valued, and (b) interpretable but unvalued. A full list of all the possible feature specifications envisioned by Pesetsky and Torrego (2007) is provided in (35).

(35) uF[val]   uninterpretable, valued
      iF[val]   interpretable, valued
      uF[ ]   uninterpretable, unvalued
      iF[ ]   interpretable, unvalued

Example (35) spells out the annotations used to describe four possible feature specifications, which consist of two probes (i.e., uF [ ], iF [ ]) and two goals (i.e., uF[val], iF[val]) for a given feature F. In order to provide a clearer graphic representation of the phi-variability encountered in these vernaculars, the annotation of items lacking a certain feature specification has also been created (*no*-F[ ]). These items, as a consequence of such a feature absence, will not be able to take part in *Agree*, either as probes or as goals. A schematic illustration of the abovementioned agreement mechanism is provided in (36), where the value introduced in the derivation by a certain item (36a) is cyclically shared across all the entries carrying the same feature specification (36b–d), leaving those lacking it unaffected.

(36) Feature sharing across categories bearing an F specification

a. *no*-F [ ] ... *u*F [ ] .... *u*F [ ]. ..... *u*F [ ] .... *i*F [**val**]
b. *no*-F [ ] ... *u*F [ ] ...... *u*F [ ]. ..... *u*F [val] ... *i*F [**val**]
c. *no*-F [ ] ... *u*F [ ] ...... *u*F [val] ... *u*F [val] ... *i*F [**val**]
d. *no*-F [ ] ⤫ *u*F [val] ... *u*F [val] ... *u*F [val] ... *i*F [**val**]

Building on Sessarego's (2014a) analysis of Spanish DPs, I assume the structure provided in (37), in which N°, Num° and D° are conceived of as the loci of interpretation for gender, number and person features, respectively (see also Carstens 2000; Simioni 2007). By virtue of the aforementioned elimination of the Valuation/Interpretability Biconditional (Pesetsky & Torrego 2007), my model does not assume that these categories will always enter the derivation with a value. Rather, the value may well be introduced into the derivation by different items, depending on the language variety. I propose that in stSp the noun comes from the lexicon fully valued for gender, number and person features, while in Afro-Andean Spanish the noun will only carry values for gender and person, so that Afro-Andean Spanish number values will be introduced by Num.

(37)

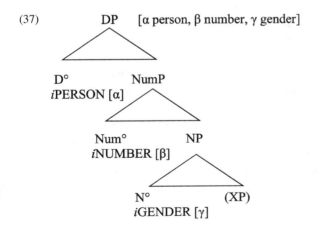

The postulation of these cross-linguistic differences in feature specifications, as already described in Sessarego (2014a: 117), allows all DP categories in both Afro-Andean varieties and standard Spanish (stSp) dialects to probe for gender and number values across the DP structure while obeying the principle of c-command, which underlies *Agree*. Thus, this solution overcomes previous technical debates on the nature of DP-internal agreement, without relying on ad hoc mechanisms such as "concord" and "co-indexation," which were designed to account for the data while circumventing c-command (Franceschina 2005; Demonte 2008; Picallo 2008; see Sessarego 2014a: 116–117 for an overview).

Given these theoretical assumptions, the phi-feature variation attested for YS, CVS and CS can be formalized by stating that certain DP categories in these dialects may be variably endowed with uninterpretable gender and number specifications. Thus, the overt morphological reductions encountered in these vernaculars can be seen as by-product of a covert lexical selection in which certain items are not specified for phi-features. A syntactic sketch of how this model is applied to my sets of Afro-Andean data is presented in (38) and (39) for gender and number agreement, respectively.

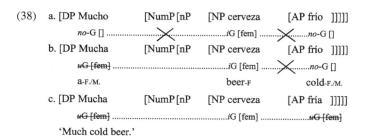

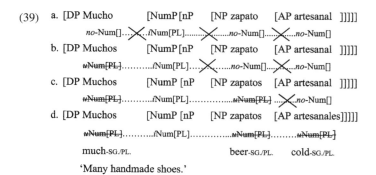

As these examples show, the proposed model can account for all the cases of gender and number agreement variability attested across the Afro-Andean DP, without having to postulate the existence of many potentially competing grammars. This model is, therefore, also well in line with the Borer–Chomsky Conjecture (Baker 2008: 156), since it identifies the lexicon with "its inventory of inflectional rules and ... grammatical formatives" as the locus of variation (Borer 1984: 29). Thus, as Adger and Smith (2005: 164) highlight, this is a very minimal solution, since speakers' selection of lexical items is a non-omittable aspect of any theory of grammar.

The quantitative findings presented in Tables 4.2–4.4 and graphically reproduced in Figures 4.1–4.3 align perfectly with the grammatical intuitions reported in Table 4.1, which may be summarized in the following statements describing the five different "grammars" (Gs) of the dialectal/idiolectal varieties detected for CS, YS and CVS (see also Gutiérrez-Rexach & Sessarego 2014: 157):

(i) G1: Gender agreement applies only to definite articles and demonstratives (example (24)).
(ii) G2: Gender agreement applies to all categories but strong quantifiers and postnominal adjectives (example (25)).
(iii) G3: Gender agreement applies to all categories (example (23)).
(iv) G4: Gender agreement applies to all categories but strong quantifiers (example (26)).
(v) G5: Gender agreement applies to all categories but postnominal adjectives (example (27)).

When these statements are compared with the sociolinguistic results, it is possible to observe that gender agreement develops across categories and generations in a systematic way. The patterns reported in G1–G5 also align with the hierarchy in (32), so that, for example, no grammar displays agreement on weak quantifiers unless definite articles and demonstratives agree too, and there is no agreement on postnominal adjectives and strong quantifiers unless prenominal adjectives and weak quantifiers also agree.

The attested evolution of gender agreement in these varieties can be explained as a gradual expansion of the agreement domain across DP categories. In resonance with Sessarego and Gutiérrez-Rexach (2011) and Sessarego (2014a), I propose the Local-Agreement Gradience Function (LAGF), which posits that agreement (sharing) obtains as the result of *Agree* applying in a local relationship and gradually expanding to less local domains. The LAGF, therefore, claims that the closest probe to the goal will get valued first and then act as the trigger for subsequent *Agree* operations to take place.

The LAGF, as formulated in Sessarego (2014a: 141), is here reproposed:

(i) If A and B are potential probes for feature F in goal C and B is closer (more local) to C than A, then *Agree* can apply between A and C only if it applies between B and C. The closer a functional head is to the noun, the more likely it is to enter into an agreement (sharing) relation with it.
(ii) Additionally, a functional element becomes a potential probe for F when it is specified as unvalued for F.
(iii) There is speaker variation with respect to the specification of F.

The LAGF delivers an evolutionary core-periphery path for the development of unvalued gender specifications across the DP. It predicts the incremental expansion of the agreement domain reflected in (32), as detected by relying on grammaticality judgments (Table 4.1) and on quantitative methodology (Tables 4.2–4.4): definite articles and demonstratives are more likely to agree with N; weak quantifiers and prenominal adjectives are less likely; and strong quantifiers and postnominal adjectives are the least likely.

Interestingly, these results are also in line with a number of SLA studies on the evolution of gender agreement. Hawkins (1998) showed that English speakers learning French present more agreement on definite articles than indefinite ones, and more agreement on determiners than adjectives. Bruhn de Garavito and White (2002) reported similar results for English L2 speakers of Spanish, in line with Franceschina (2005), who tested advanced L2 Spanish-speakers coming from a variety of L1 backgrounds (Italian, French, Portuguese, Arabic, English and German). All of these studies, besides assuming that masculine represents the default value, also share the view that agreement evolution (as any other aspect of grammar for that matter) follows incremental/ hierarchical steps.

From a biolinguistic point of view, these Afro-Andean data show how evolutionary dynamics meets dialectal variation. In line with Nowak's (2002) and Nowak, Komarova and Niyogi's (2001) proposal on the evolution of grammars, the LAGF provides a coherence measure for performance differences among a number of competing grammars (G1–G5) with respect to a given candidate grammar. More precisely, it can be observed how, in these communities, social pressure is moving the convergence point (ideal fitness) of the LAGF closer to standard Spanish (Sessarego 2014a: 141). The main consequence is a progressive application of *Agree* to less local probes, which may eventually result in a complete convergence with standard Spanish and thus in a generalized feature-sharing mechanism across the entire DP domain for younger generations of Afro-Andean speakers.

The processes exemplified in (38) and (39) can be further illustrated by deriving a DP presenting complete gender and number agreement, as in stSp (40), and then contrasting it with an Afro-Hispanic construction lacking any overt morphological redundancy for such features, such as (41) in traditional YS.

(40) stSp
Esas   pequeñas   cervezas   frías
this-F-PL small-F-PL   beer-F-PL   cold-F-PL
'These small cold beers.'

(41) YS
Ejes   pequeño   cerveza   frío
this-M-PL small-M-SG   beer-M-SG   cold-M-SG
'These small cold beers.'

The analysis of a structure like (40) would proceed as follows. The noun *cerveza* enters the derivation with an interpretable valued gender feature [*i*gen: +F], an uninterpretable valued number feature [*u*Num:+PL] and an uninterpretable valued person feature [*u*pers:+3rd]. After the application of *Merge*, the noun combines with *n*, it raises and adjoins to it.

(42)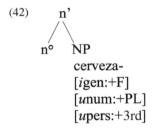
n°   NP
     cerveza-
     [*i*gen:+F]
     [*u*num:+PL]
     [*u*pers:+3rd]

In line with traditional assumptions on the distribution of adjectives across the DP (Cinque 1990, 1993, 1994), I assume that postnominal adjectives are merged earlier in the derivation than the prenominal ones. For this reason, at this point, the adjective *frí-* adjoins to the specifier projected by *n*°. The adjective comes with uninterpretable unvalued number and gender specifications, which act as probes and scan their local c-command via *Agree*. In this

88 *Variable Phi-Agreement across the Determiner Phrase*

way, they get valued, and thus number and gender values are shared between N and A.

(43)
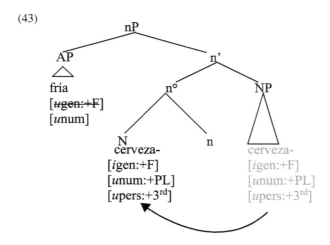

The *n*P then merges with Num, which, as indicated above, is the locus of interpretation of number, and thus carries an interpretable unvalued number feature [*u*Num:]. This specification acts as a probe and gets valued [*u*Num: +PL]. The noun moves to Num°. Num° projects a specifier in which the prenominal adjective *pequeñ-* will be merged. The uninterpretable unvalued specifications carried by this adjective will act as probes, thus resulting, once again, in the sharing of gender and number values.

(44)
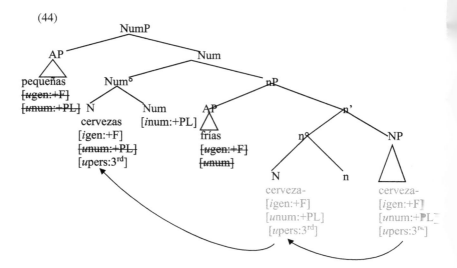

Eventually, the D head is also merged at the top of the syntactic structure. Ds are the locus of interpretation of person features. The determiner, therefore, enters the derivation with an interpretable unvalued specification for person [ipers:] and two uninterpretable unvalued ones for gender [ugen:] and number [unum:], which will get valued after the operation *Agree* applies.

(45)

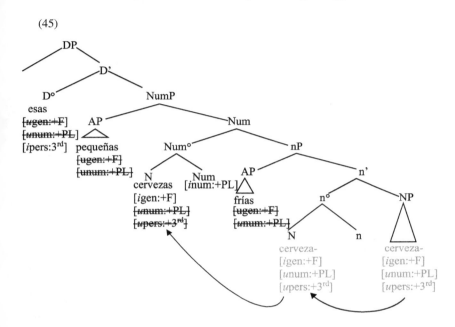

The model so far presented accounts for the agreement patterns encountered in stSp, in which all DP categories are specified for gender and number features and, consequently, result in redundant morphological marking across the DP, as in (40). Moreover, this proposal can also distinctively explain the different agreement patterns detected across the Afro-Andean varieties under analysis. In fact, with no need to postulate any modification to *Agree*, *Merge* and *Move*, it is possible to account for examples such as (41) by assuming that the YS DP categories in question lack most of the uninterpretable feature specifications found in stSp, thus resulting in default singular and masculine values, as in (46).

(46)

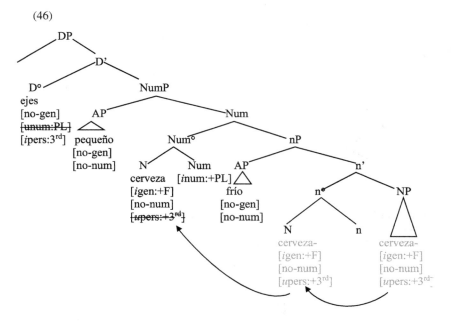

Another important distinction that must be highlighted between stSp and YS is the fact that in the Afro-Andean dialect the value for number is not introduced by N, as in stSp, but rather by Num. Note that, as far as number features are concerned, this proposal could arguably be adopted to account for the differences in agreement patterns detected between standard Brazilian Portuguese (stBP) (redundant plural marking) and popular Brazilian Portuguese (pBP) (non-redundant plural marking) as well (Scherre 1983, 1991; Simioni 2007). These two dialects, in fact, as explained by Sessarego and Ferreira (2016) and exemplified in (47) and (48), present agreement patterns that overlap with those of stSp and YS respectively.

(47) stBP
As casas vermelhas
the-F-PL house-F-PL red-F-PL
'The red houses.'

(48) pBP
As casa vermelha
the-F-PL house-F-SG red-F-SG
'The red houses.'

It is also worth stressing that the model proposed here, in which syntax remains constant and changes consist of modifications to bundles of features in the lexicon, can easily be applied to a variety of other languages, whose gender and number agreement systems have often been classified as "incomplete" or "partial." (See Stark & Pomino 2009, Pomino 2012, 2017 and Cyrino & Espinal 2019 for an overview in Romance, and Corbett 1991, 2000 for a typological perspective.) It would be of interest to see if the agreement patterns reported for these Afro-Andean dialects can also be detected across other vernaculars in contact with standard varieties. This would allow us to understand whether the agreement evolution displayed by YS, CVS and CS can also be generalized to other contact scenarios.

4.5 On the Persistence of Default Values at the Morphology–Syntax/Semantics Interface

In line with current proposals on the nature of morphological representations (Harley & Ritter 2002), I assume that agreement features, such as gender and number, obey a hierarchy of markedness, and thus are organized – according to ordered patterns – around basic or unmarked values (Battistella 1990). The idea is that for each set of feature values – such as masculine–feminine for gender and single–plural for number – there is always a default category or "elsewhere case" (Kiparsky 1973), in comparison with which the other is conceptually more marked (Corbett 2000). That is, the default value is conceived of as underspecified – or lacking feature information in a given lexical item – while the marked values imply a feature specification (Corbett 2006).

Spanish has a number system consisting of two possible values (singular vs. plural), and a gender system that is built on the masculine–feminine opposition. Singular and masculine have traditionally been classified as the default values for gender and number in Spanish (and the rest of the Romance languages) (Harris 1991; Bonet 1995; Corbett 2000). This proposal is based on a number of morphological observations. For example, in the case of number, the value 'plural' corresponds to an overt inflectional morpheme (e.g., *perros* 'dogs'), while singular does not (e.g., *perro* 'dog'). This suggests that singular is the underspecified representation for number (Croft 2003; Haspelmath 2006). A similar, but yet different, asymmetric opposition is detected for the masculine–feminine contrast. Noun coordination is one of several tests that can be done to detect the default gender value cross-linguistically (Corbett 1991). In Spanish, when nouns with different genders are coordinated, the agreeing adjective has to be masculine, as in (49) from Fuchs, Polinsky and Scontras (2014: 711), thus suggesting that the masculine value acts as the elsewhere option, while feminine is the marked category.

(49) El   libro   y   la   pintura   son   caros/*caras
      the   book.M and the   painting.F are   expensive.M.PL/expensive.F.PL
      'The book and the painting are expensive.'

Given these theoretical assumptions on the nature of morphological markedness, this section elaborates on the attested presence of non-agreeing items across the Afro-Hispanic DP, which are realized as default singular and masculine forms (Harley & Ritter 2002; McCarthy 2008). As indicated above, these elements can be conceived of as the overt morphological instantiations of a lack of phi-feature specifications in the derivation, which – for purely graphic reasons – I have depicted as "*no*-F" (see 36, 38, 39 and 46). Since these specifications are absent, no syntactic operations apply to them in narrow syntax, thus leading to overt default morphology (Adger & Smith 2005). It is important to point out that this has to be kept apart from the non-convergent computation of unvalued features, which would result in a derivational crash at Spell Out (Chomsky 1995). On the other hand, in YS, CVS and CS, these constructions are perfectly grammatical, and thus their computation does not imply any syntactic crash.

Current research on morphological theory represents features as a combination of structured grammatical nodes organized according to geometric patterns built around basic or unmarked "default" values (Harley 1994; Bonet 1995). Recent SLA proposals have adopted the notion of a hierarchy of markedness to account for the evolution of agreement configurations in interlanguage grammars (McCarthy 2008; Slabakova 2009). According to this perspective, more nodes correspond to more complex values, which, consequently, imply more processing and developmental challenges. In line with the geometrical representations adopted in McCarthy (2008: 466) and Slabakova (2009: 59), each feature is associated with a default value that is depicted as structurally bare, while more marked values are represented by richer nodal structure. Geometrical representation for 'number' and 'gender' are displayed in (50)–(51). Both 'singular' and 'masculine' are presented as default values, while 'plural' and 'feminine' are seen as more complex, given that they involve an additional node; see also Harris (1991: 44) and Sagarra and Herschensohn (2011: 174–175) on the nature of number and gender default values in Spanish, and Alemán Bañón and Rothman (2016) for event-related potential (ERP) experiments showing how plural and feminine values, being the marked specifications, imply higher cognitive processing costs.

(50)   Number values:
       SG   PL
       #   #
              |
              [>1]

(51) Gender values:
M   F
∞   ∞
    |
[Marked]

The persistence of default/unmarked values is a well-known aspect of L2 speech which can lead to fossilization phenomena and significant shortcomings in L2 inflectional morphology (White 2003b; Montrul 2004; Franceschina 2005; Lardiere 2007). The Bottleneck Hypothesis (BH) (Slabakova 2008, 2009), which suggests that the *semantics–morphology interface* represents the most challenging aspect of L2 acquisition, has borrowed the notion of hierarchical markedness to explain why singular and masculine values systematically persist in interlanguage varieties. According to Slabakova (2009: 282), "learning a second language entails learning the new configuration in which the various interpretable and uninterpretable features are mapped onto the target language inflectional morphology" and thus, when the learning output is not target-like, default values will show up.

In Chapter 1, it was mentioned that other scholars, those subscribing to the Interlanguage Hypothesis (IH), acknowledge the difficulties posed by acquiring L2 morphology but maintain that the most challenging phenomena to master in L2 acquisition are those that imply high processing demands on external interfaces (e.g., pronominal use, related to the *syntax–pragmatics interface*, Sorace 2004; Sorace & Filiaci 2006; Sorace & Serratrice 2009). I personally find both the BH and the IH equally attractive, even though I do not necessarily share the parametric assumptions on which they have been built. In fact, both proposals conceive of SLA as a sort of parameter resetting process. Slabakova (2008: 86, 117) adopts "the idea that UG-provided linguistic principles and parameters can be used to describe all stages in language development," in which the learner's "variable performance is indicative of the competition between UG-sanctioned parameter values" (see Yang 2002, 2004 on this later point). Along similar lines of reasoning, Sorace's (2011: 26) IH also embraces the P&P framework and even claims that it would be incorrect to assume "that the IH predicts the impossibility of resetting parameters" affecting phenomena related to the syntax–pragmatics interface. Rather, this hypothesis proposes that such a resetting can certainly take place, even though "the integration of syntactic and pragmatic conditions remains less than optimally efficient and gives rise to optionality."

Even though the P&P approach has shaped most of generative research for the past three decades, recent formal proposals have started to question and rethink some of the assumptions on which this theory of UG has been built

(Eguren, Fernández-Soriano & Mendikoetxea 2016). I find some of these new lines of research more empirical and convincing than the highly idealized systems envisioned by P&P (Sessarego & Gutiérrez-Rexach 2017). The fieldwork data presented in this chapter appear to be quite problematic for certain models that assume a parametrized DP, or at least for some parametric proposals – such as Ritter (1991), Picallo (1991) and Bernstein (1993), to mention just a few – which identify phi-agreement as a trigger of N-raising to explain why the Romance languages, which tend to present a rich nominal agreement system, show a word order within the DP that diverges from the word order encountered in English, where nominal agreement is highly reduced, as in (52) (see Alexiadou 2001; Wills 2006 for a discussion of some problematic aspects of a parametrized N-raising theory).

(52) a. Some   big   cold   beers   (English)
        some   big-SG   cold-SG   beer-PL
        'Some big cold beers.'
     b. Unas   grandes   cervezas frías   (Spanish)
        some-F.PL big-F.PL beer-F.PL cold-F.PL
        'Some big cold beers.'

The aforementioned theories, however, are weakened when faced with the evidence borne out by the Afro-Hispanic data. In fact, as shown in (53), even though the traditional Afro-Andean dialects present a radically reduced agreement system, this does not prevent them from showing the same adjective + noun and noun + adjective combinations encountered in standard Spanish, thus suggesting that N-raising is probably not parametrizable in terms of phi-agreement, but rather prompted by other mechanisms, such as categorical features (see also Carstens 2001; Demonte 2008).

(53) Unos   grande   cerveza   frío   (Afro-Andean Spanish)
      Some-M.PL big-M.SG   beer-M.SG cold-M.SG
      'Some big cold beers.'

Slabakova's (2009) claims on the nature of (un)interpretable features and their mapping onto L2 morphology inevitably implies an adjustment in the focus of the "bottleneck" problem. By this I mean that it may be worth considering the issue from a slightly different angle, shifting from a narrow *morphology–semantics interface* approach to a broader *morphology–syntax/semantics perspective* (see also Montrul 2011: 596 on this point). This idea, I think, is particularly relevant when analyzing the phi-agreement processes shown in the present study. In fact, agreement, as understood in minimalistic terms, implies that some features – after having gone through the syntactic

At the Morphology–Syntax/Semantics Interface 95

computation – will be read at LF (Chomsky 1995). This entails not only a mapping between semantics and morphology but, first and foremost, a dialogue between the syntactic and the semantic modules.

As maintained in Chapter 1, I propose that certain grammatical aspects of the AHLAs (i.e., their so-called "creole-like" features) may be conceived of as advanced, conventionalized L2 phenomena, which were nativized by subsequent generations of speakers. As explained in Section 4.4, current investigations on the evolution of gender agreement patterns in L2 Spanish are in line with this proposal (Bruhn de Garavito & White 2002; Franceschina 2002, 2005). Such studies, in fact, indirectly support the idea of a close parallelism between L2 development and Afro-Hispanic speech evolution. Indeed, in all of these works, agreement has been found to develop first on prenominal determiners and then, eventually, on postnominal adjectives. In particular, Díaz Collazos and Vásquez Hurtado (2017: 669) have recently decided to test the syntactic hierarchy presented in (32) (originally proposed in Sessarego & Gutiérrez-Rexach 2011) on data proceeding from college students enrolled in Spanish language courses (in class and online groups). The results of classroom students are identical to my findings, as indicated in Table 4.6.

As for the number agreement variability found in YS, CS and CVS, it must be said that similar phenomena have not only been detected in the speech of L2 Spanish speakers (White, Valenzuela, Kozlowska-Macgregor & Leung 2004; Sagarra & Herschensohn 2011), but also in several native Spanish varieties; among the most well-studied cases are the dialects of the Caribbean, Andalusia, and the Canary Islands (see Zamora Vicente 1967; Lipski 1994; Alvar 1996 for an overview). A comparison of the quantitative results

Table 4.6 *Grammatical hierarchy of gender agreement in Afro-Hispanic vernaculars compared with classroom students of Spanish*

Afro-Hispanic speech Sessarego & Gutiérrez-Rexach (2011)	Classroom students Díaz Collazos & Vásquez Hurtado (2017: 669)	Level of gender agreement
Definite articles	Definite articles	More
Demonstratives	Demonstratives	
Weak quantifiers	Weak quantifiers	
Indefinite articles	Indefinite articles	
Prenominal adjectives	Prenominal adjectives	
Strong quantifiers	Strong quantifiers	
Postnominal adjectives	Postnominal adjectives	Less

Table 4.7 *Variable rule analysis of number agreement variation in the Puerto Rican Spanish DP*

Grammatical category	Following phonological segment	Following stress
Adjective .69	Pause .65	Weak .56
Noun .57	Consonant .47	Heavy .44
Determiner .26	Vowel .37	

Statistical details (i.e., number of tokens and significance) were not provided by Poplack (1980) in the original table reproduced here.

Table 4.8 *Variable rule analysis of number agreement variation in the Popular Brazilian Portuguese DP*

(Total = 690; significance = 0.048)

Grammatical category	Following phonological segment	Following stress
Adjective .82 (N = 36)	Pause [.56] (N = 148)	Weak [.53] (N = 414)
Noun .64 (N = 356)	Vowel [.49] (N = 97)	Heavy [.46] (N = 276)
Determiner .15 (N = 298)	Consonant [.43] (N = 445)	

encountered in YS (see Table 4.5) with those reported by Poplack (1980) for Puerto Rican Spanish (see Table 4.7) shows a clear parallelism (Delicado-Cantero & Sessarego 2011). These findings are also perfectly in line with the variable number agreement patterns encountered in the popular Brazilian Portuguese vernacular spoken in Tejucupapo, a predominantly white, rural community in the State of Recife (see Table 4.8) (Sessarego & Ferreira 2016: 294).

The existence of virtually identical variable number agreement patterns across several contemporary native and non-native varieties of Spanish and Portuguese suggests that this phenomenon is better understood as a matter of natural morphological reduction, yielding a tendency toward the elimination of superfluous redundancy, as commonly occurs in vernacular speech (Chambers 2003), rather than as a surviving creole feature, as some studies may claim (i.e., Guy 1981, 2004, 2017). On this specific point, even Granda (1988a: 88), who is among the most well-known voices supporting the (de)creolization hypothesis, diverges from Guy and prefers to ascribe the reduced number agreement of the Afro-Latino varieties to internal linguistic factors that tend to preserve "maximal economy in the use of number markers"[3], since, among other things, such a tendency is also found in Paraguayan vernacular Spanish, in communities where no African presence has ever been attested (Granda 1988b).

To understand why the Afro-Hispanic vernaculars and L2 varieties tend to do away with rich agreement, it is necessary to highlight that agreement morphemes are – for the most part – redundant. Since they do not contribute to the interpretation of the utterance, they tend to be lost in situations of contact (Winford 2003). According to Chomsky (2000: 111), for whom economy is a central driver in language design, agreement might even be seen as an instance of "imperfection," superfluous for an optimal system (but see Pinker & Jackendoff 2005 on this point).

An economy-driven tendency toward lack of redundancy and preference for default values over complex values makes perfect sense from a processing perspective. The feature-geometry model, adopted by Slabakova (2009) to account for the persistence of unmarked/default forms in L2 speech, is essentially a formalization of the same concept. Such a model is also in line with the typological analysis of language universals captured by Greenberg (1963), since it makes use of structural hierarchies to account for the distribution of morphological features across languages (Harley & Ritter 2002: 5). Slabakova (2009: 60) takes this claim a step further when she states that this framework also predicts SLA tendencies in the evolution of interlanguage grammars, thus explaining why certain values would appear earlier than others in L2 speech.

This type of analysis, I think, can also help us cast light on why certain forms tend to persist in vernacular varieties (Sessarego 2011b). In particular, this model is of particular interest to the study of the Afro-Hispanic dialects, since it offers a formal explanation for why these vernaculars present reduced agreement configurations. It has to be said that the AHLAs are not the only varieties presenting default forms. Indeed, a number of non-standard languages around the world appear to show similar instances of reduced agreement, across both their nominal and verbal domains. (See Henry 2005 for Belfast English, Baptista 2002 for Cape Verdean Creole Portuguese, Sessarego & Ferreira 2016 for Popular Brazilian Portuguese, etc..) If the feature-geometry analysis is extended to these varieties, the presence of more economical/default values in such vernaculars can find a logical explanation, since more complex

---

[3] Original Spanish version: máxima economía en la utilización de los marcadores de la categoría de número.

values involve more grammatical nodes, which, in turn, are more difficult to process and acquire.

Chambers' (2001, 2003) Theory of Vernacular Universals is based on the empirical evidence that certain linguistic traits tend to recur systematically in vernacular varieties. The author points out that vernaculars appear to be in some sense more economic or "natural" than standardized languages (Kroch 1978; Gadet & Pagel 2019). It may be quite a challenge to quantify in terms of economy and/or naturalness all the linguistic traits that Chamber has identified as "vernacular roots" (Sessarego 2011b, 2014a). However, when Chambers' view on naturalness is evaluated against the Afro-Andean agreement data, it can be asserted that, since certain forms are unmarked/underspecified and thus easier to process/acquire, unless social pressure rules them out, there is no reason why they could not be conventionalized and become part of a less prestigious – but equally efficient – linguistic system.

When the linguistic analysis of reduced number/gender agreement is combined with the socioeconomic information we have for YS, CVS and CS (as shown in Chapter 2), it appears that Yungas, Chota Valley and Chincha provided the perfect environment for such a conventionalization to occur, as they were marginalized rural areas not subject to the processes of standardization driven by education and urban pressure (Sessarego 2013c, 2014b, 2014c). This claim is further supported by the recent approximation of YS, CVS and CS to more standard varieties of Spanish. When the factors preserving the traditional dialects came to disappear (essentially during the past few decades, thanks to the Land Reforms), the pressure, imposed by standardization and the linguistic norm, pushed Afro-Andean Spanish-speakers toward dropping their traditional dialects in favor of more prestigious Spanish varieties (see also Sessarego 2012b; Sessarego & Gutiérrez-Rexach 2012). This phenomenon is clearly observable when the evolution of agreement is analyzed cross-generationally (see Figure 4.1–4.3). In fact, younger generations, who did not experience the hacienda system and had more access to the standard variety, present grammars that converge more closely with the standard norm.

5 *Partial Pro-Drop Phenomena*

This chapter focuses on the presence in YS, CVS and CS of a set of grammatical constructions that, like the features analyzed in Chapter 4, have traditionally been linked to a potential creole origin for several Afro-Latino contact varieties (Otheguy 1973; Baxter, Lucchesi & Guimarães 1997; Perl & Schwegler 1998). The phenomena under study are: (a) variable subject–verb agreement, (b) non-emphatic, non-contrastive overt subjects, and (c) lack of subject–verb inversion in questions. It will be shown that these structures can be better conceived of as interface-driven, advanced, conventionalized second-language acquisition strategies which do not imply any previous creole stage for the contact vernaculars under study (Sessarego 2013b 2019b).

This analysis is not only relevant to the (de)creolization debate concerning the evolution of the AHLAs, it also has significant implications for the validity of the Null Subject Parameter (NSP) (Chomsky 1981; Rizzi 1982), since it shows that YS, CVS and CS do not conform to its universalist predictions. In fact, in line with certain other Romance varieties, such as Dominican Spanish (DS) and Brazilian Portuguese (BP) (Toribio 2000; Martínez-Sanz 2011; Barbosa et al. 2005; Camacho 2008), these Afro-Andean dialects do not clearly align with either Null Subject Languages (NSLs) or Non-Null Subject Languages (NNSLs). Consequently, their existence weakens the theoretical assumptions on which parametric syntax has been built and calls for new proposals to account for the nature of these socially stigmatized, but syntactically perfect, grammatical systems.

5.1 A Testing Ground for the Null Subject Parameter

As indicated in Chapter 3, the P&P framework (Chomsky 1976, 1981, 1986; Chomsky & Lasnik 1993) conceived of cross-linguistic variation as the result of the intersection of the universal principles of language, which would be innate and prior to language acquisition, and a finite set of binary parameters, which would be triggered by exposure to language. According to this view, to a given parametric setting (i.e., + or −) would correspond a certain cluster of properties, which – without the need to be acquired – would be automatically instantiated in the language. This specific theoretical framework would, therefore, be capable of explaining why certain superficially unrelated linguistic properties tend to group together across languages (Greenberg 1963). Moreover, it would provide a potential solution to the well-known Plato's problem, or the reason why children know so much about their language in spite of their limited amount of experience with it (Chomsky 1986: xxv). A well-known example of how an apparently unrelated group of linguistic phenomena would cluster together across languages is reflected in the predictions encapsulated by the NSP (Chomsky 1981; Rizzi 1982). The NSP divides natural languages into two macro groups, NSLs and NNSLs, depending on the NSP value. The cluster of properties associated with one or the other value, as indicated in the original formulation of the NSP, is summarized below (Roberts & Holmberg 2010: 16–18):[1]

(54) *The possibility of a silent, referential, definite subject of finite clauses*
    a. Parla italiano. (Italian, +NSP)
    b. *Speaks Italian. (English, −NSP)
    'She speaks Italian.'

(55) *Free subject inversion*
    a. Hanno telefonato molti studenti. (Italian, +NSP)
    b. *Ont téléphoné beaucoup d'étudiants. (French, −NSP)
    'Many students have telephoned.'

(56) *Absence of complementizer-trace effects*
    a. Chi hai detto che – ha scritto questo libro? (Italian, +NSP)
    b. *Who did you say that – wrote this book? (English, −NSP)
    'Who did you say wrote this book?'

(57) *Rich agreement inflection on finite verbs*
    a. Io mangio, tu mangi, etc. (Italian, +NSP)
    b. I eat, you eat, etc. (English, −NSP)

In subsequent works, as highlighted by Camacho (2008, 2013), more properties were attributed to NSLs: expletives must be null (58), and overt pronouns cannot take an arbitrary reading (59) (Suñer 1983; Jaeggli 1986).

---

[1] Recent acquisition studies have proposed that such properties do not cluster together in acquisition (Villa-García & Suárez-Palma 2016). The authors suggest that there may be an ordered effect in that property X is a prerequisite for property Y, but crucially not all properties arise concurrently in children's development.

(58) *Expletives must be null*
    a.   Llueve.   (Spanish, +NSP)
    b.   It rains.   (English, -NSP)

(59) *Overt pronouns cannot take an arbitrary reading*
    a.   Dijeron que habían venido.   (Spanish, specific or arbitrary reading)
    b.   Ellos dijeron que habían venido.   (Spanish, specific reading)
    'They said that they had come.'

A formalization of the phenomenon presented in (59) was provided by Montalbetti's (1984) Overt Pronoun Constraint (OPC). The OPC establishes that, if a language is endowed with *pro*, overt pronouns should not be interpreted as bound variables, since *pro* is the element that would take on such a reading (60) (Camacho 2008: 417–418).

(60) *Overt Pronoun Constraint*
    a.   Todo estudiante$_i$ cree que *pro$_i$* es inteligente.
    b.   Todo estudiante$_i$ cree que él$_{*i/j}$ es inteligente
    'Every student thinks that he is intelligent.'

Since its early proposal, the NSP has triggered a variety of investigations aimed at testing its predictions on a number of typologically different languages. The findings of such an empirical enterprise resulted, in some cases, in the reformulation of the original model (Jayaseelan 1999; Tomioka 2003; Saito 2004; Holmberg 2005) and, on other occasions, even in its complete refutation (Newmeyer 2004; Haspelmath 2008). In fact, the analysis of linguistic systems presenting a high degree of typological distance from the European languages on which the NSP was originally built showed that its cross-linguistic predictions can hardly be considered to be universal. An exemplification of such a problem may be represented by the study carried out by Huang (1994) on Chinese pronominal expression. Chinese, in fact, is a language lacking verbal inflection in which overt pronouns and *pro* may alternate in discourse, depending on a number of pragmatic factors.

Even within the Romance group, without going as far as analyzing highly typologically different languages, there are varieties that do not conform to the NSP predictions. In fact, certain dialects have been reported to display a combination of phenomena from both NSLs and NNSLs and, for this reason, they have often been classified as "partial pro-drop languages" (Toribio 2000; Duarte 1995; Kato & Negrão 2000; Camacho 2008, 2013; Sessarego & Gutiérrez-Rexach 2017). Their existence appears to be highly problematic for a P&P standpoint. It confounds the basic idea assuming that grammatical

102 *Partial Pro-Drop Phenomena*

properties come in well-defined clusters, which would depend on an "on/off parametric switch" (Chomsky 2000: 8).

5.2 Two Partial Pro-Drop Varieties in Ibero-Romance

A more cautious analysis of the available empirical linguistic evidence has shown that a number of languages do not conform to the original NSP predictions. Two such cases within the Romance group are DS and BP. Several works have highlighted that non-emphatic, non-contrastive overt subject pronouns are commonly encountered in these dialects, so that many of the discourse constraints differentiating null and overt pronouns in +NSP varieties have been lost (Toribio 1993a, 1993b; Duarte 1995; Modesto 2000; Ordóñez & Olarrea 2006; etc.). These high rates of overt subject pronouns also correlate with other grammatical phenomena that would place DS and BP somewhere "in between" NSLs and NNSLs. The half-way nature of these grammars has gained them the label of "partial pro-drop varieties" (Sessarego & Gutiérrez-Rexach 2017).

As for DS, Toribio (2000) has shown that this dialect does not conform to either NSLs or NNSLs, since, among other grammatical peculiarities, it displays a combination of features that, according to the NSP, should not coexist in the same language: (61) impoverished subject–verb agreement (partially due to phonetic consonant weakening), (62) presence of both overt and null subjects, and (63) overt expletive pronouns.

(61) *Verbal agreement weakening*
    a. Norm: [sal.ˈtar], [ˈsal.tas],[sal.ˈta.βãn]
    b. Santo Domingo: [sal.ˈtal], [ˈsal.ta], [sal.ˈta.βãŋ]
    c. Cibao Valley: [saj.ˈtaj], [ˈsaj.ta], [saj.ˈta.βãŋ]
    d. Southern coast: [saɾ.ˈtaɾ], [ˈsaɾ.ta], [saɾ.ˈta.βãŋ]

(62) *Presence of non-emphatic, non-contrastive overt subjects and null subjects*
    a. Si **ellos** me dicen que **yo** estoy en peligro cuando **ellos** me
       if they CL tell that I am in danger when they CL
       entren la aguja por el ombligo **yo** me voy a ver
       enter the needle through the belly-button I CL go to see
       en una situación de estrés.
       in a situation of stress
       'If they tell me that I am in danger when they put the needle in my belly-button, I am going to find myself in a stressful situation.'
    b. **Yo** no lo vi, **él** estaba en Massachusetts, ***pro*** acababa de llegar …
       I not it saw he was in Massachusetts finished of arrive
       'I did not see him, he was in Massachusetts, he just arrived …'

(63) *Overt expletive pronoun*
   a. **Ello** llegan guaguas hasta allá.
      it   arrive buses   to   there
      'Buses arrive there.'
   b. **Ello** había   mucha gente.
      it   there were many people
      'There were a lot of people.'

In addition, Toribio points out other linguistic phenomena that, even if not listed in the cluster of NSP-related grammatical properties, appear to be relevant to the analysis, since they too had to do with the use of subject pronouns: (64) lack of subject–verb inversion in questions, and (65) non-emphatic pronouns in pseudo-cleft constructions.

(64) *Lack of subject–verb inversion in questions*
   a. ¿Qué   número   tú   anotaste?
      what number   you wrote
      'What number did you write down?'
   b. ¿Qué yo les voy a mandar a esos   muchachos?
      what I CL go to send   to those boys
      'What am I going to send to those boys?'

(65) *Pseudo-cleft constructions*
   a. ¿Dónde fue que tú   estudiaste?
      where was that you studied
      'Where did you study?'
   b. ¿En qué es que tú   te vas a graduar?
      in what is that you CL go to graduate
      'What will you graduate in?'

After analyzing these and other grammatical peculiarities characterizing DS, Toribio (2000) offers an account of such phenomena that does not reject the NSP. Rather, she claims that in this dialect it would be possible to observe the coexistence of both NSL and NNSL traits because DS would be going through a process of parameter resetting (2000: 328). Thus, a dialect that was originally +NSP would gradually become −NSP. The presence of contrasting configurations in the same system would be due to the fact that DS speakers would be constantly switching between an NSL and an NNSL grammar, so that they would be "bilinguals in their native language, acquiring two grammars with opposed, competing values for the relevant parameters" (Toribio 2000: 339).

A similar yet different analysis has been provided to account for the grammatical configurations encountered in BP. Even in this dialect, in fact, it is possible to observe phenomena that, according to the predictions of the NSP,

104 *Partial Pro-Drop Phenomena*

Table 5.1 *Evolution of inflectional paradigms in Brazilian Portuguese*

Person/number	Paradigm 1	Paradigm 2	Paradigm 3
Speaker.sg	am-o	am-o	am-o
Hearer.sg	am-a-s	–	–
	am-a	am-a	am-a
Other.sg.	am-a	am-a	am-a
Speaker.pl	am-a-mos	am-a-mos	–
	–	am-a	am-a
Addressee.pl	am-a-is	–	–
	am-a-m	am-a-m	am-a-m
Other.pl	am-a-m	am-a-m	am-a-m

Table 5.2 *Evolution of the pronominal paradigm in Brazilian Portuguese*

Person/number	Pronoun		Verbal ending
Speaker.sg	Eu	Eu	am-o
Addressee.sg	Tu	Você	am-a
	Vós		
Other.sg.	Ele/Ela	Ele/Ela	am-a
Speaker.pl	Nós	A gente	am-a
Addressee.pl	Vós	Vocês	am-a
	Vocês		
Other.pl	Eles/Elas	Eles/Elas	am-a-m

should not coexist in the same language. It has also been claimed that this variety would be in the process of undergoing a major language change, consisting of the shift from an NSL to an NNSL (Camacho 2008). In fact, after surveying several studies on the "partial pro-drop" nature of BP, Camacho (2008, 2013) builds on Duarte's (1995: 19) work to point out how the rate of overt subject pronouns has been increasing steadily during the past 150 years. It went from 20 percent in 1845 to 75 percent in 1992. Such a dramatic increase appears to be associated with the weakening of subject–verb agreement morphology and to the reorganization of the pronominal system (Tables 5.1 and 5.2).

As expected, these changes triggered a system reconfiguration in BP, and thus other aspects of BP grammar had to adjust to achieve a new internal equilibrium. For example, the weakening of the agreement system resulted in the BP verbal inflection no longer being able to satisfy the Extended Projection

Principle (EPP) or the requirement for the phrase TP to have an overtly filled specifier (Chomsky 1982), much like in English. This, consequently, would have to be satisfied by an overt (weak) pronoun in Spec IP, which would allow the use of subject clitic left dislocations (SCLDs) (see Duarte 2000: 28) (66).[2]

(66) *SCLDs*
    a. A Clarinha$_i$ ela$_i$ cozinha que é uma maravilha
       the Clarinha she cooks that is a marvel
       'Clarinha, she cooks wonderfully.'
    b. Então [o Instituto de Física]$_i$ ele$_i$ manda os piores professores ...
       then the Institute of Physics it sends the worst professors
       [Os melhores]$_j$ eles$_j$ dão aula no curso de matemática.
       the best they give class in the course of mathematics
       'Then the Institute of Physics sends the worst professors ... The best ones teach mathematics.'

An additional symptom of this systemic change would be, according to Duarte and Kato (2002), the loss of subject–verb inversion in questions (67) (Silva 2001), a phenomenon that took place in BP during the nineteenth century and appears to be concomitant with the increase in overt subject pronouns. (See also Barrera-Tobón & Raña-Risso 2016 for a similar claim for New York City Spanish.)

(67) *Lack of subject–verb inversion in questions*
    a. O que a Maria leciona?
       what the Maria teaches
       'What does Maria teach?'
    b. *O que leciona a Maria?
       what teaches the Maria
    c. Onde ela leciona?
       where she teaches
       'Where does she teach?'
    d. *Onde leciona ela?
       where teaches she

Another result of such a steady increase in the use of overt subject pronouns has to do with their interpretations. In fact, by becoming so common, they would no longer be associated with emphatic speech and topicalized contexts. In addition, they can now be understood as bound variables in BP; thus, this

---

[2] See Villa-García (2018) for a similar possibility in non-Caribbean Spanish with a subject between two instances of *que* 'that': *Yo creo que Julio, que él no es así* 'I think that Julio, that he is not like this.'

dialect clearly violates Montalbetti's OPC (68) (Barbosa, Kato & Duarte 2005: 43).

(68) *Overt Pronoun Constraint violation*
    a. [Ninguém no Brasil]$_i$ acha que ele$_i$ é prejudicado pelo Governo.
        'No one in Brazil thinks that he is harmed by the government.'
    b. [Ninguém no Brasil]$_i$ acha que *pro*$_i$ é prejudicado pelo Governo.
        'No one in Brazil thinks that he is harmed by the government.'

Camacho (2008: 46) depicts the domino effects that resulted in the reconfiguration of BP grammar by providing the scheme reproduced in (69), which summarizes two possible paths of change from NSL to NNSL. In both cases, (69a) and (69b), the factor responsible for starting this chain of changes would be the aforementioned increase in the frequency of overt subject pronouns. According to the scenario depicted in (69a), this increase in the rate of overt pronouns would have triggered a reanalysis of pronominal referentiality in relation to verbal inflections, so that either the overt pronoun or the inflection would be interpreted as [+ref] (70). Such a variable interpretation of pronouns as [+/−ref] would have resulted in their appearance in Spec IP; thus, they would have become weak and satisfied the EPP. Such a system, in which the EPP could be satisfied by either a weak pronoun or by Infl, would result in the latter category becoming [−ref]. The alternative chain of changes envisioned by Camacho is exemplified in (69b). This time the outcome triggered by the higher use of overt subject pronouns would consist of Spec IP hosting them, which would satisfy the EPP and make the pronouns weak. Infl would consequently become [−ref] and lead to the variable interpretation of pronominal referentiality. Thus, (69a) and (69b) describe the same NSL-to-NNSL shift, with the only difference being that the restructuring events occur in inverted orders along the two possible paths.

(69) *Two possible paths of change from NSL to NNSL*
    a. Higher frequency → [+/−ref] pronominal → Pronominal in Spec, IP → Pronominal satisfies EPP, becomes weak, infl becomes [−ref]
    b. Higher frequency → Pronominal in Spec, IP → Pronominal satisfies EPP, becomes weak, infl becomes [−ref]→ pronominal [+/−ref]

(70) a. Él compra pan
        he buys bread
        'He buys bread.'
    b. Él compra pan
        he buys bread
        [+ref] [−ref]
    c. Él compra pan
        he buys bread
        [−ref] [+ref]

5.3 On the Nature of Partial Pro-Drop Phenomena in the AHLAs

The three varieties under inspection in this study align – to a good extent – with DS and BP. In all of them, in fact, it is possible to encounter grammatical traits that, according to the NSP predictions, should not coexist in the same language, and thus they too could be labeled as "partial pro-drop dialects." Contrary to standard Latin American Spanish varieties, YS, CVS and CS do not present a robust subject–verb agreement system. In particular, contemporary YS shows much variability in this respect. In fact, inflected and uninflected verb forms can be found in the speech of the same speaker, even within the same utterance (71) (Sessarego & Rodríguez-Riccelli 2018: 65).

(71) Yungueño Spanish
    a. Yo no tengo   plata,   yo no quiere   comprá.
       I no have-1.SG money I no want-3.SG to buy
       'I do not have money, I do not want to buy.'
    b. Nojotro fuimo   pero eyu no sabía.
       we went-1.PL   but they no knew-3.SG
       'We went but they did not know.'

Subject–verb agreement variability is also present in CVS and CS, but to a lesser extent. Indeed, it tends to be more sporadic and for the most part limited to past verb forms (72)–(73) (Sessarego 2013a: 76, 2015: 57).

(72) Chota Valley Spanish
    a. Ellos dijo   que iba al campo.
       they said-3.SG that went-3.SG to the field
       'They said they were going to the field.'
    b. Cuando yo tuvo   uso de razón.
       when   I   had-3.SG use of reason
       'When I became able to think.'

(73) Chincha Spanish
    a. Ellos comía   lo que   yo cocinaba
       they ate-3.SG it that   I cooked-1.SG
       'They used to eat what I cooked.'
    b. Nosotro vivía   con poco plata
       we lived-3.SG   with little money
       'We used to live with little money.'

Given the residuality of subject–verb lack of agreement in CVS and CS, no quantitative investigation of this phenomenon has been carried out. Conversely, a number of recent studies have provided quantitative analyses of this type for YS and have identified several internal (linguistic) and external

108 *Partial Pro-Drop Phenomena*

Table 5.3 *Variable rule analysis of the contribution of internal factors to the probability of lack of subject–verb agreement in Yungueño Spanish*

(Total = 2,160; significance = 0.000)

	Factor weight	Lack of agreement %	N	Data %
Subject				
2nd singular	.73	43	193	9
2nd/3rd plural	.60	37	1,102	51
1st plural	.45	26	258	12
1st singular	.44	21	607	28
	Range 29			
Tense				
Past	.61	34	649	30
Present	.43	22	1,511	70
	Range 18			

(social) factors that significantly affect the attested variation (Sessarego 2012a, 2017c; Sessarego & Rodríguez-Riccelli 2018).

In Tables 5.3 and 5.4, it is possible to observe the findings of the GoldVarb X runs reported in Sessarego (2017c: 174–175). Table 5.3 provides the results for the effect of internal factors on YS verbal agreement variability. The most significant internal factor group is Subject, which shows a range of 29. It can be seen that second-person singular subjects strongly favor lack of agreement (factor weight .73), while first-person singular ones disfavor the phenomenon (factor weight .44). Tense also appears to significantly affect the variation (range 18). In this case, past forms present higher levels of lack of concord than present ones (factor weights .61 vs. .43).

As far as social factors are concerned (Table 5.4), Generation is selected as the most significant factor group, with a range of 77. The eldest speakers present higher levels of agreement mismatches (factor weight .83), while the youngest informants show more subject–verb concord (factor weight .06). Education is the second most significant external factor group (range 25). As expected, illiterate speakers favor lack of agreement (factor weight .63), while literate people show more standard-like patterns (factor weight .38). Table 5.4 also indicates that the factor group Gender does not have any significant effect on the variation, thus showing that men and women present similar agreement patterns.

Table 5.4 *Variable rule analysis of the contribution of external factors to the probability of lack of subject–verb agreement in Yungueño Spanish*

(Total = 2,604; significance = 0.000)

	Factor weight	Lack of agreement %	N	Data %
Generation				
71+	.73	44	748	35
41–70	.71	34	716	33
21–40	.11	1	696	32
	Range 62			
Education				
Illiterate	.61	43	1,173	54
Literate	.37	7	987	46
	Range 24			
Gender				
Men	[.51]	27	1,203	49
Women	[.49]	27	1,401	51

Besides presenting variable degrees of subject–verb agreement, YS, CVS and CS also possess a set of additional grammatical characteristics that place them somewhere in between NSLs and NNSLs. In these dialects, in fact, overt subject pronouns may be used in non-emphatic/non-contrastive contexts (74a) while coexisting with instances of *pro* (74b) (Sessarego & Rodríguez-Riccelli 2018: 66).

(74) Yungueño Spanish
    a. **Yo** digo que **yo** lo merezco porque **yo** eso trabajé.
        I say that I it deserve because I this worked
        'I say that I deserve it because I worked for it.'
    b. Entonces, estuve yendo **yo**, me sentó mal la altura,
        therefore was going I to me felt bad the altitude
        pro no conozco más adelante, ***pro*** no *conoce*.
        no know more ahead no *know*
        'Therefore, I was going, I did not feel well due to the altitude, I do not know what is ahead, I do not know.'

In addition, it should be pointed out that in these Afro-Hispanic vernaculars it is common to find questions in which subject and verb have not been inverted (75a), as in Caribbean Spanish dialects (Villa-García, Snyder &

Riqueros-Morante 2010). Nevertheless, it has to be said that questions presenting the *wh-S-V* order are not the only ones available in YS, CVS and CS, since inverted questions can be heard too (75b) (Sessarego 2015: 58, 75).

(75) Chincha Spanish
    a. ¿Qué tú comiste en la posada?
       what you ate in the restaurant
       'What did you eat in the restaurant?'
    b. ¿Qué comes (tú)?
       what ate you
       'What did you eat?'

Moreover, findings proceeding from a set of grammaticality judgments on overt pronoun use in these dialects confirm that Montalbetti's OPC does not apply to these grammars, as exemplified in (76) for CVS.

(76) Ella$_i$ cree   que ella$_{i/k}$ es la más guapa.
     she believes that she   is the most beautiful
     'She thinks she is the most beautiful.'

5.4 Rethinking Parameters

As indicated in the previous chapters, one of the main theoretical novelties brought about by the Minimalist Program (Chomsky 1995) has to do with a new conceptualization of cross-linguistic variation. According to the traditional P&P approach (Chomsky & Lasnik 1993), language variation was determined by different combinations of a finite number of binary parameters, which, once they had been set, implied the automatic instantiation in a given language of certain interrelated grammatical properties (i.e., the setting + for the NSP would imply presence of *pro*, that-trace effect, rich agreement etc.). Conversely, more recent minimalist proposals envision linguistic variation as the result of a dissimilar distribution of grammatical features across the lexicon in different languages (Chomsky 2001; Baker 2008); thus, by leaving behind the rigidity entailed by the binary nature of P&P, they allow for more flexibility in the determination of possible grammars.

    The AHLA data evaluated in this study add further support to the aforementioned theoretical shift (Eguren, Fernández-Soriano & Mendikoetxea 2016). In fact, the proven existence of "partial pro-drop" grammars clearly weakens the validity of the NSP proposal, which, given its constrained account of cross-linguistic variation, does not allow for "in-between" varieties. Along these lines of reasoning, the analysis proposed here to account for the features encountered in YS, CS and CVS partially deviates from the models presented in the literature to explain similar phenomena in Caribbean Spanish and Brazilian Portuguese.

On the one hand, a proposal that assumes a constant code-switch between a +NSP and a −NSP grammar (Toribio 2000) does not appear to capture the nature of the variation attested in YS, CVS and CS. In fact, it does not seem feasible to think that elderly informants, who have spent their entire lives working in rural Afro-Andean villages, would have been exposed to standard varieties of Spanish to such an extent as to continuously switch between different codes. Thus, the observed variability, in this case, appears to be a typical instance of internal variation, rather than the systematic alternation of competing grammars with divergent parametric settings. On the other hand, Camacho's (2008) analysis, which proposes a case of "grammar in change" for BP, also does not completely capture the nature of the phenomena encountered in these Afro-Hispanic dialects. Even though I agree that – to some extent – all grammars are constantly evolving, in my view, the situation observed in YS, CVS and CS should not be understood as by-product of grammars transiting from a +NSP to a −NSP syntactic system (or vice versa). Thus, I do not ascribe the attested variability to syntax. Rather, here, as in Chapter 4, I assume that syntax and its operations (i.e., *Merge, Move, Agree*) remain constant, while the real locus of variation is the lexicon and its uninterpretable features (Borer 1984; Adger 2006).

The AHLA data we just analyzed are hard to reconcile with the predictions of the P&P model. Conversely, an account of variation within the framework envisioned by the Minimalist Program – as sketched in Section 3.4 and further elaborated in Section 5.5 – may offer a more suitable explanation for the "partial pro-drop" phenomena under investigation (Sessarego & Gutiérrez-Rexach 2017).

5.5 Along the Morphology–Semantics and the Syntax–Pragmatics Interfaces

The reason for the presence of variable subject–verb agreement, non-emphatic/non-contrastive overt subject pronouns, and non-inverted questions in YS, CVS, CS (and in most of the remaining AHLAs) has to do with the *grammatical processes at the root of their formation*, which, as I have suggested on multiple occasions, consist of *advanced, conventionalized SLA strategies* that do not necessarily imply a previous creole stage (Sessarego 2013a, 2015, 2019a). Besides being supported by sociohistorical data indicating that YS,

CVS and CS were probably never a creole (see Chapter 2 in this book), this proposal is also backed by contemporary research on SLA, which indicates that the so-called "creole-like" features are also easily detectable in advanced L2 Spanish varieties (Montrul 2004; Geeslin 2013).

Instances of variable subject–verb agreement are commonly encountered in L2 speech, since a full mastery of phi-features (i.e., gender, number, person) is hard to obtain, and even advanced L2 speakers may fall short of achieving a target-like proficiency in this respect (Franceschina 2002). Impoverished L2 agreement has often been linked to processing constraints applying at the *morphology–semantics interface* (White 2011: 585–586). This, as illustrated by the Bottleneck Hypothesis, would be due to the difficulty of mapping semantic concepts onto overt grammatical morphemes in SLA (Slabakova 2008), a challenge that applies not only developmentally, but also at the end-state of L2 acquisition, thus leading to fossilization phenomena consisting of significant morphological reductions (White 2003a; Franceschina 2005; Lardiere 2007).

Spanish subject–verb agreement consists of number and person morphological information appearing on the verb, in line with the number and person features expressed by the subject. As shown in Section 4.4, the category 'singular' is conceived of as the default number value, or the underspecified representation, which contrasts with the marked value 'plural'. As for the feature 'person', the possible values are three: first, second and third. The default person category is assumed to be 'third' (Kerstens 1993). In fact, the idea is that first and second values are used to refer to speech act participants, while third person is treated as the elsewhere case, or as Corbett (2006: 132) puts it, "the third person is basically what is not first and second person." In fact, Spanish DPs, with the exception of a few specific pragmatic contexts (see Corbett 2006: 133 on this point), are always understood as third person by default (77), while indefinite third-person pronouns may take on a general reading, which includes in their reference both "the speaker and hearer as well as unspecified others" (Battistella 1990: 86), as in (78).

(77) a. **La silla** es roja.
the chair be.3.SG red
'The chair is red.'
b. **Las sillas** son rojas.
the chairs be.3.PL red
'The chairs are red.'

(78) Si **uno** tiene problemas con la policía, debería llamar a su abogado.
if one have.3.SG problems with the police should.3.SG call to his.3.SG lawyer
'If anyone gets in trouble with the police, they should see a lawyer.'

Given the abovementioned nature of number and person features in Spanish, the default subject–verb agreement configuration is third-person singular (Fernández Ramírez 1986). Underspecified forms of this type tend to persist in L2 grammars (Montrul 2004: 146–152), even in the speech of students learning Spanish in formal settings, such as in second-language classrooms (Fernández-García 1999; Bruhn de Garavito & White 2002). For these reasons, encountering these patterns in the vernacular speech of communities that acquired Spanish in a naturalistic context is certainly not that surprising (Sessarego 2011b: 130–131).

YS, CVS and CS speakers show lack of subject–verb agreement to different extents, depending on a number of internal and external factors (see Tables 5.3 and 5.4 for YS). In line with the model presented by Adger and Smith (2005) to account for similar instances of variation in Buckie English, it is possible to provide an analysis of the subject–verb patterns found in the AHLAs. As for gender and number variation in the DP, I postulate that the lexical items entering the syntactic numeration may or may not be specified for certain uninterpretable features. Variation, in this way, is localized in the lexicon (Borer 1984), while the syntax and its basic operations (*Move*, *Merge*, *Agree*) remain constant (Brody 2003).

Variable subject–verb agreement is therefore conceived of as the overt byproduct of a covert computation applying to variable feature specifications. In fact, lexical items diverging only in the presence/absence of uninterpretable features will yield different overt morphological outputs, which, nevertheless, are assigned the same semantic interpretation at LF. This implies that such grammatical elements respect the "principle of sameness" (Tagliamonte 2006: 6), or the notion that speakers would have more than one way of saying the same thing.

The fact that syntax is kept invariable does not mean that social and idiolectal factors (e.g., level of education, social identity, age etc.) may not have a significant effect on variable lexical selection. This is why the current approach makes it possible to formalize the attested variability without falling back on the proposal of variable rules and/or alternating grammars (i.e., code-switching).

In the specific case of variable subject–verb agreement, it may be postulated that among the available lexical items of these Afro-Hispanic vernaculars there are two different and competing tense heads (T1 and T2). T1 carries a full set of features (number, person, tense, case), as in standard Spanish, while T2 is not endowed with number and person specifications. The application of the operation *Agree* (and *Merge*) between T1 and the subject pronoun leads to a standard-like agreement configuration, as illustrated in (79)–(80). Conversely, the lexical selection of T2 yields to a default third-person singular verb form, as formalized in (81)–(82).

(79) T1[*i*tense:PRESENT, *u*case:NOM, *u*num:, *u*pers:]...pronoun[*i*num:PL, *i*pers:1, *u*case:]
→T1[*i*tense:PRESENT, ~~*u*num:PL~~, ~~*u*pers:1~~]...pronoun [*i*num:PL, *i*pers:1, ~~*u*case:NOM~~]

(80) Spell Out: Nosotros   comemos
                 WE.NOM   eat.PRESENT.1.PL

(81) T2[*i*tense:PRESENT, *u*case:NOM]...pronoun[*i*num:PL, *i*pers:1, *u*case:]
→T2[*i*tense:PRESENT]...pronoun [*i*num:PL, *i*pers:1, ~~*u*case:NOM~~]

(82) Spell Out: Nosotros   come
                 WE.NOM   eat.PRESENT.3.SG

The subject–verb agreement operations described in (79)–(82) can easily account for the morphological alternations reported in examples (71)–(73) for the Afro-Andean dialects, in which third-person singular default forms may co-occur with different subjects. Thus, the reported verbal variability can be analyzed as the by-product of different person and number specifications on T. The phi-agreement configurations resulting from the variable selection of competing lexical entries can also be modeled by relying on a feature-geometry account (McCarthy 2008; Slabakova 2009; Sessarego & Ferreira 2016; Sessarego 2017c). In line with this approach, as highlighted in Chapter 4, morphological features can be understood as geometrical combinations of natural class nodes – which obey a precise complexity hierarchy – with more complex values corresponding to more class nodes, which, in turn, imply higher processing demands and greater acquisitional challenges (Harley & Ritter 2002; Cowper 2005).

Slabakova (2009: 59) offers a graphic sketch of how person and number features can be represented to illustrate the hierarchy of geometrical complexity involved in the acquisition of subject–verb agreement configurations. In the case of number features – as illustrated in example (50), here reproduced in (83) – singular is treated as the default category, while plural is conceived of as a more complex value. As for person features, each of the three possible values existing in Spanish is associated with a different level of complexity, which reflects the number of natural class nodes involved: a default value (third), a value involving the 'participant' node (first), and the most complex value (second), which implies the additional 'addressee' node (84).

When the subject–verb agreement operations depicted in (79)–(82) are combined with the notion of default number and person values, as shown in (83) and (84), it is possible to understand why a subject pronoun like *nosotros* 'we' may variably appear– depending on whether it agrees with T1 or T2 – with verb forms fully conjugated for number and person features [T1 *comemos*] or presenting default number (singular) and person (3rd) values [T2 *come*].

(83) Number features:
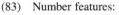

(84) Person features

Besides person and number features, in order to cast light on the nature of the verbal morphology patterns detected in the Afro-Andean varieties, it is also worth decomposing the temporal dimension of T. Cowper's (2005) feature-geometry account of 'tense' conceives of the value 'past' as more complex than 'non-past' or 'present', since it would involve the [Precedence] node (85).

(85) Tense features:
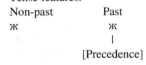

The statistical distribution of the subject–verb agreement data, as reported in Table 5.3 for YS, appears to be in line with the predictions that could be inferred by looking at the complexity hierarchies illustrated in examples (83)–(85). In fact, lack of agreement appears to be disfavored by first-person singular subjects and present tense, which are exactly the values presenting less geometrical complexity.

If we analyze the cases of subject–verb agreement variation found in the AHLAs in light of recent SLA proposals on the nature of the *morphology–semantics interface* and the relative geometrical complexity that certain morphemes present over others (Slabakova 2008, 2009; Cowper 2005; McCarthy 2008), it is not difficult to picture how certain advanced L2 patterns may have been conventionalized at the community level. All of these elements, when evaluated against the available sociohistorical information for colonial Yungas, Chota Valley and Chincha, appear to reduce the likelihood of a feasible (de)creolization hypothesis for the Afro-Hispanic vernaculars under examination.

The reduced verbal agreement system characterizing the AHLAs must have contributed indirectly to the development and stabilization in these varieties of non-emphatic, non-contrastive overt subject pronouns, which, by encapsulating person and number features, compensate for the morphological reduction of Infl. In addition, the presence of these grammatical elements in such dialects is also explainable as the result of SLA processing constraints applying at the *syntax–pragmatics interface* (Sorace 2000, 2003), since both structural and discourse-related features are involved. Indeed, null subjects (*pro*) are generally associated with old information and are used in topic-continuity and non-contrastive constructions (86) (Montrul et al. 2009: 33); thus, their proficient use implies a considerable cognitive workload on both the syntactic and the pragmatic modules of the language faculty.

(86) Juan llegó   a su casa   del trabajo.   Primero, ***pro*** se   cambió de
     Juan arrived to his house   from the work   first   CL   changed of
     ropa   y luego ***pro*** decidió   ponerse   a preparar la cena.
     clothes and then   decided   put himself   to prepare the dinner
     'Juan came home from work. First, he changed his clothes and then he decided to make dinner.'

A formalization of the difference between an overt subject pronoun and *pro* in a +NSP language has been provided by Grimshaw and Samek-Lodovici (1998), who suggest that the overt category would be endowed with a [+topic shift] feature, which would not be present in null subjects. The use in the AHLAs of overt pronouns in contexts in which *pro* would sound more pragmatically felicitous for other native varieties of Spanish appears to suggest that, in these vernaculars, such categories are not always systematically associated with [+topic shift] features. For this reason, it may be claimed that two different types of overt pronouns are available in the lexicon of these Afro-Hispanic vernaculars: type 1 would be endowed with [+topic shift] features (as in standard Spanish); type 2 would not carry such a specification, as in many advanced L2 and heritage varieties of Spanish (Rothman & Slabakova 2011; Domínguez 2013).

Note that this configuration is also in line with the solution proposed by Tsimpli et al. (2004) and Sorace (2011) to analyze overt subject pronouns in the speech of attrited/near-native speakers of Italian – as shown in Section 1.4.2 and example (16), here reproduced in (87) – for which the authors propose "optionality" or "variation" in the specification of feature values. Example (88) depicts this situation in Afro-Hispanic speech, in which subsequent instances of overt pronouns are not associated with the [+topic shift] feature that would be commonly ascribed to such elements in most Spanish dialects (Sessarego & Gutiérrez-Rexach 2017: 59).

(87) Attrited/Near-native grammar
OVERT ⇔ [+Topic Shift]
OVERT ⇔ [−Topic Shift]
NULL ⇔ [−Topic Shift]

(88) **Yo** digo que **yo** lo merezco porque **yo** eso trabajé.
[+topic shift] [−topic shift]   [−topic shift]
'I say that I deserve it because I worked for it.'

As pointed out in Chapter 1, a number of SLA studies during the past two decades have explored the vulnerability of the *syntax–pragmatics interface*, in particular, when it comes to the use of subject pronouns (Sorace 2000, 2003; Serratrice, Sorace & Paoli 2004; Rothman 2008). All of them agree that native-like proficiency in this aspect of the grammar is particularly hard to obtain, even at very advanced stages of acquisition. These findings, therefore, are in line with the model here proposed for the formation of the AHLAs, since they indirectly confirm that there is no need to postulate the existence of a more radically restructured creole variety – which would have subsequently decreolized – to explain the parallel existence of this feature in a number of contact vernaculars. Rather, it may be claimed that, being a very common and hard-to-overcome L2 phenomenon, high rates of overt subject pronouns should be expected across most contact varieties, and not just in creoles.

The use of non-emphatic, non-contrastive subject pronouns has also been linked to the presence in certain Romance varieties of non-inverted questions (see for example Toribio 2000 and Camacho 2013). The formal mechanisms underlying the nature of *wh*-questions have been a topic of copious research in generative syntax and, as far as Spanish is concerned, a number of studies have focused on the analysis of the available landing sites for subjects and *wh*-operators to refine Rizzi's (1996) *wh*-criterion (Torrego 1984; Suñer 1994; Toribio 2000; Ordóñez & Olarrea 2006).

While certain formal analyses propose that the presence/absence of subject–verb inversion would be related to the existence of a parametrized interrogative feature strength ([+wh/Q])³ in C°, which would be hard to master even in advanced L2 stages (Cuza 2013; Guerra Rivera et al. 2015), linguistic models that do not necessarily embrace the parametric/minimalist framework do acknowledge that subject–verb inversion is only mastered at advanced L2 levels of proficiency (Pienemann 1998, 2000). This fact, therefore, again suggests that this phenomenon should not be automatically associated with a previous creole stage for the AHLAs.

In YS, CVS and CS, as well as in several other AHLAs and Spanish dialects from the Caribbean, questions may present both the inverted and non-inverted subject–verb patterns, as illustrated in (89). Conversely, in the rest of the varieties of Spanish spoken in the Mainland the only configuration allowed is the one presenting inversion (i.e., *wh*-V-S), as shown in (90).

(89) Afro-Hispanic/Caribbean varieties
    a. ¿Qué tú comes?
        what you eat
        'What do you eat?'
    b. ¿Qué comes (tú)?
        what eat you
        'What do you eat?'

(90) Mainland Spanish
    a. *¿Qué tú comes?
        what you eat
        'What do you eat?'
    b. ¿Qué comes (tú)?
        what eat you
        'What do you eat?'

At this point, it is important to highlight that across both the AHLAs and the Spanish Caribbean dialects much idiolectal variation is present in relation to the types of subjects that can be inverted in these constructions. Such variability is clearly reflected in the wide range of claims made by the scholars who have studied this phenomenon. Some authors suggest that the only possible inversions in Caribbean Spanish occur with the highly frequent second-person singular informal pronoun *tú* (Davis 1971) (91); others indicate that all sorts of second-person pronouns – both singular/plural and formal/informal – would be allowed (Quirk 1972; Núñez Cedeño 1983) (92). In relation to this claim and to the overall focus of the present book, it is of interest to observe that Quirk (1972: 304) – involuntarily echoing Granda's (1968 et seq.) Decreolization

---

³ Q stands for "question."

Hypothesis for the Afro-Latino varieties of the Americas – brings up Kany's (1945) proposal to explain the origin of these constructions. Kany (1945: 125), in fact, suggested that the speech of African slaves could possibly be the source of this phenomenon and stated that "it appears to be due to Negro influence and is therefore likely to be found in other areas [besides the Greater Antilles], particularly of the Caribbean zone. The same phenomenon is current in Brazilian Portuguese."

(91) Caribbean Spanish (Davis 1971: 331)
    a. ¿Qué tú tienes?
       what you have
       'What do you have?'
    b. ¿Qué tú eres?
       what you are
       'What are you?'
    c. ¿Cuándo tú llegaste?
       when you arrived
       'When did you arrive?'

(92) Caribbean Spanish (Quirk 1972: 303)
    a. ¿Qué tú dices?
       what you.2.SG.INFORMAL say
       'What do you say?'
    b. ¿Qué usted quiere?'
       what you.2.SG.FORMAL want
       'What do you want?'
    c. ¿De dónde ustedes vienen?
       from where you.3.PL come
       'Where are you from?'

Bringing further heterogeneity to the Spanish Caribbean dataset, Lipski (1977) claims that the same speakers can easily produce inverted questions with other personal pronouns, and that the only constraint appears to be the presence of proper nouns (93). Lantolf (1980) suggests that proper nouns can be inverted as well, and that the alternation between the S–V and the V–S orders is conditioned by social factors, such as speakers' age, sex and socioeconomic class (94).[4] Toribio (1993b, 2000) introduces yet more variability to the picture and provides examples of inverted questions with full lexical DPs (95).

---

[4] In addition, it should be pointed out that non-argumental *wh*-operators lack inversion more easily than argumental ones (Torrego 1984), and that the use of proper nouns and heavy DPs preverbally tends to be facilitated by complex *wh*-phrases (*por qué, en qué lugar* etc.), while it appears more constrained by simple interrogative words (*qué, cómo, dónde* etc.) (Olarrea 1997; Ordóñez & Treviño 1999; Zubizarreta 2001; Ordóñez & Olarrea 2006). These structural

(93) Caribbean Spanish   (Lipski 1977: 61)
   a. ¿Qué él quiere?
      what he wants
      'What does he want?'
   b. *¿Qué José quiere?
      what   José wants

(94) Caribbean Spanish   (Lantolf 1980: 115)
   a. ¿Por qué Juan lo hizo?
      why   Juan it did
      'Why did Juan do it?'
   b. ¿Por qué lo hizo Juan?
      why   it did Juan
      'Why did Juan do it?'

(95) Caribbean Spanish   (Toribio 2000: 322–323)
   a. Papi, ¿qué ese letrero dice?
      Daddy what this sign says
      'Daddy, what does that sign say?'
   b. ¿Cuánto un medico gana?
      How much a doctor earns
      'How much does a doctor earn?'

More recent investigations, which have integrated a quantitative or experimental component to their studies, have acknowledged that there exists a defined hierarchy of acceptability in non-inverted questions, which appears to be influenced both by word frequency and by phonological weight. For example, Ordóñez and Olarrea (2006: 71), in their study on DS, found an acceptability rating of 100 percent with second-person singular *tú* 'you', 48 percent with first-person plural *nosotros* 'we' and a range of 11–20 percent for full DPs (the bigger or heavier the DP, the less acceptable). Very similar findings have also been reported more recently for Puerto Rican Spanish by Brown and Rivas (2011) and González-Rivera (2018), among others.

As for the AHLAs, the same pattern seems to apply. While it is relatively common to encounter non-inverted questions with the more frequent second-person singular subject pronoun, in both the formal and informal forms (96), less frequent and heavier pronouns are much more limited in use (97), while full DPs are even more constrained and thus very sporadic in Afro-Andean speech (98).[5]

---

issues add further heterogeneity to the already complex dialectal/idiolectal scenarios characterizing the nature of non-inverted questions in Caribbean Spanish.

[5] As reported in the previous footnote for Caribbean Spanish, in the AHLAs the few full DPs appearing preverbally in inverted questions also tend to co-occur with complex, non-argumental *wh*-operators, such as *por qué*.

(96) a. ¿Qué tú comiste en la posada?
         what you.SG eat in the motel
         'What did you eat in the motel?'   (Afro-Peruvian Spanish,
                                                           Sessarego 2015: 58)
     b. ¿Qué oté ta jugá?
         what are you.SG playing
         'What are you playing?' (Afro-Bolivian Spanish, Sessarego 2011a: 56)
(97) a. ¿Para qué otene truju?
         why you.PL brought
         'Why did you bring it?'   (Afro-Bolivian Spanish, Lipski 2008: 135)
     b. ¿Qué ella dijo?
         what she said
         'What did she say?'   (Afro-Peruvian Spanish, Sessarego 2015: 58)
(98) ¿Por qué el chiquito no va?
     why the kid no go
     'Why doesn't the kid go?'   (Afro-Peruvian Spanish, Cuba 2002: 37)

Some authors have tried to justify these differences in acceptability by saying that certain pronouns in Caribbean Spanish may be in the process of acting as clitics (Lipski 1977), possibly to retain person and number features on the verb, since phonological processes of consonant weakening and deletion tend to erode such information from verbal conjugations in these varieties (Contreras 1991). Lipski (1977: 64) was the first to propose the clitic-like behavior of subject pronouns in Caribbean Spanish when he stated that the "close bond between the subject pronoun and the verb may cause the words to behave as one," and thus form one single phonological unit.

Ordóñez and Olarrea (2006: 69–70), on the other hand, have pointed out that the clitic-like analysis of pronouns is questionable, since negation intervenes between the pronoun and the verb (99), thus showing that these two elements are not really acting as a single unit. In line with Cardinaletti and Stark (1999), they prefer to characterize them as weak pronouns, which, unlike clitics, may carry word stress and occur before negation, while, in contrast with strong pronouns, cannot precede a left-dislocated constituent, and cannot be either coordinated or focused.

(99) a. ¿Qué tú no comes?
         what you no eat
         'What don't you eat?'
     b. *¿Qué no tú comes?
         what no you eat

Ordóñez and Olarrea (2006) claim that inversion in Caribbean Spanish is the result of an IP containing a weak pronoun moving to a layered CP (Kayne &

Pollock 2001). In Mainland Spanish, weak pronouns would not be available, so that they would either not move (and thus remain in postverbal position) or appear preverbally via topicalization to CP. The authors do acknowledge that not all pronouns and DPs behave in the same way in inverted questions, but prefer to leave this issue of variation for future studies. In passing, they mention in a footnote that this may be a process of language change *à la* Kroch (1994) and, thus, that they will limit their analysis to second-person singular pronouns (Ordóñez & Olarrea 2006: 71–72).

Given that inverted questions appear to be conditioned by both frequency effects and phonological weight, both in the AHLAs and in Caribbean Spanish, I would like to propose, in line with González-Rivera and Sessarego (2020), the Subject-Movement Constraint, which may be stated as follows:

The heavier and less frequent the subject, the more likely it is to remain *in situ* (i.e., postverbal position).

Full DPs are heavier than pronouns, and thus they will be less likely to sound grammatically acceptable in preverbal position to AHLA/Caribbean Spanish-speakers. This also implies a range of acceptability across pronominal categories: *tú* is monosyllabic and highly frequent (and thus always acceptable), *usted* is bisyllabic and less frequent (and appears to be accepted most of the time), *nosotros/ustedes* are heavier (three syllables) and significantly less frequent in natural speech, and consequently less commonly acceptable in these dialects.

Quantitative studies on the nature of questions in Caribbean Spanish have also shown that the most common construction is actually the one presenting the *wh-V-S* order (Gutiérrez-Bravo 2008: 227 for DS). However, traditionally, the *wh-S-V* pattern has been taken to represent the Caribbean counterpart of the Mainland *wh-V-S* structure. Gutiérrez-Bravo (2005, 2007, 2008) has highlighted on several occasions how these two constructions should not be understood as equivalent questions in two different dialects. Rather, both of them are present in Caribbean Spanish and are regulated by different discourse constraints. The same constraints are encountered in Mainland Spanish, but in this variety the *wh-S-V* pattern is not an option. Its respective counterpart is expressed by examples like (100), in which the subject has been topicalized and moved to the left edge of the sentence.

(100) Tú, ¿qué comes?
 you what eat
 'What do you eat?'

Gutiérrez-Bravo (2008: 228) formulates what he calls the "Interrogative Clause Condition" to account for the EPP in questions:

A clausal Extended Projection is interrogative if the head of the highest phrase in the Extended Projection bears the feature [Q].

According to this condition, for constructions presenting the *wh-V-S* order, TP would be the highest projection. This would allow the *wh*-operator (*wh*-op) to land in [Spec, T], and T° to acquire a [Q] feature from Spec-Head agreement with *wh*-op. Such an operation would meet the EPP requirement, and thus it would allow the subject to remain in its VP internal position, as indicated in (101).

Conversely, when the *wh-S-V* structure is adopted, *wh*-op would land in [Spec, C], which results in C° acquiring [Q]. In this scenario, since [Spec, T] remains empty, a topicalized subject would be prompted to move to that position to satisfy the EPP (102). This solution, I argue, if combined with the Subject-Movement Constraint (González-Rivera & Sessarego 2020), accounts well for the inverted questions in both the AHLA and the Caribbean dialects while also providing an explanation for why not all subjects are equally acceptable in preverbal position.

(101) [TP Qué$_i$ comes$_j$ [VP tú $_{tj}$ $_{ti}$]]?
        wh   T°
        [Q] → [Q]

(102) [CP Qué$_i$ Ø [TP tú$_j$ comesk [VP $_{tj}$ $_{tk}$ $_{ti}$]]]?
        wh   C°
        [Q] → [Q]

A number of researchers have investigated the formal mechanisms underlying the L2 acquisition of *wh*-fronting and *S-V* inversion in questions (Johnson & Newport 1989; Birdsong 1992; White 1992; Martohardjono & Gair 1993; White & Juffs 1998). Results indicate that obtaining native-like mastery of these constructions may be challenging, especially if the L2 speakers proceed from an L1 background lacking these operations (e.g., in Chinese, Korean, and Japanese). The presence of the *wh-S-V* pattern in several creoles (Holm & Patrick 2007) has led some linguists to believe that the Spanish varieties presenting such a syntactic configuration would have derived from a preexisting creole language (Otheguy 1973; Perl 1998). This assumption, however, is weakened by the fact that SLA studies have shown how this pattern can also be commonly found even in quite advanced L2 varieties (Pienemann 1998, 2000; Cuza 2013; Guerra Rivera et al. 2015), thus providing indirect evidence that non-inverted questions should not necessarily be taken as an indicator of previous (de)creolization.

The existence of two different question types in the AHLAs may be perceived as an additional layer of complexity to their grammar. Such a finding is not what we would expect in the formation of contact varieties in which the emergence and conventionalization of less complex/unmarked structures is generally assumed. More historical and sociolinguistic research is certainly needed to cast light on the diachronic evolution of these two coexisting patterns in the dialects presenting such configurations (see Rosemeyer 2018 for a preliminary investigation of these issues in Caribbean Spanish). However, in the meantime, a speculative hypothesis to provide an explanation for this situation may be offered if we imagine that at a certain point during the formation of these contact vernaculars, due to processing constraints on L2 acquisition (Goodall 2004; Pienemann 2000), the linguistic output of a certain generation of L2 speakers may have presented quite variable configurations (including both *wh-S-V* and *wh-V-S* structures). The coexistence of both patterns in the speech community may have led the speakers of the following generations to discriminate between them and assign to those different word orders two dissimilar interpretations. In such a scenario, it is not unfeasible to imagine that the *wh-S-V* pattern could be adopted in the AHLA/Caribbean varieties to convey what would generally be expressed by the topicalized subject structure in the Mainland dialects.

To summarize, this section has shown how the traditional P&P perspective may be too rigid to account for the phenomena encountered in the AHLAs. In fact, the three Afro-Andean varieties analyzed here, in line with DS and BF, exhibit "partial pro-drop" grammars. The coexistence in the same language of properties belonging to both + and − NSP systems represents empirical evidence against the traditional assumption on which the P&P framework was built. For this reason, in this chapter a "rethinking" of the notion of parameter has been embraced (Eguren et al. 2016) in favor of a less rigid and more lexically oriented account of cross-linguistic variation.

In line with current minimalist proposals in the field of acquisition, the development of the lexicon and its formal features is supposed to happen gradually through a UG-driven path of possible grammars (Herschensohn 2000). For this reason, the presence of these features in the AHLAs – or a par with the gender and number variability characterizing their DP – does not necessarily have to be taken as the persisting traces of a once-spoken Pan-American Spanish creole. Conversely, it has been shown that the mastery of overt and null subject pronouns, subject–verb agreement and inverted questions depends on *advanced* L2 acquisition strategies, which are hampered by processability constraints applying at the *morphology–semantics* and *syntax–pragmatics interfaces*.

6 *Early-Peak Alignment and Duplication of Boundary Tone Configurations*

This chapter builds on recent studies focusing on Afro-Hispanic prosody (Sessarego & Rao 2016; Rao & Sessarego 2016, 2018; Knaff, Rao & Sessarego 2018; Butera, Sessarego & Rao 2019). It provides an analysis of declarative intonation for the three Afro-Andean dialects under study in terms of pitch accents and phrase boundary tones. Findings indicate that the inventory of these phonological targets in YS, CVS and CS is significantly more reduced than what has been reported for other native (non-contact) varieties of Spanish (Aguilar et al. 2009; Prieto & Roseano 2010). The Autosegmental Metrical (AM) model of intonational phonology (Pierrehumbert 1980; Hualde 2002; Ladd 2008) and the Spanish in the Tones and Break Indices (Sp_ToBI) transcriptional system (Beckman et al. 2002; Face & Prieto 2007; Estebas-Vilaplana & Prieto 2008) are adopted here to analyze the data.

The speakers of these vernaculars show evidence of duplicating nuclear pitch accents across pre-nuclear positions at the prosodic word (PW) level, as well as boundary configurations at both the intermediate and the intonational phrase levels (ip and IP). These results are interpreted as the by-product of contact-induced processes related to the nativization and conventionalization of advanced SLA strategies, which are hampered by processability constraints applying at the *pragmatics–phonology interface*. In this sense, these phenomena appear to parallel the morphosyntactic configurations analyzed in the previous chapters. In this case, however, the restructuring mechanisms are concerned with a different linguistic domain, which involves the grammatical mapping between discourse and phonological features.

6.1   Theoretical Background

Before a discussion of the details of this analysis, an overview of the AM model and the Sp_ToBI system is due. The AM model assumes a hierarchy of prosodic units, as sketched in (103). According to this framework, tones, which are generally of the high (H) and low (L) types, are understood as phonological targets corresponding with fundamental frequency (F0) peaks and valleys. They can stand individually (monotones) or can appear in sequences of two (bitones). Such tonal configurations are called pitch accents, which are associated with stressed, metrically salient syllables.

(103) Prosodic hierarchy
IP   Intonational phrase
ip   Intermediate phrase
PW   Prosodic word
F   Foot
σ   Syllable

L and H are not the only possible tones. At the phrase levels, mid (M) tones are also detectable in Spanish (Prieto & Roseano 2010) and may be used to chunk the utterance into different discourse units (D'Imperio, Eldorieta, Frota, Prieto & Vigário 2005). The most relevant levels for the current analysis are IP, ip and PW. As highlighted by Rao (2009), IPs are not isomorphic with syntax; they typically carry meaning and their boundaries tend to be limited by audible pauses (> 400 milliseconds). In most Spanish dialects, IPs end with suppressed F0 levels and final lengthening (Rao 2009, 2010). Their boundaries are transcriptionally represented with the symbol % (e.g., L%). IPs encapsulate ip sub-units, which do not necessarily convey meaning. Boundaries between ips are signaled by F0 increases through the final syllable of words, as well as F0 rise–plateau combinations, lengthening effects, F0 resets, and shorter/less audible pauses (D'Imperio et al. 2005; Eldorieta et al. 2003; Rao 2009, 2010) The symbol used to signal ip boundary tones is - (e.g., H-). Finally, PWs are associated with content words (Hualde 2002). Lexical items classified as PWs show acoustic correlates of stress such as F0 excursions (i.e., accent) and/o increases in duration and/or intensity (Ortega-Llebaria & Prieto 2010). PWs tend to show pitch accents, since they are tied to words with stressed syllables. Under certain pragmatic circumstances, some lexical items may lack pitch accent. This phenomenon is called *deaccenting* and may be driven by – among other factors – repetition in discourse and high word frequency (Rao 2009). Pragmatically, deaccenting is used in Spanish to indicate that a word is not salient.

Figure 6.1 depicts the most common pitch-accent configurations in Spanish (Aguilar, De-la-Mota & Prieto 2009). Each diagram is divided into three parts by two vertical lines. The central part consists of the stressed syllable, which is preceded and followed by the pre-tonic and post-tonic syllables, respectively. Here I will describe the most important pitch accents for the present study: $L+>H^*$, $L+H^*$ and $L+¡H^*$. For a more detailed account of the different

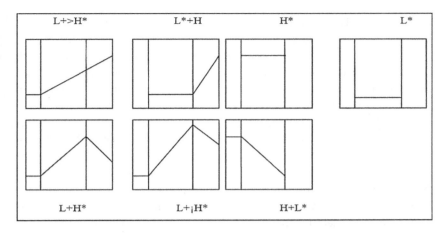

Figure 6.1 *Frequent pitch accents in Spanish*

configurations commonly encountered in Spanish, see Beckman et al. (2002), Estebas-Vilaplana & Prieto (2008), Face & Prieto (2007), Hualde (2002) and Prieto & Roseano (2010).

In each of the pitch accents depicted in Figure 6.1, the symbol * signals the tone (either L* or H*) that is associated with the stressed syllable, while the presence of the symbol > indicates that the tone is delayed, and thus associated with the post-tonic syllable, as in L+>H*. In most dialects of Spanish, in broad-focus declaratives, the configuration L+>H* is common in pre-nuclear (i.e., non-final) PWs. It consists of a valley (L) close to the beginning of the stressed syllable, followed by an incremental F0 rise that culminates in an H tone aligned with the post-tonic syllable. The configuration L+H*, on the other hand, is common for PWs in nuclear (i.e., final) position. It consists of a valley (L) followed by an H tone that appears on the stressed syllable. In broad-focus constructions, PWs in nuclear position tend to be the most salient. Spanish typically employs peak alignment configurations to signal such saliency. Thus, the peak generally aligns with the stressed syllable for salient (nuclear) PWs, while it appears on the post-nuclear syllable for non-salient (pre-nuclear) PWs. Further evidence of this peak movement strategy in Spanish is provided by the fact that peak alignment configurations may be used in pre-nuclear position in case of narrow-focus constructions when the speaker wants to put emphasis on a specific PW (Face 2001). Upstep (¡) and downstep (!) symbols are used in Figure 6.1 to show that a drastic F0 increase or decrease has taken place in the same ip in relation to the same preceding tone (e.g., L or H). For this reason, the L+¡H* pitch accent can be described as an upstepped configuration presenting a significant F0 increase of the H tone.

At the ip level, declarative constructions are characterized by a post-pitch accent F0 rise to an H- boundary tone. This specific configuration is used pragmatically to signal that the speaker is not done speaking and that more ip constituents will follow. Conversely, by the end of the utterance, at the IP level, an L% boundary tone is used to close the sentence, thus implying that the speaker has completed his or her thought (Prieto & Roseano 2010). It must be pointed out that in terms of scaling of tones across phrases, PWs at the beginning of the ip tend to present the highest F0 values, which are followed by a gradual decay in F0 levels (i.e., downstepping).

Some interesting deviations from the aforementioned standard configurations have been detected for Spanish varieties in contact with other languages. In particular, several studies have reported the systematic presence of L+H* configurations for PWs in pre-nuclear position for Spanish in contact with Basque (Elordieta 2003), Italian (Colantoni 2011; Colantoni & Gurlekian 2004), Quechua (O'Rourke 2004, 2005), Veneto (Barnes & Michnowicz 2013) and Yucatec Maya (Michnowicz & Barnes 2013).

As for the Afro-Hispanic varieties, little research has yet been carried out on their prosody. Lipski (2007) has provided an overview of some general patterns encountered in data from Chocó (Colombia), Tacarigüita (Venezuela), Curundú (Panama) and Afro-Cuban bozal Spanish, where he has pointed out the presence of H* strings in declaratives, indicating a general absence of valleys and downstepping. Similar results have also been detected in Palenquero (Spanish creole from Colombia) by Hualde and Schwegler (2008). Finally, Correa (2012) has analyzed intonational patterns in Palenquero and Kateyano (the Spanish variety used in the same region where Palenquero is spoken in Colombia) and has concluded that both varieties present a relatively reduced intonational inventory, which, among other features, is characterized by H* and L+H* configurations in narrow-focus constructions and minimal downstepping.

6.2 Methodology

The data analyzed here proceed from sociolinguistic interviews carried out from 2008 to 2013 across these Afro-Andean communities. The informants that participated in these studies were all elderly (80+ years of age) native speakers of these varieties, who did not speak any other language spoken in these regions (Quechua/Quichua and Aymara). All of them had a low

Table 6.1 *Methodological summary for declarative intonation in Yungueño Spanish, Chota Valley Spanish and Chincha Spanish*

Study	YS	CVS	CS
Years when data were collected	2008–2010	2011–2012	2012–2013
Number of informants	2	6	4
Place of origin of informants	Tocaña (North Yungas, Bolivia)	El Juncal (Chota Valley, Ecuador)	El Carmen, Guayabo, San Regis, San José (Province of Chincha, Peru)
Number of tokens (i.e., content words) analyzed	1,016	834	1,004

educational background (either completely illiterate or with minimal reading skills) and had spent all their lives in these rural communities carrying out traditional agricultural work. Table 6.1 provides a side-by-side summary of the methodology adopted to analyze declarative intonation in YS, CVS and CS.

It has to be pointed out that the data collection methodology adopted in these studies (i.e., the Labovian sociolinguistic interview) contrasts with the majority of the works that have so far been carried out on Spanish intonation, since such studies have been based, for the most part, on data from controlled tasks, which usually involved the reading of a script. The choice of this divergent methodology was in part dictated by the selection of the subjects, who would not feel at ease performing a structured task, and in part by the intention to collect more natural/vernacular speech samples, which would have been impossible to obtain by relying on more formal/controlled recording methodologies (Labov 1972b).

Given the aforementioned methodological differences, it must be acknowledged that the data collected for these Afro-Andean dialects are not strictly comparable to the results from more controlled experiments. Indeed, it has been reported that spontaneous declarative speech tends to show higher levels of deaccenting and tonic peak alignment, as well as less presence of final lowering and downstepping. These differences can be ascribed to the fact that emotions and other contextual factors (i.e., speakers' interactions) may play a significant role in spontaneous speech production, while such effects tend to be much more limited in lab speech (Face 2003).

Data were inspected using Praat (Boersma & Weenink 2014). The analysis was limited to declarative utterances that were considered to be neutral/non-emphatic. These recording fragments were obtained by excluding utterances in which the prosodic measures appeared to diverge significantly in relation to each informant's neutral-sounding declarative patterns. This selecting process had the purpose of obtaining the most representative broad-focus configurations possible, given the nature of the available data. In a second phase, the selected utterances were divided into IPs and then subsequently into ips. IP boundaries were identified by relying on a combination of final lowering, decreased intensity, final lengthening and/or long pauses, while ip cues involved instances of F0 rises, rises to plateau, lengthening effects and shorter pauses (Rao 2009, 2010).

Once IP and ip boundaries were determined, PWs were classified as being either in pre-nuclear or nuclear position. Moreover, given that F0 movement at ip boundaries is related to the ip's location within the IP, ip boundaries were analyzed as being either IP-final (i.e., final junctures) or non-IP-final (i.e., non-terminal junctures). Finally, by applying the coding schemes summarized in Figure 6.1, all lexically stressed words were assigned a pitch-accent configuration using the AM and Sp_ToBI conventions (see Prieto & Roseano 2010). A schematic representation of IP, ip and PW coding is provided in (104), where an IP is subdivided into two ips, each of which contains three PWs.

(104) Coding scheme (pn = pre-nuclear; n= nuclear; nt = non-terminal; t = terminal)
[   ]IP boundary (t)
  [   ]ip boundary (nt) [   ]ip boundary (t)
   PWpn PWpn PWn   PWpn PWpn PWn

6.3   Prosodic Findings

This section presents the prosodic findings from the phonetic inspection of the Afro-Andean data. Results have been divided into two subsections, according to the location of the prosodic configurations: pre-nuclear and nuclear positions. This was done because, as indicated in Section 6.1, previous studies on contact varieties of Spanish have reported deviations in pitch-accent configurations based on this difference, and because the nuclear position – being at the edge of phrases – also concerns an analysis of ip and IP boundary tones.

6.3.1   Pre-nuclear Position

In YS, CVS and CS the pitch-accent configurations detected in pre-nuclear position significantly deviate from the results commonly attested in this

Table 6.2 *Pre-nuclear pitch accents in Yungueño Spanish, Chota Valley Spanish and Chincha Spanish*

Pitch accents	YS (n = 467)	CVS (n = 456)	CS (n = 620)
L+(¡)H*	79.4% (371/467)	54.2% (247/456)	68.1% (422/620)
(¡)H*	18% (84/467)	40.3% (184/456)	15.2% (94/620)
(¡)H+L*	1.1% (5/467)	3.3% (15/456)	13.8% (86/620)
Other	1.5% (7/467)	2.2% (10/456)	2.9% (18/620)

context for most other native (non-contact) varieties of Spanish. Recall that in most Spanish dialects, broad-focus declaratives tend to present pre-nuclear configurations showing a post-tonic peak, like in L+>H*, while pre-nuclear peak alignment with the stressed syllable is usually interpreted as an instance of narrow focus, or emphatic speech (Prieto & Roseano 2010).

As Table 6.2 summarizes, the L+(¡)H* pitch accent, which presents alignment between the H tone and the stressed syllable, is clearly the most common configuration in YS, where it represents 79.4 percent of the data. The second most common pitch accent in this dialect is H* (18 percent), while the remaining configurations are negligible (2.6 percent all together). As for the CVS data, it can be seen that the L+(¡)H* and the (¡)H* configurations are the most favored, with 54.2 percent and 40.3 percent respectively, while the remaining pitch accents make up only 5.5 percent of the data. Finally, the CS data align – to a good extent – with the aforementioned patterns. In fact, L+(¡)H* is also the preferred pitch accent in this dialect (68.1 percent), followed by (¡)H* at 15.2 percent. This variety, nevertheless, diverges in part from the other two in that the presence of the (¡)H+L pitch accent is also detectable to a non-negligible extent (13.8 percent).

The findings, therefore, indicate that these three Afro-Andean vernaculars present very similar prosodic patterns for PWs in pre-nuclear position, which contrast strikingly with those commonly attested for most native varieties of Spanish. In fact, in all three of the data sets, post-tonic peak alignment (i.e., L+>H*), which would be the expected configuration for most Spanish dialects, is nearly absent. What can be systematically observed, on the other hand, is early-peak alignment with the stressed syllable (see Figure 6.2 for

132 *Early-Peak Alignments and Boundary Tones*

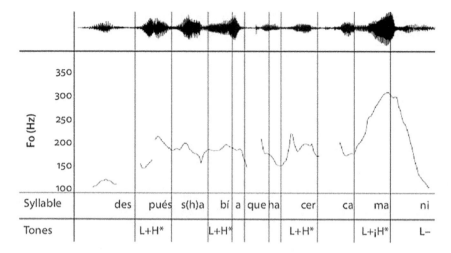

Figure 6.2 *An F0 contour for* Después había que hacer camani *'Later one had to do work' in Yungueño Spanish*

YS), which would signal narrow-focus/nuclear position (i.e., emphatic speech) in standard Spanish.

These results are, therefore, in line with previous studies on other Afro-Hispanic varieties (Lipski 2007; Hualde & Schwegler 2008; Correa 2012), since aligned pitch accents are the most common configurations. Moreover, as in those vernaculars, the rate of deaccenting appears to be significantly low: 5 percent for YS, 4 percent for CVS and 6 percent for Afro-Peruvian Spanish. This is quite remarkable, since in other varieties of Spanish deaccented tokens tend to represent some 20 percent of the lexical items and are used pragmatically to signal that certain words are not salient since they can be easily recovered from the context (Rao 2009).

6.3.2 Nuclear Position

When we look at the nuclear patterns at the ip boundaries that are not IP-final (Table 6.3), the H- configuration, which would be the preferred pattern in most varieties of Spanish, appears to be quite rare, with rates of 19.5 percent in YS, 0 percent in CVS and 10.1 percent in CS. Conversely, it is possible to systematically observe the L- tone. This is definitely surprising, since at this point of the utterance the speaker is not done speaking and more ips will follow. On the other hand, at the PW level, tones appear to follow standard patterns, since they systematically align with the stressed syllables, thus

Table 6.3 *Nuclear configurations in non-IP-final ips in Yungueño Spanish, Chota Valley Spanish and Chincha Spanish*

Configurations	YS (n = 251)	CVS (n = 197)	CS (n = 149)
L+(¡)H*L-	53.8% (135/251)	35.5% (70/197)	53.7% (80/149)
L*L-		20.8% (41/197)	
H*L-		18.3% (36/197)	
(¡)H+L*L-			13.4% (20/149)
L+H*H-	19.5% (49/251)		10.1% (15/149)
Other L-	26.7% (67/251)	25.4% (50/197)	22.8% (34/149)

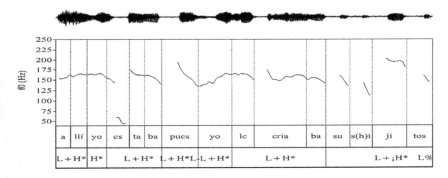

Figure 6.3 *An F0 contour for* Allí yo estaba pues, yo le criaba a sus hijitos *'There I was, well, I would take care of their children' in Chincha Spanish*

pragmatically signaling the saliency of words in nuclear position; in this position they also tend to present systematic upstep (¡) (see Figure 6.3 for CS).

An analysis of the prosodic configurations encountered in nuclear position at the IP boundary (i.e., in terminal position) shows how the L% boundary tone prevails in each dialect (see Figure 6.4 for CVS). An interesting difference concerning the CS data set in this case is a somewhat high level of H% boundary tones (16.8 percent), which is not generally expected in these constructions, given the declaratory nature of the utterances under study. In fact, H% boundary tones are more common in questions. A potential account

134   Early-Peak Alignments and Boundary Tones

Table 6.4 *IP-final configurations in Yungueño Spanish, Chota Valley Spanish and Chincha Spanish*

Configurations	YS (n = 204)	CVS (n = 122)	CS (n = 220)
L+(¡)H*L%	63.2% (129/204)	33.6% (41/122)	50.9% (112/220)
L*L%	17.7% (36/204)	56.6% (69/122)	
(¡)H+L*L%			18.2% (40/220)
L+(¡)H*H%			16.8% (37/220)
Other L%	19.1% (39/204)	9.8% (12/122)	14.1% (31/220)

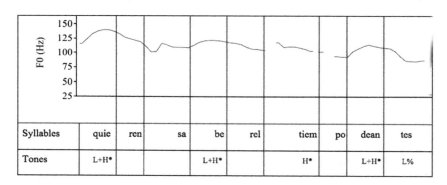

Figure 6.4 *An F0 contour for* Quieren saber el tiempo de antes *'They wanted to know about the past' in Chota Valley Spanish*

of this phenomenon has been provided by Butera et al. (2019: 10), who suggested that, due to the spontaneous nature of the interviews, certain speech fragments in that specific data set were at time disjointed and, consequently, may have favored more H% boundary tone realizations (see also Bustin, Fenton & Muntendam 2017).

Across these Afro-Andean dialects, at the PW level, the most common pitch-accent types in this position are L+(¡)H* and L*, as expected (Prieto & Roseano 2010). In this regard, YS and CS favor the first pattern, with 63.2 percent and 50.9 percent, respectively, while in CVS the L* configuration is preferred (56.6 percent).

6.4 An Analysis along the Pragmatics–Phonology Interface

One of the most striking findings for nuclear PWs in these Afro-Andean dialects is the widespread use of L+H* and the almost complete absence of the L+>H* pitch accent, which, in contrast, is the preferred configuration in most native (non-contact) varieties of Spanish (Rao & Sessarego 2016). While natural data have been reported to show more pitch alignment configurations than lab speech (Face 2003), the systematic presence of L+H* in pre-nuclear position across all three dialects cannot be dismissed as just a methodological issue. In fact, interestingly, L+H* is a configuration that tends to occur in nuclear position in most Spanish dialects, a location that in broad-focus declaratives is generally associated with prosodic heads and relative prominence. The same configuration, in fact, is also used in Spanish to signal emphasis in narrow-focus constructions. These peculiar results, therefore, appear to indicate that a prominent/more salient pattern, which would typically occur only in nuclear positions and narrow-focus constructions, has here been generalized to all pre-nuclear locations, falling back on what appears to be a cyclical copy-and-paste strategy (Sessarego & Rao 2016). As a result, the typical phonological distinction between L+H* and L+>H*, which is used in Spanish to signal a pragmatic difference in contextual prominence, does not appear to be part of the pitch-accent inventory system of these Afro-Andean dialects. Along the same lines of reasoning, it could also be argued that deaccenting, as a pragmatic strategy that avoids highlighting non-salient lexical items, seems not to apply to these Afro-Andean vernaculars, since this phenomenon appears at much lower levels across these varieties than other Spanish dialects (Face 2003).

When the configurations at the PW level in nuclear positions are analyzed in YS, CVS and CS, it is possible to observe that L+H* is the most common pitch accent at both the ip- and IP-edges. At the ip-edge, the L+H* configuration is generally preferred in most Spanish dialects because the boundary tone tends to impede peak displacement. At the IP-edge, several Spanish dialects fall back on suppression to L*, while others prefer circumflex contours with an L+H* configuration (Rao & Sessarego 2016). As for the Afro-Andean vernaculars analyzed here, CVS appears to align more closely with the varieties preferring L*, while YS and CS are more similar to the dialects favoring L+H*. All of them, moreover, favor the L% IP boundary tone to pragmatically indicate that the speaker is done speaking, a strategy that is in line with normative Spanish. Overall, therefore, these findings point to a cohesiveness in the data that allows for some degree of variation – possibly related to subtle pragmatic effects – while aligning for the most part with standard Spanish patterns. It is quite surprising, therefore, to find a significant presence of L- at non-terminal junctures across these Afro-Andean vernaculars. This suggests that this pragmatic strategy, which is used in most varieties of Spanish to signal that the speaker is not done speaking (i.e., H- at the ip boundary), is not part of these grammars. Indeed, the systematic use of L- may be due to a generalization of the preferred IP-level configuration to the lower level. This, in turn, represents another instance of a copy-and-paste strategy by which a prominent category (i.e., the terminal L tone) has been copied to all other positions: the non-terminal ip junctures.

Instances of contact-driven restructuring may lead to reductions in certain aspects of a grammar. This tends to be the case for grammatical structures implying high processing demands on linguistic interfaces, since they put extra effort into modular coordination. Nevertheless, such reductions do not necessarily impoverish the communicative power of a language, which tends to always be preserved. This is due to the systemic nature of grammars, or the fact that each language leans toward preserving its own internal equilibrium. Remember that in Chapter 5 it was observed that a reduction in the verbal morphology of these Afro-Hispanic varieties triggered a higher usage of overt subject pronouns to preserve the information encoded in person and number features. Keeping in mind the presence of these systemic mechanisms, after taking a closer look at the pitch accents detected across YS, CVS and CS, I would like to propose that a compensatory reconfiguration of the phono-pragmatic system of these dialects has taken place.

We know that Spanish-speakers often employ peak alignment movement to convey a pragmatic distinction between broad and narrow focus. That is done by phonologically displacing the peak across the horizontal axis. Thus, in standard Spanish a post-tonic peak generally conveys broad focus, while a tonic one signals narrow focus/emphatic speech. On the other hand, in these vernaculars, peaks are always systematically aligned with stressed syllables, and thus the aforementioned peak alignment strategy cannot be used to express emphasis. The result of this phenomenon pragmatically translates to what speakers of many other varieties of Spanish would perceive as an overgeneralization of narrow focus or emphatic speech.

It may be proposed that for these contact varieties a compensatory adjustment has taken place along the *pragmatics–phonology interface*, so that narrow focus is here conveyed by falling back on phonetic (rather than phonological) processes. Indeed, in these dialects, emphasis can still be expressed. Nevertheless, Afro-Andean speakers do not seem to do so by

At the Pragmatics–Phonology Interface   137

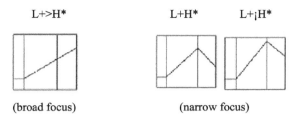

Figure 6.5 *Common Spanish broad and narrow-focus strategies (via phonology with the possibility of phonetic upstep)*

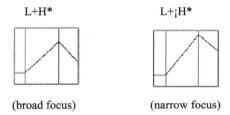

Figure 6.6 *Suggested Afro-Andean broad and narrow-focus strategies (via phonetics only)*

displacing the peak via phonological tonal alignment (along the horizontal axis); rather, they appear to employ phonetic F0 movements – resulting in upstepped configurations – along the vertical axis (i.e., L+¡H*). This, in turn, provides a potential account for the systematic presence of upstepped pitch accents (especially in nuclear position, see Figure 6.3) across these data sets (see Butera et al. 2019 on this point). Figures 6.5 and 6.6 provide a schematic representation of the proposed phono-pragmatic reconfiguration, in which the narrow-focus strategies in standard Spanish and Afro-Andean Spanish are compared.

Some authors have argued that certain prosodic patterns found across the Afro-Hispanic varieties may be related to a potential substrate effect, possibly due to some non-specified Bantu languages (Hualde & Schwegler 2008). On the other hand, in line with recent proposals (Sessarego & Rao 2016; Rao & Sessarego 2016), I would like to suggest that the prosodic configurations systematically detected across these Afro-Andean dialects may be better explained, again, as advanced L2 strategies, which are neither necessarily linked to any specific substrate language nor to a previous (de)creolization phase for YS, CVS and CS.

Michnowicz and Barnes (2013) and Barnes and Michnowicz (2013) have proposed an SLA-driven simplification process to account for the pre-nuclear use of L+H* pitch accent in Spanish varieties in contact with Veneto and Maya. My Afro-Andean data further support this SLA-based account, since it can offer a logical explanation for why a number of Spanish contact dialects with highly heterogeneous substrates tend to converge on the same prosodic patterns (see Elordieta 2003 for Basque; Colantoni 2011, Colantoni & Gurlekian 2004 for Italian; O'Rourke 2004, 2005 for Quechua). In fact, the replication and simplification of phonological targets can be associated with the historical evolution of these Afro-Andean speech communities, whose members at some point acquired Spanish as a second language in a non-tutored plantation context. Given such a peculiar setting, it is possible to imagine that the first generation of slaves acquiring Spanish in this environment may have experienced some communicative challenges and, even though their L2 speech generally converged with Spanish quite closely, certain aspects of this contact variety inevitably diverged from the target language. As a result of this contact-driven restructuring process, more emphatic/salient phonological targets may have overridden other configurations involving nuanced pragmatic meanings.

Another potential account for these diverging prosodic patterns would be to claim that colonial Spanish already presented these specific configurations, so that such features might have been preserved in these rural, isolated Afro-Hispanic communities. Given that we do not have direct access to colonial Spanish data of this kind, this hypothesis cannot be completely ruled out, especially if we consider that a few archaic morphosyntactic features (such as the use of *ser* 'to be' as an auxiliary verb in certain contexts, and the preservation of a few now-disused verb forms) have been detected for some contemporary Afro-Hispanic dialects (Cuba 2002; Sessarego 2015, 2017c, 2019a). Nevertheless, the fact that the aforementioned prosodic patterns have also been encountered in a number of other Spanish contact varieties, which are neither rural nor isolated, strongly suggests that these features are more likely to be the result of contact, rather than the traces of intonational archaisms.

Overall, these findings point to a reduced set of phonological targets across the PW, ip and IP levels. The result, as we saw, is an overgeneralization of L+H* and L configurations, which appear to have been driven by a copy-and-paste strategy. The following examples schematically depict the same broad-focus declarative constructions in most non-contact varieties of Spanish and in the three Afro-Andean dialects examined here. These examples represent six PWs distributed across two ips, which are embedded within an IP. As we have

At the Pragmatics–Phonology Interface   139

seen, the Afro-Andean example diverges from standard Spanish in that at the PW level the L+H* configuration has been copied to each position, while the tonal L configuration has been generalized from the terminal IP-edge to the non-terminal ip boundary tones.

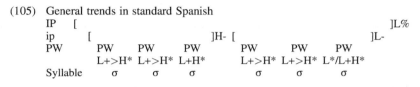

The results for YS, CVS and CS are remarkably similar. The model proposed here to account for such findings suggests that those parallelisms are the result of universal SLA strategies, which are driven by processing constraints applying at the *pragmatics–phonology interface*. Therefore, in parallel with the instances of variable phi-agreement and the partial pro-drop phenomena analyzed in the previous chapters, I argue that a fundamental aspect of the development of these tonal configurations was the input of advanced L2 speakers of Spanish to the following generations of Afro-Andean speakers, who nativized such L2 varieties and conventionalized them at the community level. For this reason, all of the Afro-Hispanic features analyzed in this book can be seen as the consequence of *advanced, conventionalized L2 processes*, which left an unquestionable trace in these grammars.

7 Final Considerations

The Afro-Hispanic languages of the Americas (AHLAs) are rich in structures and prosodic patterns that would be considered either ungrammatical or pragmatically infelicitous in standard Spanish. Some of these linguistic deviations from the norm have traditionally been classified as the traces of a once-existing creole language, which would have almost completely dissolved after a process of decreolization. This hypothesis, according to several scholars (Granda 1968 et seq.), would be the only reasonable explanation to account for the parallel presence in these contact varieties of the same peculiar "creole-like" features.

The present book was written out of the conviction that the Decreolization Hypothesis is on the wrong track and that such "creole-like" features can actually be explained as the result of common contact-driven processes, which tend to occur every time Spanish is acquired as a second language. In particular, this study has suggested that the AHLAs might be seen as the result of *advanced* SLA strategies that were nativized and conventionalized at the community level, without necessarily envisioning any (de)creolization phase for these vernaculars.

This book is based on data collected during several years of fieldwork research in the Afro-Andean communities of Yungas (Bolivia), Chota Valley (Ecuador) and Chincha (Peru). It combines both sociolinguistic and formal techniques of data gathering and analysis to provide more fine-grained, empirically testable generalizations. Results have shown how these contact varieties represent an extremely rich testing ground for formal theories, which have usually been built on standardized language data.

In Chapter 2, a sociohistorical analysis of the Black Diaspora to the Andes has been offered in order to cast light on the origins of YS, CVS and CS. Findings indicate that, due to series of geographic, economic and demographic factors, the Afro-descendant population in these regions never achieved the large numbers observed in other parts of the Americas. Moreover, most of the blacks who entered this territory were not directly brought from Africa; rather

Final Considerations 141

they were predominantly *criollo* captives, who, in all likelihood, could speak vernacular varieties of Spanish natively. The overall sociodemographic patterns detected for the Andean region have also been encountered for the more specific realities of colonial Yungas, Chota Valley and Chincha. In those communities, in fact, large-scale plantations never existed and the social dynamics characterizing life on such haciendas do not support the feasibility of a (de)creolization model.

While Chapter 2 was primarily concerned with showing that a (de)creolization phase for these vernaculars is not likely from a sociohistorical point of view, Chapters 3 to 6 have addressed the same issue from a linguistic perspective. In particular, it has been demonstrated that all of the so-called "creole-like" elements, often mentioned in relation to these dialects, can actually be conceived of as the result of *advanced L2 traits*, which are related to processing constraints applying at the *interface* between different language modules (Sessarego 2013b, 2019b).

Chapter 3 offered an overview of the main theoretical perspectives on the study of inter- and intra-speaker language variation. In fact, paving the way for the linguistic analyses that are developed in the rest of the book, this chapter has highlighted that, even though the generative and sociolinguistic traditions have generally adopted diametrically divergent views on this matter (Chomsky 1957, 1966, 1986; Labov 1972a, 1972b), in more recent times some efforts have been made to reconcile these two fields. In particular, formalist analyses of diachronic language change have opened the doors of generative research to the use of performance data (Kroch 1989, 1994), and the development of microparametric enquiry on non-standard dialects has further enhanced a more empirical approach to data gathering (Kayne 1996; Barbiers & Cornips 2001). During the past 15 years or so, partially thanks to the derivational shift brought about by the Minimalist Program (Chomsky 1995, 2001), the study of inter- and intra-speaker speech variability has become more central to formal analyses (Adger & Smith 2005; Adger 2006), to the point that several works have proposed models that conceive generative theorizing and sociolinguistic methodologies as complementary, rather than contrasting (Sessarego 2013d; Sessarego & Gutiérrez-Rexach 2011; Parrott 2007, 2009; Adger & Smith 2010), with the goal of producing more fine-grained generalizations for stigmatized varieties – such as the AHLAs – for which relying exclusively on grammaticality judgments and other formal methodologies may prove particularly hard or even impossible (Sessarego 2014a).

Chapter 4 presented an analysis of variable gender and number agreement across the Determiner Phrase of these vernaculars. The reduced agreement systems of these varieties are analyzed as a by-product of linguistic constraints concerning the *morphology–semantics interface*, which, according to some recent theoretical accounts, may be envisioned as the "bottleneck" of acquisition (Slabakova 2008, 2009). As for these specific dialects, results show a case of cross-generational change, consisting of the systematic substitution of stigmatized basilectal Afro-Andean features with more prestigious standard Spanish ones. The approach adopted here, in line with the theoretical trend described in Chapter 3, strives to combine insights from minimalist syntax and variationist sociolinguistics. In so doing, it adopts current formal proposals on the nature of feature valuation and checking while treating variation as a matter of presence/absence of uninterpretable features in a derivation (Pesetsky & Torrego 2007; Adger & Smith 2005). The proposed analysis presents an account that diverges from theories embracing a parametrized N-raising DP (Ritter 1991; Picallo 1991; Bernstein 1993). Rather, it backs a rethinking of the rigid notion of parameter in favor of a more flexible approach, in which the locus of variation resides in the lexicon (Eguren et al. 2016).

In line with the same theoretical perspective, Chapter 5 shows that YS, CVS and CS are characterized by phenomena that do not align with the predictions of the Null Subject Parameter (NSP) (Rizzi 1982), since they present structures that belong to both null and non-null subject languages. In particular, it is shown how – owing to compensatory mechanisms always at work in language – a reduction in verbal morphology in the formation of these varieties corresponded to an increase in the overt rates of subject pronouns, which allowed for person and number features to be explicitly expressed. This readjustment in grammar shows how the erosion of verbal conjugations, a process primarily related to the difficulty of mapping semantic concepts onto bond morphology (i.e., *morphology–semantics interface*), had a triggering effect on overt subject expression and subject placement in questions, phenomena that pertain to the *syntax–pragmatics interface*, which is considered by a number of scholars as one of the most challenging aspects to master in SLA (Sorace & Filiaci 2006; Tsimpli & Sorace 2006; Belletti, Bennati & Sorace 2007; Sorace 2000, 2003).

Several instances of systemic contact-driven restructuring have also been detected across the Afro-Andean *phonology–pragmatics interface*. Chapter 6 shows how narrow focus in Afro-Andean Spanish is expressed via phonetic rising, by employing upstepped configurations, rather than by relying on phonological tone alignment as in standard Spanish. This reconfiguration appears to have been prompted by the fact that – owing to the more limited pitch-accent configurations available in these varieties – all tones tend to systematically align with the stressed syllable, so that the tonal peak can no longer be moved across syllables to express emphasis (Sessarego & Rao 2016). This almost categorical tone alignment appears to be by-product of a copy-and-paste strategy by which, at some point in the evolution of these varieties, L2 Spanish-speakers managed to master the most prominent/ emphatic prosodic configuration at the PW level in declarative constructions (i.e., the L + H* pitch accent in nuclear position) and then reproduced it for each single PW. A parallel process occurred at higher prosodic levels, where the prominent L boundary tone has been copied from the final IP position (i.e., L%) to be replicated at each ip boundary edge, thus resulting in widespread L- configurations across the utterance.

A close look at YS, CVS and CS grammars has shown how their so-called "creole-like" features can actually be conceived of as common instances of contact-induced change, which can be encountered – to different extents – in virtually all contact varieties of Spanish. The study of these varieties has also offered an ideal "testing ground" for formal hypotheses, which have traditionally been built on standardized language data (e.g., the NSP and the Parametrized N-raising DP). In so doing, this book has shown the vast research potential that these contact varieties encompass.

This book is also meant to contribute to the (Spanish) Creole Debate, both from the sociohistorical and the linguistic perspectives. Indeed, from a sociohistorical point of view, it is fascinating to observe that the varieties that have traditionally been classified as Spanish creoles in the Americas (Papiamento and Palenquero) are spoken in two rather circumscribed regions (the Netherlands Antilles and the Colombian village of San Basilio de Palenque) by a relatively reduced number of people, in sharp contrast with the French- and English-based creoles, which are significantly more widespread across the Caribbean and other parts of the American continent. It is also of particular interest to notice that Papiamento and Palenquero are spoken exactly were no Spanish law ever applied in colonial times (in a former Dutch colony and in a Maroon community, which – by definition – was not subject to the Spanish rule). The Legal Hypothesis of Creole Genesis (LHCG) (Sessarego 2015, 2017a, 2019a) has addressed these issues by proposing that, besides certain economic, social, religious and demographic factors, Spanish colonial slave law – being the only system that provided slaves with legal personhood – had a significant effect on preventing Spanish creoles from forming or being preserved in the Americas.

The present study has integrated sociohistorical and linguistic analyses to cast further light on the AHLAs. The future of creole studies, I believe, would benefit greatly from a stronger interdisciplinary collaboration capable of combining linguistic, legal, and historical insights to better understand the nature and evolution of these languages. I hope this project may serve as a source of inspiration for other researchers who may decide to combine different disciplines – maybe along the lines of the LHCG – to further explore the nature and origins of these and other contact varieties.

From a linguistic perspective, this book has also highlighted the importance of SLA processes in the formation of both creole languages and the AHLAs. In particular, it has shown how processes of borrowing, imposition and grammatical reduction played – to different extents, depending on the specific contact scenario – a key role in shaping these grammars. Above all, it has argued that grammars are not robustly transmitted during the emergence of creoles (in contrast to Blasi et al. 2017), given that morphosyntactic and tonal features tend not to be inherited during creolization and are difficult to master completely, even in advanced stages of L2 acquisition. Moreover, it has also been claimed that creoles are not the simplest world's languages (in contrast with McWhorter 2001), since they may inherit a good number of syntactic, semantic and phonological distinctions from their substrate languages, which may result in systems presenting a relatively high level of complexity in certain aspects of their grammars.

In conclusion, this project has embraced an approach to linguistic analysis that rests squarely on the cross-fertilization of ideas and methodologies proceeding from a number of fields (e.g., SLA, creolistics, generative theorizing, sociolinguistics and social history). It aims at a cohesiveness in language science that lies in the incorporation of multifaceted fieldwork techniques coupled with current theoretical proposals on the nature of linguistic interfaces, language processing and sociolinguistic dynamics. The findings of the current study, as well as the integrated research approach on which they were built, can now be applied to and tested in other contact scenarios. The next step is to investigate how different contact settings – potentially involving a number of dissimilar social factors and linguistic inputs – may have shaped the grammars of other contact varieties. This book, therefore, not only casts light on the nature of Afro-Andean Spanish and the rest of the AHLAs, it also provides a new set of theoretical and methodological perspectives to approach in a more integrated manner the study of contact-driven restructuring across language interfaces and linguistic domains.

References

Aboh, E. 2015. *The Emergence of Hybrid Grammars*. Cambridge: Cambridge University Press.
  2016. Creole distinctiveness: A dead end. *Journal of Pidgin and Creole Languages*, 31.2: 400–418.
Aboh, E., & M. DeGraff 2016. A null theory of creole formation based on Universal Grammar. In Roberts, I. (ed.), *The Oxford Handbook of Universal Grammar*, 401–458. Oxford: Oxford University Press.
Adger, D. 2006. Combinatorial variability. *Journal of Linguistics*, 42: 503–530.
  2007. Variability and modularity: A response to Hudson. *Journal of Linguistics*, 43, 695–700.
  2010. A minimalist theory of feature structure. In Kibort, A., & G. Corbett (eds.), *Features: Perspectives on a Key Notion in Linguistics*, 185–218. Oxford: Oxford University Press.
Adger, D., & J. Smith 2005. Variation and the minimalist program. In Cornips, L., & K. P. Corrigan (eds.), *Syntax and Variation. Reconciling the Biological and the Social*, 149–178. Amsterdam: John Benjamins.
  2010. Variation in agreement: A lexical feature-based approach. *Lingua*, 120.5: 1109–1134.
Adger, D., & P. Svenonius 2011. Features in minimalist syntax. In Boeckx, C. (ed.), *Handbook of Linguistic Minimalism*, 27–51. Oxford: University Press.
Adger, D., & G. Trousdale 2007. Variation in English syntax: Theoretical implications. *English Language and Linguistics*, 11.2: 261–278.
Aguilar, L., C. De-la-Mota & P. Prieto 2009. Sp_ToBI training materials. http://prosodia.upf.edu/sp_tobi.
Aguirre Beltrán, G. 1946. *La población negra en México: Estudio etnohistórico*. Mexico City: Ediciones Fuente cultural.
Aguirre, C. 1997. Peru. In Rodríguez, J. (ed.), *The Historical Encyclopedia of World Slavery*, 501–502. Santa Barbara, CA: ABC-CLIO.
Alarcón, I. 2011. Spanish grammatical gender under complete and incomplete acquisition: Early and late bilinguals' linguistic behavior within the noun phrase, *Bilingualism: Language and Cognition*, 14.3: 332–350.
Alemán Bañón, J., & J. Rothman 2016. The role of morphological markedness in the processing of number and gender agreement in Spanish: An event-related potential investigation. *Language, Cognition and Neuroscience*, 31.10: 1273–1298.

References

Alexiadou, A. 2001. Adjective syntax and noun raising: Word order asymmetries in the DP as the result of adjective distribution. *Studia Linguistica*, 55.3: 217–248.

Alleyne, M. 1980. *Comparative Afro-American: An Historical-Comparative Study of English-Based Afro-American Dialects of the New World*. Ann Arbor, MI: Karoma.

Alvar, M. 1996. *Manual de dialectología hispánica*. Madrid: Grupo Planeta.

Álvarez, A., & E. Obediente. 1998. El español caribeño: Antecedentes sociohistóricos y lingüísticos. In Pearl M., & A. Schwegler (eds.), *América negra: Panorámica actual de los estudios lingüísticos sobre variedades hispanas, portuguesas y criollas*, 40–61. Madrid/Frankfurt: Iberoamericana/Vervuert.

Álvarez Nazario, M. 1974. *El elemento afronegroide en el español de Puerto Rico*. San Juan: Instituto de Cultura Puertorriqueña.

Andersen, R. 1980. Creolization as the acquisition of a second language as a first language. In Valdmann, A., & A. Highfield (eds.), *Theoretical Orientations in Creole Studies*, 273–295. San Diego, CA: Academic Press.

Andersen, R. (ed.) 1983. *Pidginization and Creolization as Language Acquisition*. Rowley, MA: Newbury House.

Andrien, K. 1995. *The Kingdom of Quito, 1690–1830: The State and Regional Development*. Cambridge: Cambridge University Press.

Baker, M. 2008. *The Syntax of Agreement and Concord*. Cambridge: Cambridge University Press.

Baker, P. 1990. Off target? *Journal of Pidgin and Creole Languages*, 5: 107–119.

Bakker, P., C. Levisen & E. Sippola (eds.) 2016. *Phylogenetic Approaches to Creole Languages*. Amsterdam/Philadelphia: John Benjamins.

Bakker, P., A. Daval-Markussen, M. Parkvall & I. Plag 2011. Creoles are typologically distinct from non-creoles. *Journal of Pidgin and Creole Languages*, 26.1: 5–42.

Baptista, M. 2002. *The Syntax of Cape Verdean Creole*. Amsterdam: John Benjamins.

Barbiers, S. 2009. Locus and limits of syntactic microvariation. *Lingua*, 119.11: 1607–1623.

Barbiers, S., & L. Cornips 2001. Introduction to syntactic microvariation. In Barbiers, S., L. Cornips and S. van der Kleij (eds.), *Syntactic Microvariation*, 1–11. Meertens Institute Electronic Publications in Linguistics. www.meertens.knaw .nl/projecten/sand/synmic/.

Barbosa, P., M. A. Kato & M. E. Duarte 2005. Null subjects in European and Brazilian Portuguese. *Journal of Portuguese Linguistics*, 4: 11–52.

Barnes, H., & J. Michnowicz 2013. Peak alignment in semi-spontaneous bilingual Chilipo Spanish. In Carvalho, A., & S. Beaudrie (eds.), *Selected Proceedings of the 6th Workshop on Spanish Sociolinguistics*, 109–122. Somerville, MA: Cascadilla Proceedings Project.

Barrera-Tobón, C., & R. Raña-Risso 2016. A corpus-based sociolinguistic study of contact-induced changes in subject placement in the Spanish of New York City bilinguals. In Sessarego, S., & F. Tejedo-Herrero (eds.), *Spanish Language and Sociolinguistic Analysis*, 323–342. Amsterdam: John Benjamins.

References

Battistella, E. 1990. *Markedness: The Evaluative Superstructure of Language*. Albany, NY: State University of New York Press.
Baxter, A., Lucchesi, D. & M. Guimarães 1997. Gender agreement as a "decreolizing" feature of an Afro-Brazilian dialect. *Journal of Pidgin and Creole Languages*, 12:1: 1–57.
Beckman, M., M. Díaz-Campos, J. McGory & T. Morgan 2002. Intonation across Spanish, in the Tones and Break Indices framework. *Probus* 14: 9–36.
Béjar, S. 2008. Conditions on phi-agree. In Harbour, D., D. Adger & S. Béjar (eds.), *Phi Theory*, 130–154. Oxford: Oxford University Press.
Belletti, A., Bennati E. & A. Sorace 2007. Theoretical and developmental issues in the syntax of subjects: Evidence from near-native Italian. *Natural Language & Linguistic Theory*, 25: 657–689.
Bello, A. 1847[1988]. *Gramática castellana destinada al uso de americanos*. [edited by R. Trujillo]. Madrid: Arco Libros.
Benincà, P. 1989. *Dialect Variation and the Theory of Grammar*. Dordrecht: Foris.
  1994. *La variazione sintattica: Studi di dialettologia romanza*. Bologna: Il Mulino.
Bentley, W. 1887. *Dictionary and Grammar of the Kongo Language, as Spoken at San Salvador, the Ancient Capital of the Old Kongo Empire, West Africa*. London: Baptist Missionary Society.
Bernstein, J. 1993. The syntactic role of word markers in null nominal constructions. *Probus*, 5: 5–38.
Bickerton, D. 1981. *Roots of Language*. Ann Arbor, MI: Karoma.
Birdsong, D. 1992. Ultimate attainment in second language acquisition. *Language*, 68: 706–755.
Black, J., & V. Motapanyane (eds.) 1996. *Microparametric Syntax and Dialect Variation*. Amsterdam: John Benjamins.
Blasi, D., S. Michaelis & M. Haspelmath. 2017. Grammars are robustly transmitted even during the emergence of creole languages. *Nature Human Behaviour*, 1: 723–729.
Boersma, P., & D. Weenink 2014. Praat: Doing phonetics by computer. www.praat.org/.
Bonet, E. 1995. The feature structure of Romance clitics. *Natural Language and Linguistic Theory*, 13: 607–617.
Borer, H. 1984. *Parametric Syntax. Case Studies in Semitic and Romance Languages*. Dordrecht: Foris.
Bouisson, E. 1997. Esclavos de la tierra: Los capesinos negros del Chota-Mira, siglos XVII–XX. *Procesos, Revista Ecuatoriana de Historia*, 11: 45–67.
Bowser, F. 1974. *The African Slave in Colonial Peru, 1524–1650*. Stanford, CA: Stanford University Press.
Bridikhina, E. 1995. El tráfico de esclavos negros a La Paz a fines del siglo XVIII. *Estudios Bolivianos*, 1: 183–191.
Brockington, L. 2006. *Blacks, Indians, and Spaniards in the Eastern Andes*. Lincoln, NE/London: University of Nebraska Press.
Brody, M. 2003. *Lexico-Logical Form*. Cambridge, MA: MIT Press.

References

Brown, E., & J. Rivas. 2011. Subject–verb word-order in Spanish interrogatives: A quantitative analysis of Puerto Rican Spanish. *Spanish in Context*, 8.1: 23–49.

Browne, R. 2017. *Surviving Slavery in the British Caribbean*. Philadelphia, PA: University of Pennsylvania Press.

Bruhn de Garavito, J., & L. White 2002. The second language acquisition of Spanish DPs: The status of grammatical features. In Pérez-Leroux, A. T., & J. M. Liceras (eds.), *The Acquisition of Spanish Morphosyntax: The L1/L2 Connection*, 153–178. Dordrecht: Kluwer.

Bryant, K. 2005. Slavery and the context of ethnogenesis: African, Afro-Creoles, and the realities of bondage in the kingdom of Quito, 1600–1800. PhD Dissertation, Ohio State University.

Burnard, T., & J. Garrigus 2018. *The Plantation Machine Atlantic Capitalism in French Saint-Domingue and British Jamaica*. Philadelphia, PA: University of Pennsylvania Press.

Busdiecker, S. 2006. We are Bolivians too: The experience and meaning of blackness in Bolivia. PhD Dissertation, University of Michigan.

Bustin, A., E. Fenton & A. Muntendam 2017. Controlled elicitation of Afro-Peruvian Spanish intonation of broad focus declaratives. Paper presented at the 11th International Symposium on Bilingualism, University of Limerick, Ireland (June 11–15).

Butera, B., S. Sessarego, S. & R. Rao. 2019. Afro-Peruvian Spanish declarative intonation: Analysis and implications. In Campos, H., et al. (eds.), *Proceedings of the Hispanic Linguistics Symposium 2016*, 230–247. Amsterdam: John Benjamins.

Butera, B., S. Sessarego, 2020. Afro-Peruvian Spanish declarative intonation: Analysis and implications. In Morales-Font, A., M. Ferreira, R. Leow & C. Sanz (eds.) *Hispanic Linguistics: Current Issues and New Directions*, 229–248. Amsterdam. Philadelphia: John Benjamins.

Camacho, J. 2008. Syntactic variation: The case of Spanish and Portuguese subjects *Studies in Hispanic and Lusophone Linguistics*, 1.2: 415–433.

2013. *Null Subjects*. Cambridge: Cambridge University Press.

Cardinaletti, A. 1997. Subjects and clause structure. In Haegeman, L. (ed.), *The New Comparative Syntax*, 33–63. New York, NY: Longman.

Cardinaletti, A., & M. Starke. 1999. The typology of structural deficiency: A case study of the three classes of pronouns. In van Riemsdijk, H. (ed.), *Clitics in the Languages of Europe*, 145–233. Berlin: Mouton de Gruyter.

Carstens, V. 2000. Concord in minimalist theory. *Linguistic Inquiry*, 31.2: 319–355.

2001. Multiple agreement and case-deletion: Against Φ-incompleteness. *Syntax*, 4: 147–163.

Centurión Vallejo, H. 1954. *Esclavitud y manumisión de negros en Trujillo*. Trujillo: Imprenta de la Universidad de Trujillo.

Chambers, J. 2001. Vernacular universals. In Fontana, J. M., L. McNally, T. M. Turell & E. Vallduví (eds.), *Proceedings of ICLaVE, the First International Conference on Language Variation in Europe*, 52–60. Barcelona: Universitate Pompeu Fabra.

2003. *Sociolinguistic Theory: Linguistic Variation and Its Social Significance*. Malden and Oxford: Blackwell Publishers.

2004. Dynamic typology and vernacular universals. In Kortmann, B. (ed.), *Dialectology Meets Typology: Dialect Grammar from a Cross Linguistic Perspective*, 127–145. Berlin: Mouton de Gruyter.

Chomsky, N. 1957. *Syntactic Structures*. The Hague: Mouton.

1965. *Aspects of the Theory of Syntax*. Cambridge, MA: MIT Press.

1966. *Cartesian Linguistics*. New York, NY: Harper and Row.

1976. *Reflections on Language*. London: Temple Smith.

1981. *Lectures on Government and Binding*. Dordrecht: Foris.

1982. *Some Concepts and Consequences of the Theory of Government and Binding*. Cambridge, MA: MIT Press.

1986. *Knowledge of Language: Its Nature, Origin and Use*. New York, NY: Praeger.

1988. *Language and Problems of Knowledge: The Managua Lectures*. Cambridge, MA: MIT Press.

1995. *The Minimalist Program*. Cambridge, MA: MIT Press.

2000. Minimalist inquiries: The framework. In Martin, R, D. Michaels & J. Uriagereka (eds.), *Step by Step*, 89–156. Cambridge, MA: MIT Press.

2001. Derivation by phase. In Kenstowicz, M. (ed.), *Ken Hale: A Life in Language*, 1–52, Cambridge, MA: MIT Press.

2006. *Language and Mind*. 3rd ed. Cambridge, MA: MIT Press.

Chomsky, N., & H. Lasnik. 1993. The theory of principles and parameters. In Joachim J., A. von Stechow, W. Sternefeld & T. Vennemann (eds.), *Syntax: An International Handbook of Contemporary Research, Vol. 1*, 506–569. Berlin: Walter de Gruyter.

CHSJ 2012. *Casa Hacienda San José*. www.havciendasanjose.com.pe.

Cinque, G. 1990. Ergative adjectives and the lexicalist hypothesis. *Natural Language and Linguistic Theory*, 8: 1–40.

1993. On the evidence for partial N-movement in the Romance DP. *Venice Working Papers in Linguistics*, 3.2: 21–40.

1994. On the evidence for partial N movement in the Romance DP. In Cinque, G., J. Koster, J.-Y. Pollock, L. Rizzi & R. Zanuttini (eds.), *Paths towards Universal Grammar*, 85–110. Washington, DC: Georgetown University Press.

Clementi, H. 1974. *La abolición de la esclavitud en América Latina*. Buenos Aires: Editorial La Pléyade.

Clements, C. 2009. *The Linguistic Legacy of Spanish and Portuguese*. Cambridge: Cambridge University Press.

Colantoni, L. 2011. Broad-focus declaratives in Argentine Spanish contact and non-contact varieties. In Gabriel, C., & C. Lleó (eds.), *Intonational Phrasing in Romance and Germanic: Cross-Linguistic and Bilingual Studies*, 183–212. Amsterdam: John Benjamins.

Colantoni, L., & J. Gurlekian. 2004. Convergence and intonation: Historical evidence from Buenos Aires Spanish. *Bilingualism: Language and Cognition*, 7(2): 107–119.

Colmenares, G. 1997. *Historia Económica y Social de Colombia – II Popayán una Sociedad Esclavista 1680–1800*. Cali: TM editores, Universidad del Valle, Banco de la República, Colciencias.

Contreras, H. 1991. On the position of subjects. In Rothstein, S. (ed.), *Perspectives on Phrase Structure: Heads and Licensing, Syntax and Semantics 25*, 63–80. New York, NY: Academic Press.
Corbett, G. (1991). *Gender.* Cambridge: Cambridge University Press.
(2000). *Number.* Cambridge: Cambridge University Press.
(2006). *Agreement.* Cambridge: Cambridge University Press.
(2012). *Features.* Cambridge: Cambridge University Press.
Cornips, L., & C. Poletto 2005. On standardising syntactic elicitation techniques (part 1). *Lingua*, 115: 939–957.
Coronel Feijóo, R. 1991. *El valle sangriento de los indígenas de la coca y el algodón a la hacienda cañera jesuita, 1580–1700*. Quito: ABYA-YALA.
Correa, J. A. 2012. La entonación del palenquero y del keteyano hablado en Palenque (Colombia). In Maglia, G., & A. Schwegler (eds.), *Palenque (Colombia): Oralidad, identidad y resistencia*, 31–56. Bogotá: Pontificia Universidad Javeriana/Instituto Caro y Cuervo.
Cowper, E. 2005. The geometry of interpretable features: Infl in English and Spanish. *Language*, 81: 10–46.
Crespo, A. 1995. *Esclavos negros en Bolivia*. La Paz, Bolivia: Librería Editorial Juventud.
Croft, W. 2003. *Typology and Universals*. Cambridge: Cambridge University Press.
Cuba, M. 2002. *El castellano hablado en Chincha*. Lima: Talleres Gráficos de Angélica Tapia.
Cushner, N. 1980. *Lords of the Land: Sugar, Wine, and the Jesuit Estates of Coastal Peru*. Albany, NY: State University of New York Press.
1982. *Farm and Factory: The Jesuit and the Development of Agrarian Capitalism in Colonial Quito, 1600–1767*. Albany, NY: State University of New York Press.
Cuza, A., 2013. Crosslinguistic influence at the syntax proper: Interrogative subject–verb inversion in heritage Spanish. *International Journal of Bilingualism*, 17: 71–96.
Cuza, A., & R. Pérez-Tattam 2016. Grammatical gender selection and phrasal word order in child heritage Spanish: A feature re-assembly approach. *Bilingualism: Language and Cognition*, 19.1: 50–68.
Cyrino, S., & M. T. Espinal. 2019. The syntax of number in Romance. *Studia Linguistica*, 1–39.
D'Imperio, M., G. Elordieta, S. Frota, P. Prieto & M. Vigário 2005. Intonational phrasing in Romance: The role of syntactic and prosodic structure. In Frota, S., M. Vigário & M. J. Freitas (eds.), *Prosodies*, 59–98. Berlin: Mouton de Gruyter.
Davis, C. 1971. Tú, ¿qué tú tienes? *Hispania*, 54: 331–332.
De Janvry, A., E. Sadoulet & W. Wolford 1998. The changing role of the state in Latin American land reforms. CUDARE Working Paper No. 852. Berkeley, CA: Department of Agriculture and Resource Economics and Policy.
De Vogelaer, G. 2006. Actuation, diffusion, and universals: Change in the pronominal system of Dutch dialects. *Zeitschrift für Dialektologie und Linguistik*, 3: 259–274.

References

DeCamp, D. 1971. Towards a generative analysis of a post-creole continuum. In Hymes, D. (ed.), *Pidginization and Creolization of* Cambridge: Cambridge University Press.

DeGraff, M. 2003. Against creole exceptionalism. *Language*, 79.2: 391–410.

2005. Linguists' most dangerous myth: The fallacy of Creolist Exceptionalism. *Language in Society*, 34: 533–591.

Delicado-Cantero, M., & S. Sessarego 2011. Variation and syntax in number expression in Afro-Bolivian Spanish. In Ortiz-López, L. (ed.), *Selected Proceedings of the 13th Hispanic Linguistics Symposium*, 42–53. Somerville, MA: Cascadilla Press.

Demonte, V. 2008. Meaning–form correlations and adjective position in Spanish. In Kennedy, C., & L. McNally (eds.), *The Semantics of Adjectives and Adverbs*, 71–100. Oxford: Oxford University Press.

Díaz-Campos, M., & C. Clements 2005. Mainland Spanish colonies and Creole genesis: The Afro-Venezuelan area revisited. In Lotfi, S., & M. Westmoreland (eds.), *Proceedings of the Second Workshop on Spanish Sociolinguistics*, 41–53. Somerville, MA: Cascadilla Press.

2008. A Creole origin for Barlovento Spanish? A linguistic and sociohistorical inquiry. *Language in Society*, 37: 351–383.

Díaz Collazos, A. M., & D. Vásquez Hurtado 2017. Gender agreement in online versus classroom students of first-semester Spanish. *Open Linguistics*, 3: 656–672.

Domínguez, L. 2013. *Understanding Interfaces*. Amsterdam: John Benjamins.

Donaldson, B. 2011. Nativelike right-dislocations in near-native French. *Second Language Research*, 27: 361–390.

Duarte, M. E. 1995. A perda do princípio "Evite pronome" no português brasileiro. PhD Dissertation, UNICAMP.

2000. The loss of the 'Avoid Pronoun' principle in Brazilian Portuguese. In Kato, M., & E. Negrão (eds.), *Brazilian Portuguese and the Null Subject Parameter*, 17–36. Madrid/Frankfurt: Iberoamericana/Vervuert.

Duarte, M. E., & M. Kato 2002. A diachronic analysis of Brazilian Portuguese WH-questions. *Santa Barbara Portuguese Studies*, 6: 326–340.

D'Alessandro, R., & M. van Oostendorp 2017. On the diversity of linguistic data and the integration of the language sciences. *Frontiers in Psychology*, 8: 1–4.

Eguren, L., O. Fernández-Soriano & A. Mendikoetxea (eds.) 2016. *Rethinking Parameters*. Oxford: Oxford University Press.

Elordieta, G. 2003. The Spanish intonation of speakers of a Basque pitch-accent dialect. *Catalan Journal of Linguistics*, 2: 67–95.

Elordieta, G., S. Frota, P. Prieto & M. Vigário 2003. Effects of constituent length and syntactic branching on intonational phrasing in Ibero-Romance. In Solé, M.-J., D. Recasens & J. Romero (eds.), *Proceedings of the XVth International Congress of Phonetic Sciences*, 487–490. Barcelona: Futurgraphic.

Epstein, S., S. Flynn & G. Martohardjono 1996. Second language acquisition: Theoretical and experimental issues in contemporary research. *Behavioral and Brain Sciences*, 19: 677–714.

Estebas-Vilaplana, E., & P. Prieto. 2008. La notación prosódica del español: una revisión del Sp_ToBI. *Estudios de Fonética Experimental*, 17: 263–283.

References

Face, T. 2001. Intonational marking of contrastive focus in Madrid Spanish. PhD Dissertation, Ohio State University.

2003. Intonation in Spanish declaratives: Differences between lab speech and spontaneous speech. *Catalan Journal of Linguistics*, 2: 115–131.

Face, T., & P. Prieto 2007. Rising accents in Castilian Spanish: A revision of Sp_ToBI. *Journal of Portuguese Linguistics*, 6.1: 117–146.

Fernández-García, M. 1999. Patterns in gender agreement in the speech of second language learners. In Gutiérrez-Rexach, J., & F. Martínez-Gill (eds.), *Advances in Hispanic Linguistics*, 25–39. Somerville, MA: Cascadilla.

Fernández Ramírez, S. 1986. *Gramática Española. 4. El verbo y la oración*. Madrid Arco Libros.

Flores Galindo, A. 1984. *Aristocracia y plebe: Lima 1760–1830 (Estructura de clases y sociedad colonial)*. Lima: Mosca Azul.

Frampton, J., & S. Gutmann 2000. Agreement is feature sharing. www.math.neu.edu/ling /pdffiles/agrisfs.pdf.

Franceschina, F. 2002. Case and φ-feature agreement in advanced L2 Spanish grammars. In Foster-Cohen, S., T. Ruthenberg & M. Poschen (eds.), *EUROSLA Yearbook*, 71–86. Amsterdam: John Benjamins.

2005. *Fossilized Second Language Grammars*. Amsterdam: John Benjamins.

Fuchs, Z., M. Polinsky & G. Scontras. 2014. The differential representation of number and gender in Spanish. *Linguistic Review*, 32: 703–737.

Gadet, F., & S. Pagel. 2019. On the notion of 'natural' in ecological linguistics. In Ludwig, R., P. Mühlhäusler & S. Pagel (eds.), *Linguistic Ecology and Language Contact*, 43–74. Cambridge: Cambridge University Press.

Geeslin, K. 2013 (ed). *The Handbook of Spanish Second Language Acquisition*. Malden, MA: Wiley-Blackwell.

González-Rivera, M. 2018. Sobre el sujeto preverbal en oraciones exclamativas. Paper presented at Hispanic Linguistics Symposium, University of Texas at Austin, Austin, TX (October).

González-Rivera, M., & S. Sessarego. 2020. La inversión del sujeto en el español caribeño: el caso de las oraciones exclamativas. Paper presented at Congreso Retorno al Español del Caribe 2020, Pontificia Universidad Católica Madre y Maestra, Santo Domingo (November 4–7).

Goodall, G. 2004. On the syntax and processing of Wh-questions in Spanish. In Schmeiser, B., V. Chand, A. Kelleher & A. Rodriguez (eds.), *Proceedings of the 23rd West Coast Conference on Formal Linguistics*, 237–250. Somerville, MA: Cascadilla Press.

Granda, G. de. 1968. La tipología criolla de dos hablas del área lingüística hispánica. *Thesaurus*, 23: 193–205.

1977. *Estudios sobre un área dialectal hispanoamericana de población negra: las tierras bajas occidentales de Colombia*. Bogotá: Publicaciones del Instituto Caro y Cuervo.

1978. *Estudios lingüísticos afrohispánicos y criollos*. Madrid: Gredos.

1988a. *Lingüística e historia: Temas afro-hispánicos*. Valladolid: Universidad de Valladolid.

1988b. *Sociedad, historia y lengua en el Paraguay*. Bogotá: Instituto Caro y Cuervo.
Greenberg, J. 1963. Some universals of grammar with particular reference to the order of meaningful elements. In Greenberg, J. (ed.), *Universals of Grammar*, 73–113. Cambridge, MA: MIT Press.
Grimshaw, J., & V. Samek-Lodovici 1998. Optional subjects and subject universals. In Barbosa, P., D. Fox, P. Hagstom, M. McGinnis & D. Pesetsky (eds.), *Is the Best Good Enough? Optimality and Competition in Syntax*, 192–219. Cambridge, MA: MIT Press.
Guamán Poma de Ayala, F. 1615[2006]. *El primer nueva corónica y buen gobierno*. Buenos Aires: Siglo Ventiuno.
Guerra Rivera, A., Coopmans, P., & S. Baauw 2015. On the L2 acquisition of Spanish subject–verb inversion. *Procedia – Social and Behavioral Sciences*, 173: 37–42.
Gutiérrez-Bravo, R. 2005. *Structural Markedness and Syntactic Structure*. New York, NY: Routledge/Taylor and Francis.
  2007. Prominence scales and unmarked word order in Spanish. *Natural Language and Linguistic Theory*, 25: 235–271.
  2008. Topicalization and preverbal subjects in Spanish wh-interrogatives. In Bruhn de Garavito J., & E. Valenzuela (eds.), *Selected Proceedings of the 10th Hispanic Linguistics Symposium*. Somerville, MA: Cascadilla Proceedings Project, 225–236.
Gutiérrez-Rexach, J., & S. Sessarego 2014. Morphosyntactic variation in three Afro-Andean dialects: The evolution of gender agreement in DP. *Lingua*, 151.B: 142–161.
Guy, G. 1981. Linguistic variation in Brazilian Portuguese: Aspects of the phonology, syntax, and language history. PhD Dissertation, University of Pennsylvania.
  2004. Muitas linguas: The linguistic impact of Africans in colonial Brazil. In Curto, J., & P. Lovejoy (eds.), *Enslaving Connections: Changing Cultures of Africa and Brazil During the Era of Slavery*, 125–137. New York, NY: Humanity Books.
  2005. Grammar and usage: A variationist response. *Language*, 81: 561–563.
  2017. The African diaspora in Latin America. In Cutler, C., Z. Vrzić & P. Angermeyer (eds.), *Language Contact in Africa and the African Diaspora in the Americas*, 49–78. Amsterdam: John Benjamins.
Harley, H. 1994. Hug a tree: Deriving the morphosyntactic feature hierarchy. In Carnie, A., & H. Harley (eds.), *MIT Working Papers in Linguistics 21*, 289–320. Cambridge, MA: MIT Press.
Harley, H., & E. Ritter 2002. Person and number in pronouns: A feature-geometric analysis. *Language*, 78: 482–526.
Harris, J. 1991. The exponence of gender in Spanish. *Linguistic Inquiry*, 22.1: 27–62.
Haspelmath, M. 2006. Against markedness (and what to replace it with). *Journal of Linguistics*, 42.1: 25–70.
  2008. Parametric versus functional explanations of syntactic universals. In Biberauer T., & A. Holmberg (eds.), *The Limits of Syntactic Variation*. Amsterdam: Benjamins.
Hassaurek, F. 1867. *1831–1885: Four Years among Spanish-Americans*. New York, NY: Hurd and Houghton.

References

Hawkins, R. 1998. The inaccessibility of formal features of functional categories in second language acquisition. Paper presented at the Pacific Second Language Research Forum, Tokyo (March).

Helps, A. 1900. *The Spanish Conquest in America and Its Relation to the History of Slavery and to the Government of Colonies, 1855–1861*, 4 vols. London: John Lane.

Henry, A. 2005. Ideolectal variation and syntax theory. In Cornips, L., & K. Corrigan (eds.), *Syntax and Variation: Reconciling the Biological and the Social*, 109–122. Amsterdam: John Benjamins.

Hernández, T. 2013. *Racial Subordination in Latin America: The Role of the State, Customary Law, and the New Civil Rights Response*. Cambridge: Cambridge University Press.

Herschensohn, J. 2000. *The Second Time Around: Minimalism and L2 Acquisition*. Amsterdam: John Benjamins.

Holm, J. 1992. Popular Brazilian Portuguese: A semi-creole. In D'Andrade, E., & A. Kihm (eds.), *Actas do colóquio sobre crioulos de base lexical portuguesa*, 37–66. Lisbon: Colibri.

Holm, J. A., & P. L. Patrick (eds.) 2007. *Comparative Creole Syntax. Parallel Outlines of 18 Creole Grammars*. London: Battlebridge.

Holmberg, A. 2005. Is there a little *pro*? Evidence from Finnish. *Linguistic Inquiry*, 36: 533–564.

Hualde, J. I. 2002. Intonation in Spanish and the other Ibero-Romance languages. In Wiltshire, C., & J. Camps (eds.), *Romance Philology and Variation*, 101–115. Philadelphia, PA: John Benjamins.

Hualde, J. I., & A. Schwegler 2008. Intonation in Palenquero. *Journal of Pidgin and Creole Languages*, 23: 1–31.

Huang, Y. 1994. *The Syntax and Pragmatics of Anaphora: A Study with Special Reference to Chinese*. Cambridge: Cambridge University Press.

Ivanov, I. 2009. Second language acquisition of Bulgarian object clitics: A test case for the interface hypothesis. PhD Dissertation, University of Iowa.

2012. L2 acquisition of Bulgarian clitic-doubling: A test case for the Interface Hypothesis. *Second Language Research*, 28.3: 345–368.

Jackendoff, R. 1997. *The Architecture of the Language Faculty*. Cambridge, MA: MIT Press.

2002. *Foundations of Language: Brain, Meaning, Grammar, Evolution*. Oxford: Oxford University Press.

Jaeggli, O. 1986. Arbitrary plural pronouns. *Natural Language and Linguistic Theory*, 4: 43–76.

Jayaseelan, K. 1999. Empty pronoun in Dravidian. In Jayaseelan, K. (ed.), *Parametric Studies in Malayalam Syntax*, 14–25. New Delhi: Allied Publishers.

Johnson, J., & E. N. Newport. 1989. Critical period effects in second language learning: The influence of maturational state on acquisition of English as a second language. *Cognitive Psychology*, 21: 60–99.

Kany, C. 1945. *American–Spanish Syntax*. Chicago, IL: University of Chicago Press.

Kato, M., & E. Negrão (eds.) 2000. *Brazilian Portuguese and the Null Subject Parameter*. Frankfurt/Madrid: Vervuert/Iberoamericana.
Kato, M., & F. Ordóñez (eds.) 2016. *The Morphosyntax of Portuguese and Spanish in Latin America*. Oxford: Oxford University Press.
Kayne, R. 1996. Microparametric syntax: Some introductory remarks. In Black, J., & V. Motapanyane (eds.), *Microparametric Syntax and Dialect Variation*, ix–xxviii. Amsterdam: John Benjamins.
   2000. *Parameters and Universals*. Oxford: Oxford University Press.
Kayne, R., & J.-Y. Pollock. 2001. New thoughts on stylistic inversion. In Hulk, A. & J.-Y. Pollock (eds.), *Subject Inversion in Romance and the Theory of Universal Grammar*, 107–162 Oxford: Oxford University Press.
Kempen, G., & E. Hoenkamp. 1987. An incremental procedural grammar for sentence formulation. *Cognitive Science*, 11: 201–258.
Kerstens, J. 1993. *The Syntax of Number, Person and Gender*. Berlin: Mouton de Gruyter.
King, R. 2005. Morphosyntactic variation and theory: Subject–verb agreement in Acadian French. In Cornips, L., & K. Corrigan (eds.), *Syntax and Variation: Reconciling the Biological and the Social*, 199–229. Amsterdam: John Benjamins.
Kiparsky, P. 1973. "Elsewhere" in phonology. In Stephen A., & P. Kiparsky (eds.), *A Festschrift for Morris Halle*, 93–106. New York, NY: Holt, Rinehait and Winston.
Klee, C. A., & Lynch, A. 2009. *El español en contacto con otras lenguas*. Washington, DC: Georgetown University Press.
Klein, H., & B. Vinson. 2007. *African Slavery in Latin America and the Caribbean*. Oxford: Oxford University Press.
Knaff, C., R. Rao & S. Sessarego 2018. Future directions in the field: A look at Afro-Hispanic prosody. *Lingua*, 202: 76–86.
Kroch, A. 1978. Toward a theory of social dialect variation. *Language in Society*, 7.1: 17–36.
   1989. Function and grammar in the history of English: Periphrastic "do." In Fasold, R., & D. Schiffrin (eds.), *Language Change and Variation*, 133–172. Amsterdam: Benjamins.
   1994. Morphosyntactic variation. In Beals, K. (ed.), *Proceedings of the Thirtieth Annual Meeting of the Chicago Linguistics Society, 2*, 180–201. Chicago, IL: Chicago Linguistics Society.
   2000. Syntactic change. In Baltin, M., & C. Collins (eds.), *The Handbook of Contemporary Syntactic Theory*, 629–739. Oxford: Blackwell Publishing.
Kouwenberg, S., & P. Patrick (eds.) 2003. *Reconsidering the Role of SLA in Pidginization and Creolization*. Studies in Second Language Acquisition. Cambridge: Cambridge University Press.
Labov, W. 1966. *The Social Stratification of English in New York City*. Washington, DC: Center for Applied Linguistics.
   1969. Contraction, deletion and inherent variability of the English copula. *Language*, 45: 715–762.

1972a. *Sociolinguistic Patterns*. Philadelphia, PA: University of Pennsylvania Press.

1972b. *Language in the Inner City*. Philadelphia, PA: University of Pennsylvania Press.

1974. Language change as a form of communication. In Silverstein, M. (ed.), *Human Communication: Theoretical Explorations*, 221–256. Hillsdale, NJ: Lawrence Erlbaum Associates

1984. Field methods of the project on linguistic change and variation. In Baugh, J., & J. Sherzer (eds.), *Language in Use*, 84–112. Englewood Cliffs, NJ: Prentice Hall.

Ladd, D. Robert 2008. *Intonational Phonology*. Cambridge: Cambridge University Press.

Lantolf, J. 1980. Constraints on interrogative word order in Puerto Rican Spanish. *Bilingual Review*, 7–8: 113–122.

Lapesa, R. 1981. *Historia de la lengua española*. Madrid: Gredos.

Lardiere, D. 2005. On morphological competence. In Dekydtspotter, L., R. A. Sprouse & A. Liljestrand (eds.), *Proceedings of the 7th Generative Approaches to Second Language Acquisition Conference*, 178–192. Somerville, MA: Cascadilla Proceedings Project.

2007. *Ultimate Attainment in Second Language Acquisition: A Case Study*. Mahwah, NJ: Erlbaum.

2000. Mapping features to forms in second language acquisition. In Archibald, J. (ed.), *Second Language Acquisition and Linguistic Theory*, 102–129. Oxford: Blackwell.

Laurence, K. 1974. Is Caribbean Spanish a case of decreolization? *Orbis*, 23: 484–499.

Lavandera, B. 1988. The study of language in its socio-cultural context. In Newmeyer, F. (ed.), *Linguistics: The Cambridge Survey IV. Language: The Socio-cultural Context*, 1–13. Cambridge: Cambridge University Press.

Leal, T., J. Rothman & R. Slabakova. 2014. A rare structure at the syntax–discourse interface: Heritage and Spanish-dominant native speakers weigh in. *Language Acquisition*, 21.4: 411–429.

Lefebvre, C. 1998. *Creole Genesis and the Acquisition of Grammar*. Cambridge: Cambridge University Press.

Lefebvre, C., L. White & C. Jourdan (eds.) 2006. *L2 Acquisition and Creole Genesis*. Amsterdam: John Benjamins.

Levelt, W. J. M. 1989. *Speaking: From Intention to Articulation*. Cambridge, MA: MIT Press.

Lipski, J. 1977. Preposed subjects in questions: Some considerations. *Hispania*, 60: 61–67.

1993. On the non-creole basis for Afro-Caribbean Spanish. www.personal.psu.edu/jml34/noncreol.pdf.

1994. *Latin American Spanish*. New York, NY: Longman.

2005. *A History of Afro-Hispanic Language. Five Centuries, Five Continents*. Cambridge: Cambridge University Press.

2006a. Morphosyntactic implications in Afro-Hispanic language: New data on creole pathways. www.personal.psu.edu/jml34/afmorph.pdf.

2006b. Afro-Bolivian Spanish and Helvécia Portuguese: Semi-creole parallels. *PAPIA: Revista Brasileira de Estudos Crioulos e Similares*, 16: 96–116.

2007. Castile and the hydra: The diversification of Spanish in Latin America. www.personal.psu.edu/jml34/hydra.pdf.

2008. *Afro-Bolivian Spanish*. Madrid/Frankfurt: Iberoamericana/Vervuert.

2009. Afro-Choteño speech: Towards the (re)creation of "Black Spanish". *Negritud*, 2: 99–120.

Lockhart, J. 1968. *Spanish Peru, 1532–1560: A Social History*. Madison, WI: University of Wisconsin Press.

Luna Desola, D. 1978. Algunos aspectos ideológicos de la independencia latinoamericana. *Anuario de Estudios Centroamericanos*, 4.1: 79–92.

Macera, Pablo. 1966. *Instrucciones para el Manejo de las Haciendas Jesuitas del Perú, ss. XVII/XVIII*. Lima: Universidad Nacional Mayor de San Marcos.

MacLean y Estenós, R. 1947. *Negros en el nuevo mundo*. Lima: PTCM.

Martínez-Sanz, C. 2011. Null and overt subjects in a variable system: The case of Dominican Spanish. PhD Dissertation, University of Ottawa.

Martohardjono, G., & J. W. Gair. 1993. Apparent UG inaccessibility in SLA: Misapplied principles or principled misapplications? In F. R. Eckman (ed.), *Conference: Linguistics, Second Language Acquisition and Speech Pathology*, 79–103. Amsterdam: John Benjamins.

Mayén, N. 2007. Afro-Hispanic linguistic remnants in Mexico: The case of the Costa Chica region of Oaxaca. PhD Dissertation, Purdue University.

McCarthy, C. 2008. Morphological variability in the comprehension of agreement: An argument for representation over computation. *Second Language Research*, 24.4: 459–486.

McWhorter, J. 1998. Identifying the creole prototype: Vindicating a typological class. *Language*, 74: 788–818.

2000. *The Missing Spanish Creoles. Recovering the Birth of Plantation Contact Languages*. Berkeley, CA: University of California Press.

2001. The world's simplest grammars are creole grammars. *Language Typology*, 5: 125–166.

2014. A response to Mufwene. *Journal of Pidgin and Creole Languages*, 29.1: 172–176

2018a. *The Creole Debate*. Cambridge: Cambridge University Press.

2018b. Why neither demographics nor feature pools can explain the missing Spanish plantation creoles. *Lingua*, 201: 4–12.

Megenney, W. 1993. Elementos criollo-portugueses en el español dominicano. *Montalbán*, 15: 3–56.

1999. *Aspectos del lenguaje afronegroide en Venezuela*. Madrid/Frankfurt: Iberoamericana/Vervuert.

Mellafe, R. 1984. *La introducción de la esclavitud negra en Chile: Tráfico y rutas*. Santiago: Editorial Universitaria.

Michnowicz, J., & H. Barnes. 2013. A sociolinguistic analysis of pre-nuclear peak alignment in Yucatan Spanish. In Howe, C., S. Blackwell & M. Lubbers Quesada (eds.), *Selected Proceedings of the 15th Hispanic Linguistics Symposium*, 221–235. Somerville, MA: Cascadilla Proceedings Project.

Migge, B. 2003. *Creole Formation as Language Contact: The Case of the Suriname Creoles*. Amsterdam: John Benjamins.

Mintz, S. 1971. The socio-historical background to pidginization and creolization. In Hymes, D. (ed.), *Pidginization and Creolization of Languages*, 481–498. Cambridge: Cambridge University Press.

Modesto, M. 2000. Null subject without 'rich' agreement. In Kato, M., & E. Negrão (eds.), *Brazilian Portuguese and the Null Subject Parameter*, 147–174. Madrid/Frankfurt: Iberoamericana/Vervuert.

Montalbetti, M. 1984. After binding: On the interpretation of pronouns. PhD Dissertation, Massachusetts Institute of Technology.

Montrul, S. 2004. *The Acquisition of Spanish*. Amsterdam: John Benjamins.

2011. Multiple interfaces and incomplete acquisition. In Rothman, J., & R. Roumyana (eds.), *Acquisition at the Linguistic Interfaces [Lingua* Special Issue, 121.4], 567–688. New York, NY: Elsevier.

Montrul, S., R. Prince & A. Thomé-Williams 2009. Subject expression in the non-native acquisition of Brazilian Portuguese. In Pires, A., & J. Rothman (eds.), *Minimalist Inquiries into Child and Adult Language Acquisition: Case Studies across Portuguese*, 301–325. Berlin: Mouton DeGruyter.

Mufwene, S. 1997. Jargons, pidgins creoles and koines: What are they? In Spears A., & Winford D. (eds.), *The Structure and Status of Pidgins and Creoles*, 35–70. Amsterdam: John Benjamins.

2001. *The Ecology of Language Evolution*. Cambridge: Cambridge University Press.

2014. The case was never closed: McWhorter misinterprets the ecological approach to the emergence of creoles. *Journal of Pidgin and Creole Languages*, 29.1: 157–171.

Muysken, P. 1997. Media Lengua. In Thomason, S. (ed.), *Contact Languages: A Wider Perspective*, 365–426. Amsterdam: John Benjamins.

Mühlhäusler, P. 1986. *Pidgin and Creole Linguistics*. Oxford: Basil Blackwell.

Nebrija, A. 1981[1492]. *Gramática de la lengua castellana* [edited by A. Quilis]. Madrid: Editora Nacional.

Newmeyer, F. 2003. Grammar is grammar and usage is usage. *Language*, 79.4: 682–707.

2004. Against a parameter-setting approach to language variation. *Linguistic Variation Yearbook*, 4: 181–234.

2017. Where, if anywhere, are parameters? A critical historical overview of parametric theory. In Bowern, C., L. Horn & R. Zanuttini (eds.), *On Looking into Words (and Beyond)*, 547–569. Berlin: Language Science Press.

Nowak, M. 2002. Computational and evolutionary aspects of language. *Nature*, 417: 611–617.

Nowak, M., N. Komarova & P. Niyogi 2001. Evolution of Universal Grammar. *Science*, 291: 114–118.

Núñez Cedeño, R. 1983. Pérdida de trasposición de sujeto en interrogativas pronominales del español del Caribe. *Thesaurus*, 38: 35–57.

Olarrea, A. 1997. Pre- and postverbal subject positions in Spanish: A minimalist account. PhD Dissertation, University of Washington.
O'Rourke, E. 2004. Peak placement in two regional varieties of Peruvian Spanish intonation. In Auger, J., J. C. Clements & B. Vance (eds.), *Contemporary Approaches to Romance Linguistics*, 321–341. Amsterdam: John Benjamins.
2005. Intonation and language contact: A case study of two varieties of Peruvian Spanish. PhD Dissertation, University of Illinois at Urbana-Champaign.
Ordóñez, F., & A. Olarrea. 2006. Microvariation in Caribbean/Non-Caribbean Spanish interrogatives. *Probus*, 18: 59–96.
Ordóñez, F., & E. Treviño. 1999. Left dislocated subjects and the pro-drop parameter: A case study of Spanish. *Lingua*, 107: 38–68.
Ortega-Llebaria, M., & P. Prieto 2010. Acoustic correlates of stress in Central Catalan and Castilian Spanish. *Language and Speech*, 54.1: 73–97.
Otheguy, R. 1973. The Spanish Caribbean: A creole perspective. In Bailey, C.-J., & R. Shuy (eds.), *New Ways of Analyzing Variation in English*, 323–339. Washington, DC: Georgetown University Press.
Parrott, J. 2007. Distributed morphological mechanisms of Labovian variation in morphosyntax. PhD Dissertation, Georgetown University.
2009. Danish vestigial case and the acquisition of vocabulary in distributed morphology. *Biolinguistics*, 3: 2–3, 270–304.
Penny, R. 2002. *A History of the Spanish Language*. Cambridge: Cambridge University Press.
Peñaherrera de Costales, P., & A. Costales Samaniego 1959. *Coangue o historia cultural y social de los negros del Chota y Salinas*. Quito: Llacta.
Perez, D. 2015. Traces of Portuguese in Afro-Yungueño Spanish? *Journal of Pidgin and Creole Languages*, 30.2: 307–343.
Perez, D., S. Sessarego & E. Sippola 2017. Afro-Hispanic varieties in comparison: New light from phylogeny. In Bakker, P., C. Levisen & E. Sippola (eds.), *Phylogenetic Approaches to Creole Languages*, 269–292. Amsterdam/Philadelphia: John Benjamins.
Perl, M. 1998. Introduction. In Perl, M., & A. Schwegler (eds.), *América negra: Panorámica actual de los estudios lingüísticos sobre variedades hispanas, portuguesas y criollas*, 1–24. Madrid/Frankfurt: Iberoamericana-Vervuert.
Perl, M., & A. Schwegler (eds.), 1998. *América negra: Panorámica actual de los estudios lingüísticos sobre variedades hispanas, portuguesas y criollas*. Madrid/Frankfurt: Iberoamericana-Vervuert.
Pesetsky, D., & E. Torrego 2001. T to C movement: Causes and consequences. In Kenstowicz, M. (ed.), *Ken Hale: A Life in Language*, 355–426, Cambridge, MA: MIT Press.
2007. The syntax of valuation and the interpretability of features. In Karimi, S., V. Samiian & W. K. Wilkins (eds.), *Phrasal and Clausal Architecture: Syntactic Derivation and Interpretation*, 262–294. Amsterdam: John Benjamins.
Philippaki-Warburton, I. 1987. The theory of empty categories and the pro-drop parameter in Modern Greek. *Journal of Linguistics*, 23: 289–318.
Picallo, C. 1991. Nominals and nominalizations in Catalan. *Probus*, 3: 279–316.

2008. Gender and number in Romance. *Lingue e Linguaggio*, 1: 47–66.
Pienemann, M. 1998. *Language Processing and Second Language Development: Processability Theory*. Amsterdam/Philadelphia, PA: John Benjamins.
Pienemann, M. (ed.) 2000. *Cross-Linguistic Aspects of Processability Theory*. Amsterdam/Philadelphia, PA: John Benjamins.
Pierrehumbert, J. 1980. The phonology and phonetics of English intonation. PhD Dissertation, Massachusetts Institute of Technology.
Pinker, S. 1994. *The Language Instinct*. New York, NY: William Morrow.
Pinker, S., & R. Jackendoff 2005. The faculty of language: What's special about it? *Cognition*, 95: 201–236.
Plag, I. 2008a. Creoles as interlanguages: Inflectional morphology. *Journal of Pidgin and Creole Languages*, 23.1: 109–130.
  2008b. Creoles as interlanguages: Syntactic structures. *Journal of Pidgin and Creole Languages*, 23.2: 307–328.
  2009a. Creoles as interlanguages: Phonology. *Journal of Pidgin and Creole Languages*, 24.1: 119–138.
  2009b. Creoles as interlanguages: Word-formation. *Journal of Pidgin and Creole Languages*, 24.2: 339–362.
Poletto, C. 2000. *The Higher Functional Field: Evidence from Northern Italian Dialects*. Oxford: Oxford University Press.
Pollard, C., & I. Sag 1994. *Head-Driven Phrase Structure Grammar*. Chicago, IL: University of Chicago Press.
Pomino, N. 2012. Partial or complete lack of plural agreement. In Gaglia, S., & M-O. Hinzelin (eds.), *Inflection and Word Formation in Romance Languages*, 201–229. Amsterdam: John Benjamins.
  2017. Gender and number. In Dufter, A., & E. Stark (eds.), *Manual of Romance Morphosyntax and Syntax*, 691–725. Berlin: Walter de Gruyter.
Poplack, S. 1980.The notion of the plural in Puerto Rican Spanish: Competing contrasts on (s) deletion. In Labov, W. (ed.), *Locating Language in Time and Space*, 55–67. New York, NY: Academic Press.
Portugal Ortiz, M. 1977. *La esclavitud negra en las épocas colonial y nacional de Bolivia*. Instituto Boliviano de Cultura, La Paz.
Preminger, O. 2014. *Agreement and Its Failures*. Cambridge, MA: MIT Press.
Prieto, P., & P. Roseano (eds.), 2010. *Transcription of Intonation of the Spanish Language*. Munich: LINCOM.
Quirk, R. 1972. On the extent and origin of questions in the form ¿Qué tú tienes? *Hispania*, 55: 303–304.
R Core Team 2016. *R: A Language and Environment for Statistical Computing*. Vienna: R Foundation for Statistical Computing. www.R-project.org/.
Rao, R. 2009. Deaccenting in spontaneous speech on Barcelona Spanish. *Studies in Hispanic and Lusophone Linguistics*, 2.1: 31–75.
  2010. Final lengthening and pause duration in three dialects of Spanish. In Ortega-Llebaria, M. (ed.), *Selected Proceedings of the 4th Conference on Laboratory Approaches to Spanish Phonology*, 69–82. Somerville MA: Cascadilla Proceedings Project.

Rao, R., & S. Sessarego 2016. On the intonation of Afro-Bolivian Spanish declaratives: Implications for a theory of Afro-Hispanic creole genesis. *Lingua*, 174: 45–64.

2018. The intonation of Chota Valley Spanish: Contact-induced phenomena at the discourse–phonology interface. *Studies in Hispanic and Lusophone Linguistics*, 11.1: 163–192.

Reinhart, T. 2006. *Interface Strategies: Reference-Set Computation*. Cambridge, MA: MIT Press.

Restall, M. 2000. Black conquistadors: Armed Africans in early Spanish America. *The Americas*, 57.2: 171–205.

Režač, M. 2004. Elements of cyclic syntax: Agree and Merge. PhD Dissertation, University of Toronto.

Ritter, E. 1991. Two functional categories in noun phrases: Evidence from Modern Hebrew. In Rothstein, S. (ed.), *Perspectives on Phrase Structure: Heads and Licensing*, 37–62. San Diego, CA: Academic Press.

Rizzi, L. 1982. *Issues in Italian Syntax*. Dordrecht: Foris

1996. Residual verb second and the Wh-criterion. In Belletti, A., & L. Rizzi (eds.), *Parameters and Functional Heads*, 63–90. Oxford: Oxford University Press.

Roberts, I., & A. Holmberg. 2010. Introduction: parameters in minimalist theory. In Biberauer, T., A. Holmberg, I. Roberts & M. Sheehan (eds.), *Null Subjects: The Structure of Parametric Variation*, 1–57. Cambridge: Cambridge University Press.

Rodríguez Tocarruncho, L. 2010. *La marca de plural y otros aspectos morfológicos y sintácticos del español del Pacífico de Colombia*. Madrid: Consejo Superior de Investigaciones Científicas.

Romero, R., & S. Sessarego (2018). Hard come, easy go: Linguistic interfaces in Istambul Judeo-Spanish and Afro-Ecuadorian Spanish. In King, J., & S. Sessarego (eds.), *Language Variation and Contact-Induced Change: The Spanish Language across Space and Time*, 83–110. Amsterdam/Philadelphia: John Benjamins.

Rosenblat, A. 1954. *La población indígena y el mestizaje en America*. Buenos Aires: Editorial NOVA.

Rosemeyer, M. 2018. The pragmatics of Spanish postposed wh-interrogatives. *Folia Linguistica*, 52.2: 283–317.

Rostworowski Tovar de Díez Canseco, M. 1999. *Historia de los Incas*. Lima: Editorial Bruño.

Rothman, J. 2008. How pragmatically odd! Interface delays and pronominal subject distribution in L2 Spanish. *Studies in Hispanic and Lusophone Linguistics*, 1: 317–339.

2009 Pragmatic deficits with syntactic consequences: L2 pronominal subjects and the syntax–pragmatics interface. *Journal of Pragmatics*, 41: 951–973.

Rothman, J., & R. Slabakova 2011 (eds.), *Acquisition at the Linguistic Interfaces* [*Lingua* Special Issue, 121.4]. New York, NY: Elsevier.

Sagarra, N., & J. Herschensohn 2011. Proficiency and animacy effects on L2 gender agreement processes during comprehension. *Language Learning*, 61.1: 80–116.

Saito, M. 2004. Ellipsis and pronominal reference in Japanese clefts. *Studies in Modern Grammar*, 36: 1–44.

Scherre, M. M. P. 1988. Reanálise da concordância nominal em português. PhD Dissertation, Federal University of Rio de Janeiro.

1991. A concordância de número nos predicativos e nos particípios passivos. *Organon*, 18: 52–70.

Schumann, J. 1978. *The Pidginization Process: A Model for Second Language Acquisition*. Rowley, MA: Newbury House.

Schwartz, B. 1996. Now for some facts, with a focus on development and an explicit role for L1. *Behavioral and Brain Sciences*, 19: 739–740.

1998. The second language instinct. *Lingua*, 106, 133–160.

Schwartz, B., & R. Sprouse. 1996. L2 cognitive states and the full transfer/full access model. *Second Language Research*, 12, 40–72.

Schwegler, A. 1991a. La doble negación dominicana y la génesis del español caribeño. *Lingüística*, 3: 31–88.

1991b. El español del Chocó. *América Negra*, 2: 85–119.

1993. Rasgos (afro-)portugueses en el criollo del Palenque de San Basilio (Colombia). In Alayon, C. D. D. (ed.), *Homenaje a José Pérez Vidal*, 667–696. La Laguna, Tenerife: Litografía A. Romero S. A.

1996. *Chi ma nkongo: Lengua y rito ancestrales en El Palenque de San Basilio (Colombia)*. 2 vols. Frankfurt/Madrid: Vervuert Verlag.

1999. Monogenesis revisited: The Spanish perspective. In Rickford J., & S. Romaine (eds.), *Creole Genesis, Attitudes and Discourse*, 235–262. Amsterdam/Philadelphia, PA: John Benjamins.

2010. State of the Discipline. Pidgin and creole studies: Their interface with Hispanic and Lusophone linguistics. *Studies in Hispanic and Lusophone Linguistics*, 3.2: 431–481.

2014. Portuguese remnants in the Afro-Hispanic diaspora. In Amaral, P., & A. M. Carvalho (eds.), *Portuguese-Spanish Interfaces: Diachrony, Synchrony, and Contact*, 403–441. Amsterdam: John Benjamins.

Seiler, G. 2004. On three types of dialect variation, and their implications for linguistic theory: Evidence from verb clusters in Swiss German dialects. In Kortmann, B. (ed.), *Dialectology Meets Typology. Dialect Grammar from a Cross-Linguistic Perspective*, 367–399. Berlin: Walter de Gruyter.

Serratrice, L., A. Sorace, F. Filiaci & M. Baldo 2009. Bilingual children's sensitivity to specificity and genericity: Evidence from metalinguistic awareness. *Bilingualism: Language and Cognition*, 12.2: 239–257.

Serratrice, L., A. Sorace & S. Paoli. 2004. Crosslinguistic influence at the syntax–pragmatics interface: Subjects and objects in English–Italian bilingual and monolingual acquisition. *Bilingualism: Language and Cognition*, 7.3: 183–205.

Sessarego, S. 2011a. *Introducción al idioma afroboliviano: Una conversación con el awicho Manuel Barra*. Cochabamba/La Paz: Plural Editores.

2011b. On the status of Afro-Bolivian Spanish features: Decreolization or vernacular universals? In Michnowicz, J. (ed.), *Proceedings of the 5th International Workshop on Spanish Sociolinguistics*, 125–141. Somerville, MA: Cascadilla.

2012a. Non-creole features in the verb system of Afro-Hispanic languages: New insights from SLA studies. *International Journal of Linguistics*, 4.1: 146–157.
2012b. Vowel weakening in Yungueño Spanish: Linguistic and social considerations. *PAPIA: Revista Brasileira de Estudos Crioulos e Similares*. 22.2: 279–294.
2013a. *Chota Valley Spanish*. Madrid: Iberoamericana
2013b. Afro-Hispanic contact varieties as conventionalized advanced second languages. *IBERIA*, 5, 1: 96-122.
2013c. On the non-creole bases for Afro-Bolivian Spanish. *Journal of Pidgin and Creole Languages*, 28.2: 363–407.
2013d. Enhancing dialogue between quantitative sociolinguistics and minimalist syntax. *Studies in Hispanic and Lusophone Linguistics*, 5.2: 79–97.
2014a. *The Afro-Bolivian Spanish Determiner Phrase: A Microparametric Account*. Columbus, OH: Ohio State Press.
2014b. On Chota Valley Spanish origin: Linguistic and sociohistorical evidence. *Journal of Pidgin and Creole Languages*, 29.1: 86–133.
2014c. Afro-Peruvian Spanish in the context of Spanish creole genesis. *Spanish in Context*, 11.3: 381–401.
2015. *Afro-Peruvian Spanish: Spanish Slavery and the Legacy of Spanish Creoles*. Amsterdam: John Benjamins.
2016a. On the Non-(de)creolization of Chocó Spanish: A linguistic and sociohistorical account. *Lingua*, 184: 122–133.
2017a. The legal hypothesis of Creole genesis: Presence/absence of legal personality, a new element to the Spanish creole debate. *Journal of Pidgin and Creole Languages*, 32.1: 1–47.
2017b. Extracts from 'Solving the Spanish Creole puzzle: The legal hypothesis of creole genesis', in *Afro-Peruvian Spanish: Spanish Slavery and the Legacy of Spanish Creoles* (Amsterdam/Philadelphia: John Benjamins, 2015), pp. 120–121, 139–145, 156–157. In Farquharson, J., & B. Migge (eds.), *Pidgins and Creoles. Vol. 1*, 172–181. London: Routledge.
2017c. A feature-geometry account for subject–verb agreement phenomena in Yungueño Spanish. In Colomina-Almiñana, J. (ed.), *Contemporary Studies on Theoretical and Applied Linguistics of Spanish Variation*, 265–282. Columbus, OH: Ohio State University Press.
2017d. Chocó Spanish and the missing Spanish creole debate: Sociohistorical and linguistic considerations to solve the puzzle. *Language Ecology*, 1.2: 213–241.
2017e. Chocó Spanish double negation and the genesis of the Afro-Hispanic dialects of the Americas. *Diachronica*, 34.2: 219–252.
2018a. *La schiavitù nera nell'America spagnola*. Genova: Marietti Editore.
2018b. Enhancing dialogue in the field: Some remarks on the status of the Spanish creole debate. *Journal of Pidgin and Creole Languages*, 33.1: 197–203.
2018c. On the importance of legal history to Afro-Hispanic linguistics and creole studies. In Sessarego, S. (guest ed.), *Current Trends in Afro-Hispanic Linguistics* [*Lingua* Special Issue, 202], 13–23. Amsterdam: Elsevier.

2019a. *Language Contact and the Making of an Afro-Hispanic Vernacular: Variation and Change in the Colombian Chocó.* Cambridge: Cambridge University Press.

2019b. Universal processes in contact-induced syntactic change: Evidence from the Afro-Hispanic varieties. In Darquennes, J., J. Salmons & W. Vandenbussche (eds.), *Language Contact. An International Handbook,* 24–38. Berlin: Mouton de Gruyter.

2019c. Chocó Spanish: An Afro-Hispanic language on the Spanish frontier. In Ortiz-López, L. (ed.), *Hispanic Contact Linguistics: Theoretical, Methodological and Empirical Perspectives,* 219–252. Amsterdam/Philadelphia, PA: John Benjamins.

2020. Not all grammatical features are robustly transmitted during the emergence of creoles. *Humanities & Social Sciences Communications,* 7.130: 1–8.

Sessarego, S., B. Butera & R. Rao 2019. Aspectos de la entonación afroperuana. *Cuadernos de la Asociación de Lingüística y Filología de América Latina,* 11.1: 199–215.

Sessarego, S., & L. Ferreira 2016. Spanish and Portuguese parallels: Impoverished number agreement as a vernacular feature of two rural dialects. In Sessarego, S., & F. Tejedo-Herrero (eds.), *Spanish Language and Sociolinguistic Analysis,* 283–304. Amsterdam: John Benjamins.

Sessarego, S., & J. Gutiérrez-Rexach 2011. A minimalist approach to gender agreement in the Afro-Bolivian DP: Variation and the specification of uninterpretable features. In DeVogelaer, G., & M. Janse (eds.), *The Diachronic of Gender Marking* [Special issue of *Folia Linguistica,* 45.2], 465–488. Berlin: Mouton de Gruyter.

2012. Variation universals and contact induced change: Language evolution across generations and domains. In González-Rivera, M., & S. Sessarego (eds.), *Current Formal Aspects of Spanish Syntax and Semantics,* 251–270. Newcastle upon Tyne: Cambridge Scholars.

2017. Revisiting the Null Subject Parameter: New insights from Afro-Peruvian Spanish. *Isogloss,* 3.1: 43–68.

Sessarego, S., & R. Rao 2016. On the simplification of a prosodic inventory: The Afro-Bolivian Spanish case. In Cuza, A., L. Czerwionka & D. Olson (eds.), *Inquiries in Hispanic Linguistics,* 171–190. Amsterdam: John Benjamins.

Sessarego, S., & A. Rodríguez-Riccelli 2018. Formal issues in Afro-Hispanic morphosyntax: The Afro-Bolivian Spanish case. In Sessarego, S. (guest ed.), *Current Trends in Afro-Hispanic Linguistics* [*Lingua* Special Issue, 202], 58–75. Amsterdam: Elsevier.

Seuren, P., & H. Wekker 1986. Semantic transparency as a factor in Creole genesis. In Muysken, P., & N. Smith (eds.), *Substrata versus Universals in Creole Genesis,* 57–70. Amsterdam: John Benjamins.

Siegel, J. 2008. Pidgin/Creoles and second language acquisition. In Kouwenberg, S., & J. V. Singler (eds.), *The Handbook of Pidgin and Creole Studies,* 189–218. Oxford: Blackwell.

Silva, G. 2001. *Word Order in Brazilian Portuguese.* Berlin: De Gruyter.

References 165

Simioni, L. 2007. A concordância de número no DP: Propostas minimalistas. *Estudos Lingüísticos*, 36.1: 117–125.

Slabakova, R. 2008. *Meaning in the Second Language*. Berlin: Mouton de Gruyter.

2009. What is easy and what is hard to acquire in a second language? In Bowles, M., T. Ionin, S. Montrul & A. Tremblay (eds.), *Proceedings of the 10th Generative Approaches to Second Language Acquisition Conference*, 280–294. Somerville, MA: Cascadilla Press.

2013. What is easy and what is hard to acquire in a second language: A generative perspective. In García Mayo M., M. J. Gutiérrez Mangado & M. Martínez-Adrián (eds.), *Contemporary Approaches to Second Language Acquisition*, 5–28. Amsterdam/Philadelphia, PA: John Benjamins.

2016. *Second Language Acquisition*. Oxford: Oxford University Press.

2019. "L" stands for language. *The Modern Language Journal*, 103: 152–160.

Slabakova, R., & I. Ivanov 2011. A more careful look at the syntax–discourse interface. *Lingua*, 121: 637–651.

Sorace, A. 2000. Syntactic optionality in non-native grammars. *Second Language Research*, 16: 93–102.

2003. Near-nativeness. In Doughty, C., & M. Long (eds.), *The Handbook of Second Language Acquisition*, 130–153. Oxford: Blackwell.

2004. Native language attrition and developmental instability at the syntax–discourse interface. *Bilingualism: Language and Cognition*, 7: 143–145.

2005. Selective optionality in language development. In Cornips, L., & K. Corrigan (eds.), *Syntax and Variation: Reconciling the Biological and the Social*, 55–80. Amsterdam: John Benjamins.

2011. Pinning down the concept of "interface" in bilingualism. *Linguistic Approaches to Bilingualism*, 1.1: 1–33.

Sorace, A., & F. Filiaci 2006. Anaphora resolution in near-native speakers of Italian. *Second Language Research*, 22.3: 339–368.

Sorace, A., & F. Keller 2005. Gradience in linguistic data. *Lingua*, 115: 1497–1524.

Sorace, A., & L. Serratrice 2009. Internal and external interfaces in bilingual language development. *International Journal of Bilingualism*, 13.2: 195–210.

Sorace, A., L. Serratrice, F. Filiaci & M. Baldo 2009. Discourse conditions on subject pronoun realization: Testing the linguistic intuitions of bilingual children. *Lingua*, 119: 460–477.

Stark, E., & N. Pomino 2009. Adnominal adjectives in Romance. Where morphology seemingly meets semantics. In Espinal, M. T., M. Leonetti & L. McNally (eds.), *Proceedings of the IV Nereus International Workshop: Definiteness and DP Structure in Romance Languages*, 113–135. Konstanz: Fachbereich Sprachwissenschaft der Universität Konstanz.

Suñer, M. 1983. proarb. *Linguistic Inquiry*, 14: 188–191.

1994. V-movement and the licensing of argumental wh-phrases in Spanish. *Natural Language and Linguistic Theory*, 12: 335–372.

Svenonius, P. 2002. Icelandic case and the structure of events. *Journal of Comparative Germanic Linguistics*, 5: 197–225.

166 References

Tagliamonte, S. 2006. *Analyzing Sociolinguistic Variation*. Cambridge: Cambridge University Press.
    2012. *Variationist Sociolinguistics: Change, Observation, Interpretation*. Hoboken, NJ: John Wiley & Sons.
    2016. Quantitative analysis in language variation and change. In Sessarego, S., & F. Tejedo-Herrero (eds.), *Spanish Language and Sociolinguistic Analysis*, 1–32. Amsterdam: John Benjamins.
Tardieu, J.-P. 2006. *El negro en la Real Audiencia de Quito: Siglos XVI–XVIII*. Quito: Abya-Yala.
Távara, S. 1855. *Abolición de la esclavitud*. Lima: Imprenta del Comercio.
Thompson, R. 1961. A note on some possible affinities between the creole dialects of the Old World and those of the New. In Le Page, R. B. (ed.), *Creole Language Studies 2*, 107–113. London: Macmillan.
Tomioka, S., 2003. The semantics of Japanese null pronouns and its cross-linguistic implications. In Schwabe, K., & S. Winkler (eds.), *The Interfaces: Deriving and Interpreting Omitted Structures*, 321–340. Amsterdam, John Benjamins.
Toribio, A. J. 2000. Setting parametric limits on dialectal variation in Spanish. *Lingua: International Review of General Linguistics*, 110.5: 315–341.
    1993a. Lexical subjects in finite and non-finite clauses. *Cornell Working Papers in Linguistics*, 11: 149–178.
    1993b. Parametric variation in the licensing of nominals. PhD Dissertation, Cornell University.
Torrego, E. 1984. On inversion in Spanish and some of its effects. *Linguistic Inquiry*, 15.1: 102–129.
Torres Saldamando, E. 1900[1967]. *Apuntes Históricos sobre las encomiendas en el Perú*. Lima: UNMSM.
Tremblay, A. 2005. On the use of grammaticality judgments in linguistic theory: theoretical and methodological perspectives. *Second Language Studies*, 24: 129–167.
Tsimpli, I., & A. Sorace. 2006. Differentiating interfaces: L2 performance in syntax–semantics and syntax–discourse phenomena. *Proceedings of the 30th Annual Boston University Conference on Language Development*, 653–664. Somerville, MA: Cascadilla.
Tsimpli, I., A. Sorace, C. Heycock & F. Filiaci 2004. First language attrition and syntactic subjects: A study of Greek and Italian near-native speakers of English. *International Journal of Bilingualism*, 8.3: 257–277.
Valenzuela, E., 2006. L2 end state grammars and incomplete acquisition of the Spanish CLLD constructions. In Slabakova, R., S. Montrul & P. Prévost (eds.), *Inquiries in Linguistic Development: In Honor of Lydia White*, 283–304. Amsterdam: John Benjamins.
Valkhoff, M. 1966. *Studies in Portuguese and Creole*. Johannesburg: Witwatersrand University Press.
Van Coetsem, F. 1988. *Loan Phonology and the Two Transfer Types in Language Contact*. Berlin: De Gruyter Mouton.

References 167

Villa-García, J. 2018. Properties of the extended verb phrase: Agreement, the structure of INFL, and subjects. In Geeslin, K. (ed.), *The Cambridge Handbook of Hispanic Linguistics*, 329–350. Cambridge: Cambridge University Press.

Villa-García, J., W. Snyder & J. Riqueros-Morante 2010. On the analysis of lexical subjects in Caribbean and Mainland Spanish: Evidence from L1 acquisition. Proceedings of the 34th Annual Boston University Conference on Language Development (BUCLD 34), 2: 433–444.

Villa-García, J., & I. Suárez-Palma 2016. Early null and overt subjects in the Spanish of simultaneous English–Spanish bilinguals and crosslinguistic influence. *Revista Española de Lingüística Aplicada*, 29.2: 250–395.

Weinreich U., W. Labov & M. Herzog 1968. Empirical foundations for a theory of language change. In Lehmann, W. P., & Y. Malkiel (eds.), *Directions for Historical Linguistics*, 95–188. Austin, TX: University of Texas Press.

Weiss, H. 2001. On two types of natural languages: Some consequences for linguistics. *Theoretical Linguistics*, 27: 87–103.

Whinnom K. 1965. Origin of European-based creoles and pidgins. *Orbis*, 14: 510–527.

White, L. 1992. Subjacency violations and empty categories in L2 acquisition. In Goodluck, H., & M. Rochement (eds.), *Island Constraints*, 445–464. Dordrecht: Kluwer.

2003a. *Second Language Acquisition and Universal Grammar*. Cambridge: Cambridge University Press.

2003b. Fossilization in steady state L2 grammars: Persistent problems with inflectional morphology. *Bilingualism: Language and Cognition*, 6.2: 129–141.

2011. Second language acquisition at the interfaces. *Lingua*, 121.4: 577–590.

White, L., & A. Juffs. 1998. Constraints on wh-movement in two different contexts of non-native language acquisition: Competence and processing. In Flynn, S., G. Martohardjono & W. O'Neil (eds.), *The Generative Study of Second Language Acquisition*, 111–129. Mahwah, NJ: Lawrence Erlbaum.

White, L., E. Valenzuela, M. Kozlowska-Macgregor & Y.-K. Leung 2004. Gender and number agreement in nonnative Spanish. *Applied Psycholinguistics*, 25.1: 105–133.

Wills, D. 2006. Against N-raising and NP-raising analyses of Welsh noun phrases. *Lingua*, 116: 11: 1807–1839.

Wilner, J. 2007. *Wortubuku fu Sranan Tongo*. Paramaribo: SIL International.

Winford, D. 1997. Property items and predication in Sranan. *Journal of Pidgin and Creole Languages*, 12: 237–302.

2000. "Intermediate" creoles and degrees of change in creole formation: The case of Bajan. In Neumann-Holzschuh, I., & E. W. Schneider (eds.), *In Degrees of Restructuring in Creole Languages*, 215–246. Amsterdam/Philadelphia, PA: John Benjamins.

2003. *An Introduction to Contact Linguistics*. Malden, MA: Blackwell.

2008. Atlantic creole syntax. In Kouwenberg, S., & Singler, J. (eds.), *The Handbook of Pidgin and Creole Studies*, 19–47. Malden, MA: Wiley-Blackwell.

Winford, D., & B. Migge 2008. Surinamese creole: Morphology and syntax. In Schneider, E. W. (ed.), *Varieties of English, Vol. 2: The Americas and the Caribbean*, 693–731. Berlin: Mouton de Gruyter.

Yang, C. 2002. *Knowledge and Learning in Natural Language*. Oxford: Oxford University Press.
 2004. Universal grammar, statistics, or both? *Trends in Cognitive Science*, 8.10: 451–456.
Zamora Vicente, A. 1967. *Dialectología española*. Madrid: Gredos.
Zubizarreta, M. L. 2001. The constraints on preverbal subjects in Romance interrogatives. In Hulk, A., & J.-Y. Pollock (eds.), *Subject Inversion in Romance and the Theory of Universal Grammar*, 183–204. Oxford: Oxford University Press.

Index

abolition of slavery, 3, 37, 49
acquisitional barriers, 28
advanced SLA processes, 16, 18, 20, 32, 34–35
affixation, 9
African Diaspora to the Americas, 32
African languages, 9, 11, 14, 16, 36, 44, 46
African substrate languages, 8, 12
African-born captives, 43
Afro-Andean grammars, 37, 68, 74
Afro-Andean Spanish, ix, 35, 83, 94, 98, 137, 142, 144
Afro-Bolivian Spanish, 4, 121
Afro-descendants, 37–44, 48–49, 52–54, 52, 67, 140
Afro-Ecuadorian, 71
Afrogenesis Hypothesis, 36–37
Afro-Hispanic features, 139
Afro-Hispanic languages of the Americas (AHLAs), 6, 140
Afro-Hispanic linguistics, 3
Afro-Hispanic vernaculars, 3, 8, 34, 36, 51, 65, 67, 97, 109, 113, 115–116
Afro-Iberian creole, 4
Afro-Latino linguistics, 5
Afro-Latino varieties of the Americas, 4, 119
Afro-Lusophone creole substrate, 36
Afro-Lusophone vernaculars, 4, 66
Afro-Mexican Spanish, 6
Afro-Peruvian Spanish, 71, 121
Afro-Puertorican Spanish, 6
Afro-Venezuelan Spanish, 4
alcabalas, 42
almojarifazgos, 42
anaphoric subject pronouns, 26
Andalusia, 95
Angola, 52
Antilles, 2–3, 5, 119, 143
Arabic, 86

Argentina, 41, 74
Articulatory-Perceptual system, 24
Aruba, 2
asientos, 41
Atlantic creoles, 3
Atlantic Ocean, 41
attrition, 26–27
Aymara, 69, 128

Bantu, 9, 137
Barlovento Spanish, 5–6
basilectal features, 4, 20, 23, 35, 67, 142
Basque, 128, 138
Belfast English, 79, 97
bilingualism, 14, 26
bilinguals, 12–14, 103
Bioprogram Hypothesis, 21–23
Bolivian Spanish, 36
Bonaire, 2
Borer–Chomsky Conjecture, 85
borrowing, 10–15, 18, 144
bottleneck, 11, 66
boundary configurations, 34, 125
bozales, 3, 6, 41–47, 53, 56, 128
Brazilian Portuguese, 4, 65, 90, 95–98, 99, 104, 111
Buckie English, 64–65, 80, 113
Buenos Aires, 41
Bulgarian, 28

Canary Islands, 95
Cape Verdean Creole Portuguese, 97
Caribbean islands, 2
Caribbean Spanish, 3–4, 109–111, 118–122, 124
Cartagena, 4–5, 41
castle factories, 36
Catholic Church, 38, 46

170　Index

Cerro Rico, 42
chacras, 47–48, 55
Chinese, 101, 123, 154
Chocó Spanish, 4, 5–6
Christian indoctrination, 47
chronicle, 38
Chulumani, 51–52
clitic, 28, 105, 121
code-switching, 80, 113
co-indexation, 84
Colombia, 1–5, 41, 54, 128, 143
colonial Spanish, 5, 18, 138
colonization, 17, 37, 44
colony, 45–48, 52, 55, 143
Company of Jesus, 38, 46–48, 54–55
comparative historical linguistics, 5
competence/performance dichotomy, 57
Conceptual-Intentional system, 24
Congo, 9
conquistadores, 37–39
contact-induced processes, 8, 125
continuum, 17–20
conventionalization, 21, 23, 98, 124–125
conventionalized advanced second languages, 20
copula, 15, 22
copy-and-paste strategy, 135–139, 143
creole thermometer, 17
creole umbrella, 17
creolistics, 17, 19, 23, 144
creolization, 9, 11–14, 35, 44, 53, 144
criollos, 43–46, 53–56
crystallized aspects of an L2, 32
Cuban Spanish, 5
Cuenca, 43
Curaçao, 2

declarative intonation, 33, 125, 129
(de)creolization, 3, 4–5, 8, 10, 17, 19, 29, 36–37, 53, 55, 66, 96, 99, 116, 124, 137, 140–141
decreolization, 2–3, 18, 35–36, 56, 140
Decreolization Hypothesis, 3, 5, 19, 37, 119, 140
Department of La Paz, 51
diasystem, 5, 8
discrimination, 38, 67
Dominican Spanish, 5, 99, 120
downstepping, 128–129
Dutch Antilles, 2

E(xternal)-language, 57, 59, 61–62, 74
early-peak alignment, 6
ecological factors, 9
ecological linguistics, 23
education, 23, 32, 37, 50, 67, 78, 81, 98, 113
English-based creoles, 143
environmental factors, 9
European languages, 1, 9–15, 32, 67, 101
Extended Projection, 104, 123

feature valuation and checking, 24, 33, 80, 142
freedmen, 37–39
French, 28, 31, 42, 46, 55, 86, 100
French-based languages, 1, 3, 143

Gbe, 14–15
geminates, 30
GoldVarb, 60, 75, 108
grammatical intuitions, 61, 70, 73–74, 85
grammatical reduction, 11–12, 14, 144
grammatical restructuring, 10, 13, 17, 35, 50
grammatical transmission, 10
grammaticality judgments, x, 33, 59, 68–69, 73–74, 86, 110, 141, 167
grammaticalization, 9
Greek, 27
Guayaquil, 43

haciendas, 32, 36–38, 44–56, 67, 78, 98, 141, 150
Haitian French, 31
Highland Bolivian Spanish. *See* Bolivian Spanish
highland mining centers, 44
highlands, 41–42
Hispaniola, 41
historical linguistics. *See* comparative historical linguistics
hybrid variety, 14
hybridization, 14

I(nternal)-language, 57, 59, 61, 80
imposition, 10–15, 144
impoverished subject–verb agreement, 33, 102
indigenous workforce, 41
innovations, 5, 12
Interlanguage Hypothesis, 19–20, 23, 93
intermediate creoles, 17

Interpretable features, 24, 63
interrogative, 20, 117, 123
intonational phrases, 34, 125
Italian, 27, 67, 86, 100, 117, 128, 138
Italian Syntactic Dialect Atlas, 62

Japanese, 123
Jesuits. *See* Company of Jesus

Kateyano, 128
Kikongo, 13–14
Korean, 123
Kwa, 9

L1 acquisition, 23, 25–26, 31–32
L2 morphology, 93–94
La Paz. *See* Department of La Paz
ladinos, 38, 43, 46–47
Land Reforms, 37, 49–50, 56, 67, 78, 98, 151
language change, 6, 9, 104, 122, 141
language restructuring, 30–31, 66
language shift, 50, 67
large-scale plantations, 44, 46, 141
Latin, 30
Latin American Spanish, 50, 107
lenition, 29–30
lexical borrowing, 18
lexicon, 1, 11–14, 24–26, 29–30, 36, 65, 81, 83, 85, 91, 110–111, 113, 116, 124, 142
lexifier, 10–12, 14–15, 17–18, 32
Lima, 41–45
linguistic norm, 23, 32, 35, 67–68, 70, 78, 98, 135, 140
Local-Agreement Gradience Function, 85
Logical Form, 24–25, 63

Mainland Spanish, 118, 122
manumission, 5, 53
maroon community, 2, 5, 143
marriage, 47, 55
Maya, 138
Media Lengua, 13–14
medium-sized plantations, 46
mestizos, 43, 46, 49, 52–53, 55
microparameters, 61–62, 62, 80
microparametric syntax, 60
microvariationist syntax, 61
Minimalist Program, 23–24, 62–63, 110–111, 141, 149
mit'a, 42–44

mixed languages, 13–14
mobility, 50, 67, 78
modular multibody systems, 31
Monogenesis Hypothesis, 1
Monogenesis-Decreolization Hypothesis, 3
monopoly, 41, 45
morphemes, 28, 31, 66, 97, 112, 116
morphological reduction, 18, 84, 96, 112, 116
morphology–semantics interface, 28, 33, 94, 112, 115, 142
morphosyntactic variability, 29
morphosyntax, 13
mulattoes, 43, 52

nativization, 31, 125
natural class nodes, 114
New York City Spanish, 105
Niger, 9
non-inverted questions, 33, 111, 117, 120, 124
non-null subject languages, 142
non-standard languages, 97
N-raising, 94, 142–143
null subject languages, 27, 99
numeration, 64, 81, 113

Observer's Paradox, 69
Old Spanish, 30
operationalized structures, 63
overt expletive pronouns, 102
Overt Pronoun Constraint, 101, 106

Pacific creoles, 3
Palenquero, 2, 5, 13–14, 18, 128, 143
Palo Monte, 4
Panama, 128
Papiamento, 1, 5, 18, 143
Paraguayan vernacular Spanish, 97
parameter switch, 26
partial pro-drop languages, 101
performance errors, 63, 73–74
phi-features, 66, 81, 84, 92, 112
phonemes, 16, 30
phonetic consonant weakening, 102
phonological targets, 34, 125–126, 138
phrase boundary tones, 33, 125
pidginization, 19
pidgins, 9, 17, 19, 21–22, 31, 36
piezas, 45, 56
pitch-accent configurations, 6, 130
plantation societies, 9, 52–53, 55

Popayán, 54
Popular Brazilian Portuguese. *See* Brazilian Portuguese
Potosí, 42
Praat, 130
pre-nuclear pitch accents, 34
principle of sameness, 64, 81
Principles & Parameters model, 26, 58
probabilistic modeling, 59
Processability Theory, 19–20, 23
prosodic patterns, 16, 131, 137–138, 140
proto-creole, 7
proto-language, 1, 3
pseudo-cleft constructions, 103
psycholinguistic models, 19
quantitative sociolinguistics, 59

Quechua, 68, 128, 138
Quichua, 13–14, 68, 128
Quito, 39, 43

R simulations, 9, 12
radical creoles, 20, 32
R-brul, 60
rebellions, 48
religious ceremonies, 47
Romance languages, 91, 94

San Basilio de Palenque, 2, 5, 143
semi-creole, 17
simplification, 30
slave markets. *See* slave trafficking
slave trafficking, 41, 45, 53
sociodemographics, 4, 36, 44, 47, 56
sociolinguistic interview, 57, 68–69, 73–75, 128
Spanish Crown, 5, 41–42
Sranan, 15–16
Sranan Tongo, 15, 31
standard languages, 3

standard norm. *See* linguistic norm
standardization, 4, 21, 23, 32, 35, 74, 98
standardized language, 7, 34, 62, 140, 143
statistical tools, 60
stigma, 67–68
stigmatized vernaculars, 33
stressed syllable, 6, 126, 131, 143
subject–verb inversion, 6, 99, 103, 105, 117, 150, 153
substrate languages. *See* African substrate languages
sugarcane industry, 46
Surinam, 15
Syntactic Atlas of Dutch Dialects, 62
Syntactic Atlas of Spanish, 62

Temporalidades, 38, 48, 56
topical subjects, 26
topicalization, 122
Tumbes, 38
typological class, 8, 17

underspecified forms, 113
uninterpretable features, 24, 63–64, 81, 89, 93, 111, 113, 142, 164
Universal Grammar, 23

Valuation/Interpretability Biconditional, 82–83
Varbrul, 60
Veneto, 128, 138
Venezuela, 4, 128
vernacular roots, 21–23
Viceroy Toledo, 42

West African languages, 9, 12
Western European languages, 9, 12

Yucatec Maya, 128